Bearsted and Thurnham Remembered

Bearsted and Thurnham Remembered

Kathryn Kersey

with contributions
from

**Rosemary Pearce
Michael Perring
and
Roger Vidler**

First published in 2005 by Kathryn Kersey
Reprinted 2005
Reprinted with corrections and revisions 2006

Kathryn Kersey
5 Greensand Road, Bearsted, Maidstone, Kent, ME15 8NY

ISBN 0954583124

Front and back covers:
An impression of Bearsted and Thurnham in former times in watercolours by Richard Odell

Text digitally set in 11, 12, 14 and 16pt Garamond, 8 and 10pt Times New Roman
Printed and bound in Great Britain by Parchment (Oxford) Limited

Acknowledgements

Once again, I thank most gratefully Stuart Bligh and the staff at the Centre for Kentish Studies in Maidstone in assisting my many document requests, Simon Lace and Veronica Tonge at Maidstone Museum, Maidstone Reference Library, the very helpful staff at Medway Archives and especially the staff at the Bearsted and Madginford branches of the Kent Library Service, also John Meakins and the wonderful staff at the Kent Fire Brigade Museum, Tovil.

I have been able to include some photographs and reports through the courtesy and generosity of Denis Fowle, Downs Mail, and the Kent Messenger newspaper group. Extracts from the Saddlers' Company archives are published by kind permission of the Master and Wardens of the Worshipful Company of Saddlers. I also thank Eleanor Seymour, a most generous archivist at the Saddlers' Company.

Special thanks must also go to Laurence Allen for supplying glimpses into a changed social world and thus enabling, what I hope, is a balanced piece of writing to be achieved. Both of us are indebted to Pearl Anderson of Robert Runcie House, Maidstone, for tirelessly producing piles of Annual Reports and other paperwork in response to many research queries. Additional thanks to Michelle Goodman of the City of Westminster Archives Centre.

Immense thanks and deep appreciation to Richard Odell for his exquisite watercolour impressions of Bearsted and Thurnham in former times, and for most generous permission to use them on the front and back covers.

I would like to acknowledge the kind assistance, together with most generous permission to quote and use as a source of information/illustrations, the following people and organisations:

Brenda Ansett (née Mercer), Rosemary Arbiter (née Brook), Mary Baker (née Palmer), Vera Banner (née Croucher), Bearsted and District Local History Society, Bearsted Green Women's Institute, Bearsted Scout Group, Bearsted and Thurnham Women's Institute, all the staff at Bearsted Medical Practice, BJW Computers, John Blamire Brown, Sister Mary Margaret OHP (née Margaret Blamire Brown), Irene Bourne (née Keay), Joyce Bourne (née Palmer), Barbara Brears (née Grout), Doris Britcher (née Bentley), John Bynoe, the late Ella Cardwell (née Foster), Allan Carr, Centre for Kentish Studies, Anthony Chadwick, Ina Chester, Terry Clarke, Trevor Cleggett, the late Edith Coales, Roy Cooks, Alf and Marjorie Cork (née Amos), Alan Croucher, Ian Dalziel, Roy Datson, Brenda Donn, Heather Downer, Alan and Mary Duke, Theresa and David Elliott, Martin Elms, Deborah Evans, Rowland and Janet Fairbrass, Audrey and the late Eddie Fermor, Alison and Vernon Finch, Geoffrey Fletcher, Barbara Foster (née Westall), Sheila and the late Tony Foster, Evelyn Fridd (née White), Sue Frith, Ron Fullex, Peter Gentry, Margery Gibson (née Pearce), Pam Gibson, the late Thomas Gilbert, Norah Giles (née Pettipiere), Jonathan Glenister, Barbara Gosden, Peter Green, Pat Grimes (née Robbins), Violet Hale (née Pollard), John Hardy, Winifred Harris (née Guest), Jane Heard, Marion and Peter Hebblethwaite, Philip Hesketh, the late Mary Hirst, Holy Cross church, Joy Hope, Jenni Hudson (née Howard), Christine Hughes, Felix Hull, Chris and Sue Hunt, Richard Hunt, Jane Jarett, Trudy Johnson (née Penney), Jean Jones (née Hodges), Babs and Sian Jossi, Kent Archaeological Society, the Kent Messenger Newspaper Group, Ian Lambert, Bruce Leiper, Tony Long, Judith Lovelady, Hamish Mackay Miller, Madginford Women's Institute, Robin Martin, John and Betty Mills (née Pearson), Maidstone Museum and Bentlif Art Gallery Pretty Bequest 1865, Meresborough Books, James Moore, Dr Martin Moss, Jackie Nicholas, Richard Odell, the estate of Sara Orczy, Baroness Brown, the late Jessie Page (née Brook), Dr Frank Panton, Ian Payne, Margaret Peat (née Lang), Medway Archives, Mick Patterson, Evelyn Pearce (née Harnett), Margaret Plowright (née White), The Postal History Society, Rowland Powell, Lesley Reynolds (née Datson), Andrew Richardson, Norman Rickwood, Roseacre Women's Institute, Peter Rosevear, the Worshipful Company of Saddlers, Maureen Shettle, Janet and Louie Smith, the late Mildred Sierakowski, Pam Skinner, Jean Spendley, Miriam Stevens (née Gardener), Thomas Tate, Marion and the late John Thompson, Joan Thorne (née Palmer), Lesley Thorne, Thurnham History Group, Nora Tolhurst, Jo Tuck, Rosemary Vellender, Graham Walkling, the late Hetty Walkling, Martin Weeks, Doug and Anona Wilkinson (née Hadley), Karen and Steve Williams, Ted Wingrove, and the late Barbara Wraight.

I thank my fellow contributors – Michael, Roger and Rosemary, for all their hard work and endeavours: some of the research undertaken together for this book has been a mutual voyage of discovery about surroundings long since considered familiar. I particularly thank Michael Perring for his special memories of his favourite place and an encyclopaedic knowledge of all things Thurnham.

Every reasonable effort has been made to contact the copyright holders of images from the Kay Carlton Hill Film Studio, and information about the Rose Mount Nursing Home, but I have been wholly unsuccessful. I would welcome the opportunity to contact them in order that formal permission may be obtained for using information from these sources. I would be pleased to insert the appropriate acknowledgement in any subsequent re-printing of this book.

I thank my long-suffering husband, Malcolm for further technological erudition. I also thank James and George and all the members of my family for their positive encouragement together with their patient endurance of domestic disruption and quite joyous sense of humour.

I thank, and acknowledge, an award by the Allen Grove Local History Fund of the Kent Archaeological Society, which was of financial assistance in the research required in preparing this book for publication.

Editorial Note

Where there is a particularly helpful description of events or an explanation of circumstances, it has been incorporated into the main body of the text for reasons of greater clarity and ease of reading. Any inclusions are subject to a note to indicate that the source used and that the words should not be regarded as written by one of the contributors - by this means it is hoped to avoid all accusations of that particular horror of all writers: inadvertent plagiarism.

Where an original document has been transcribed, the original spelling is given. The only deviation from this policy has been instances where a greater clarity is required.

Addresses given are all in Bearsted or Thurnham and place names are in Kent, unless otherwise stated.
St Mary's church, Thurnham is referred to as St Mary's church. Holy Cross church, Bearsted is referred to as Holy Cross church.

Abbreviations Used

CCRC	Medway Archives Centre, Civic Centre, Strood
CKS	Centre for Kentish Studies, County Hall, Maidstone
KAS	Kent Archaeological Society, library located in Maidstone Museum
NA	National Archives, Kew, London (previously known as the Public Record Office)

Latin
Ibid.	In the same place and refers to the previously named publication.
Op.cit.	In the publication already named.
Passim	Wording used that is dispersed through the text rather than a direct quotation.

Contents

Introduction

If I had to think of a single word or phrase that summed up this book, I would probably opt for 'a glorious gallimaufry' - that wonderful word that means rather a jumble or medley of things.

Whilst I was undertaking the research for my earlier book on Bearsted School, I discovered many interesting facts. Some of the information did not strictly concern the school, but involved the wider community within Bearsted and Thurnham. This is not surprising as the school was a 'village' school'. It was clear though that there had been very little oral history recorded concerning ordinary village life together with the experiences of local craftsmen and tradesmen. One former resident, born in Bearsted in the 1920s commented, 'When I was a child, the coming of the railway was a recent and living memory. There are few people now left in Bearsted and Thurnham that can recount the community memories'. The community memories and other photographs from older residents of Bearsted and Thurnham were just far too interesting to remain unrecorded.

I was truly delighted to discover that Rosemary, Michael and Roger are also fascinated by local history. It is an enormous pleasure to include their contributions in this book.

Here then, is some of the most interesting local information that we discovered, organised into a rather loose chronological arrangement, just as in modern life we look forwards and back with a series of random connections throughout every day.

We hope that you have as much enjoyment and pleasure in sharing this gallimaufry of information as we did when we started to research the two villages of Bearsted and Thurnham.

Introduction to revised edition

Since the first edition of this book was published in 2005, many people have taken up my invitation to correct inadvertent errors which had crept into the text. I have also received further details to some of the original information. Inaccurate historical research is of little help to anyone and so I have undertaken some revision as appropriate. However, I remain conscious that there will remain further errors in some of the information and I still welcome corrections and further advice.

Kathryn Kersey

1 A brief overview of Bearsted and Thurnham

The term 'village' has attracted many definitions and descriptions. Many of these include the phrase, 'a collection of houses all in the same area, but smaller than a town.' Until recent times, generations of inhabitants living in those houses resided in the same area, shared employment, experiences, and devised their own entertainment.

It is generally agreed by historians and archaeologists that most settlements in Kent were originally linear. It is difficult to imagine this today as the image of Bearsted is usually conveyed by the houses situated around the Green. Four hundred years ago, parts of the parishes of Bearsted and Thurnham were still in separate linear areas. Crismill, Roundwell, Sutton Street, the Green, Ware Street, Roseacre Street and Thurnham Lane were all hamlets that more or less functioned independently. They were loosely united by the two churches of Holy Cross and St Mary's.

In 1798, the historian, Edward Hasted described the two villages:[1]

> BERSTED... The PARISH lies mostly on what may be called high ground, a pleasant, and the greatest part of it, a dry situation; the soil is in general a deep sand, although towards the south west part it partakes of the quarry rock, and on the south side of the Lenham river a black moorish soil of fertile meadow ground. This river parts it toward the south from Otham, another smaller stream, which rises near Boxley, separates it on the western side from that parish and Maidstone, leaving within the bounds of it, a part of the hamlet of Maginford. Besides the above, this parish is watered by two or three other smaller rivulets, which rise northward, and run here into the Lenham river the easternmost of them separating it from Hollingborne and Leeds.
>
> The high road from Ashford and Lenham towards Maidstone, runs along the northern boundaries of it, passing over Berstead-green, the houses round which form the parish village. Near it stands the church; besides this there are two other hamlets called Ware and Roseacre-streets. In the south east part of the parish is the seat of Milgate, pleasantly situated and well-clothed with trees, at the back of which the ground descends to the river, and at a small distance, that of Lower Milgate, so called from its lower situation, still nearer the river...
>
> ...The PARISH of Thurnham, though healthy, is yet from the nature of its soil an unpleasant situation, and is rather an unfrequented place, of little thoroughfare; the high ridge of chalk hills cross it, close to the foot of which is the church with the court-lodge and parsonage and at a small distance eastward Aldington court, having a double avenue of trees leading from it, almost to Bersted-green, to which this parish joins southward, near which the soil approaches the chalk, where the inclosures are large and open, having but few trees in the hedge-rows to shelter them, and the land poor and flinty...
>
> From hence, on the hill northward, the country is wild and dreary, lying high and much exposed to the bleak northern aspect; the soil here is very poor and wet, a heavy tillage land of a kind of red earth, covered with quantities of flints...In the north-east part is a large quantity of wood-land, called Binbury wood, near which the high road from Maidstone through Detling leads on towards Stockbury valley and Key-street. Through this part of Thurnham, on the west side of this road, just before you descend to the low country is Binbury manor pound, and at a field or two distance behind it, the house itself.

Hasted noted the main geographical characteristics of Bearsted and Thurnham were sited around areas of chalk, sand and clay. The land was sufficient to support small communities and their associated industries.

A detail from the map that accompanied Hasted's description:

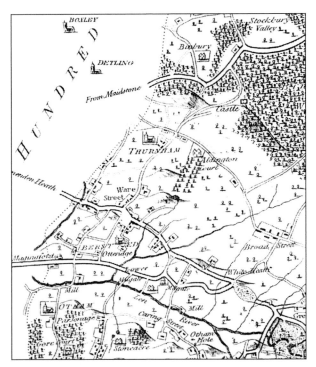

Reproduced courtesy of the Kent Archaeological Society

In 1831 a census recorded Bearsted inhabitants as 594, and Thurnham 571. As Hasted indicates, the main road to, from, and through Bearsted would have been Ware Street from a junction with the Sittingbourne Road as it progresses out of Maidstone. Today, the name of the road changes from Bearsted Road to Ware Street and then to The Street. The road to Ashford existed but it was not a main thoroughfare. The traffic that passed though Bearsted and Thurnham was on foot, or riding a horse and cart.

Trade directories for the area show that with just over a thousand local inhabitants, Bearsted and Thurnham were not huge communities in the Eighteenth and Nineteenth centuries; but there was a great variety of occupations. The population began to expand as people moved into the villages, drawn by the need for employment and the labour demands of agriculture and other industries. Some of the industries evolved and diversified: the village blacksmith later became a mechanic and garage owner. Tile-makers in Thurnham and Bearsted adapted to changes in building techniques by manufacturing and supplying bricks to local builders. Other trades and professions, such as the staff at the railway station, the master at the village school and some shopkeepers were deliberate introductions.

In 1871, the census return recorded that the population of Bearsted and Thurnham was just over a thousand people. The number of houses had slightly increased as some were built in the villages during Queen Victoria's reign. However, the majority of ordinary people did not own their home; they rented property or lived in tied accommodation. Housing in quantity began in the Roseacre area at the end of the First World War. Tower Lane was built, followed by parts of Plantation Lane, The Grove and some houses in The Landway. Development continued along the Ashford Road but this came to a standstill during the Second World War.[2]

Farm land was built upon at Cross Keys in the 1950s to address an urgent need for accommodation in Bearsted. In the 1960s the development of land on Madginford farm estate also began. Thurnham's recent development began with the construction of Sandy Mount in the middle 1960s and was followed by Bearsted Park and Grove Green estates in the 1980s: the latter almost completely enclosing Weavering Street. Grove Green was originally on the outskirts of the Thurnham parish and was an independent hamlet complete with church and school. Due to these recent developments, Thurnham parish has now changed shape, size and population once more.

Many inhabitants made a contribution to the communities: some are still remembered to this day. It is a remarkably rich heritage for a small area.

2 Ware Street, Thurnham

Many of these memories of the people living in Ware Street and their houses were recalled by Mr Thomas Gilbert and Mrs Emma Smith. Thomas Gilbert was usually known as Tom. He was around ninety years old when his recollections were recorded by the now disbanded Thurnham History Group. Emma is normally known as Louie, after her middle name, Louisa. She was born in Smart's Cottages, which are on the Green in Bearsted, and has spent at least eighty five years in Bearsted and Thurnham. Some of her great-grandparents also lived in Ware Street, so her connections date back at least 150 years.

This photograph was taken around 1917 and shows Louie as a small child with her parents Charles Earl, Elizabeth Lydia (née Baker) and her older brother, Charles:

Photograph courtesy of Louie Smith (née Earl)

Tom clearly recalled his arrival in Ware Street because it coincided with a train travelling over the railway bridge. Around 1900 the Gilbert family were on their way to a new home beyond the top of Bell Lane. He thought that there was a huge iron monster living on the bridge, making a terrible noise. He was very scared as he knew nothing about trains and arrived at the new house as a frightened small boy.

The front of Tom's house looked out on a meadow which sloped down to the railway. Two wooded and high banks formed a valley which ended at the bottom of Romney Hill on the main Ashford to Maidstone Road. Tom later knew that it was called 'Banky Meadow'. At the top of the hill there was a gate which led to a farm and an old quarry working known as 'Bell Hole' which even then was overgrown with bushes and trees. This was a short distance from an old cart track which led to some cottages where his family and their neighbours, Mrs Betts and her two sons, lived.

The summer evenings were particularly quiet in Ware Street. If Tom stood outside the Methodist Chapel, he often heard a nightingale singing in the woods and bushes beyond the railway station. There were also occasions when he heard the distinctive call of the nightjar from over a mile away. The bird was in a wooded area beyond the golf course. It was many years before he realised that the sound he heard was similar to a short burst of machine gun fire.

Many local children roamed the fields and woods. If they were lucky enough to discover a pheasant or partridge nest then they would tell Mr Attwood, who was the local gamekeeper. Mr Attwood paid threepence for the information about a nest and was known to pay up to sixpence if the eggs were brought to him. There were other opportunities to earn some money. On Saturday mornings, Tom often played by the railway bridge at Ware Street. Horse-drawn coaches with high seats would pass under it on a day out. From the bridge he would call 'Throw out your rusties'. If he was lucky, a handful of pennies would be thrown out for collection.

When Tom was a child, autumn was an important time. For around six weeks nearly everyone in the village worked to harvest hops. Whole families participated as the joint effort boosted earnings. The cash was used to buy shoes and clothes for the winter. He recalled that the local name for receiving the money was 'The Pay Off'.

During the First World War, Tom's father was in the Army. The wages were low, and as many men were serving their country, money was scarce. In 1916, Tom's family decided that he should leave school. He was aged 12½ when he went to work. His first wages were six shillings a week and in the absence of his father, he was regarded as the 'man of the house'. The chores he had to perform included tending the garden and allotment.

A diagram that accompanies these next memories from Tom and Louie about Ware Street can be found on the next page.

From the village green on the North Side of Ware Street

Golf Course

The first hole of the golf course was in the corner next to the railway and on the bank above there was a man-made pond. West of it, the ground and clay bank looked as if it had once been excavated. Stories persisted that house tiles had once been made there. The pond was known as 'Cal Pond'. The sand pit at the entrance to the golf course was quite deep and formed a fairly high cliff.

Brick Field

There were two kilns; each held thousands of bricks. Freshly-made and unfired, they were known as 'green bricks'. They were loaded in a furnace with spaces between. The furnaces held six or seven fires each. The fire covers were swung into position over the furnace openings and sealed with a slurry mixture of clay and Fullers Earth, before firing. The clay and Fullers Earth mixture was an efficient sealant. Both ingredients were obtained from a nearby meadow. The fires burned for some days. Tom worked there for a short while in the 1920s before the brick field closed down around 1926.

Neatherton Cottages

This is a pair of cottages which are also known as 10 and 12 Ware Street. Tom recalled that 10 Ware Street was occupied by Mr Webb and two sisters called Esther and Sally. 12 Ware Street was occupied by Mr and Mrs Cook and two daughters.

Church Cottages

These were occupied by four families by the name of Flood, Simmonds, Summers and Attwood.

An interpretation of Tom Gilbert and Louie Smith's memories of the north side of Ware Street:
(not to scale)

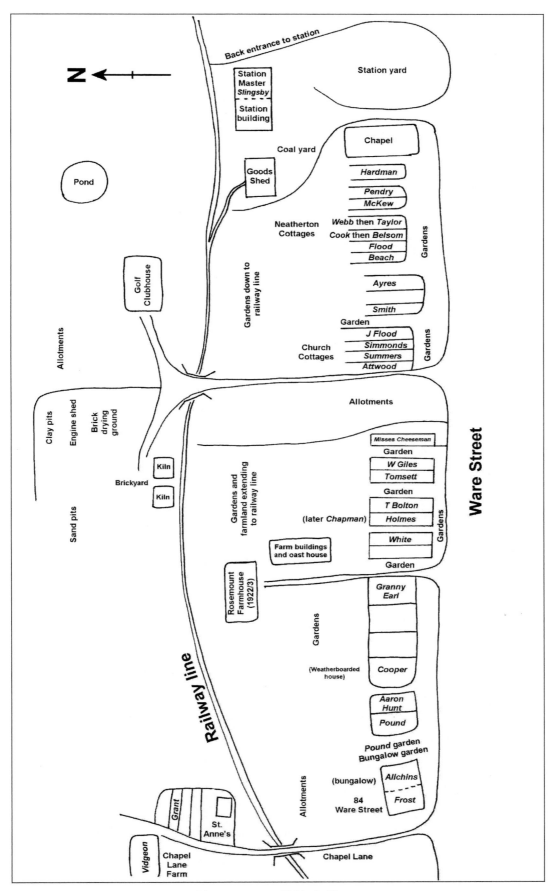

Diagram courtesy of Malcolm Kersey

Ware Street by the road next to the Golf Course

Some of the land was used for allotments. Nearby were two houses, the second of which was the home of the Misses Cheeseman who ran a small laundry. Their neighbours were the Giles and Tomsett families and Tommy Bolton. Tommy Bolton was a local carrier who undertook daily journeys to Maidstone. His garden was really a jumble of buildings. These were used to accommodate his horse and cart. Tommy had three children: a daughter known as 'Topsy' and twin boys, whose nick-names were 'Alike' and 'Similar'. The Holmes family lived next to the Bolton family. Mr and Mrs Chapman and their daughter, who was known as 'Rene' were also neighbours.

By 1939, Louie had married Jack Smith and they had moved into 48 Ware Street so that Jack could work for Mr Hodges at Rosemount Dairy farm. He earned seventeen shillings a week as a waggoner, milking the cows and delivering the milk. Louie was able to work in the fields of local farms whenever the demands of her family allowed. She was particularly skilled in putting up the strings on wooden poles for such vegetable crops as peas and runner beans. She recalled regularly undertaking this work on farming land which bordered the south side of the Ashford Road, where Shirley Way was later built.

The ground floor of 48 Ware Street comprised one large downstairs room with a scullery at the back. There was still an iron pump for water but it was not used as the house had a piped supply. There was no electricity and no mains drainage. Meals were cooked an iron range. There was an outside lavatory which was emptied on a Saturday morning by a vehicle known as a 'honey wagon'. It was operated by two men who undertook this operation whilst cheerfully eating their sandwiches; quite oblivious to the awful smell! Louie recalled that the inhabitants of other properties in Ware Street sorted out sewage matters for themselves. This usually meant that the men of the family dug an enormous pit at the bottom of the garden for the lavatory drainage and when it was full up, another one was dug. Luxuriant rhubarb usually grew on the top of the filled pits.

Further down Ware Street were three cottages and garden by a track leading to the Rosemount Dairy. The yard for the dairy was adjacent to a house adjacent which was occupied by an old lady known as 'Granny Earl'; Louie's great grandmother. She lived in the house with a son and grandson. Her grandson, Charles, was Louie's father. In the summer, Granny Earl sold lemonade from her house.

Around 1930, Tom's family moved into another house in Ware Street. At the end of their property was a weather-boarded house which was occupied by the Cooper family. Next door to the Cooper family, on the right hand side, was a rather dilapidated house believed to date from medieval times. On the other side of the Cooper's house was a tile-hung property run as a shop by Aaron Hunt and his daughters, Ethel, Maude and Adelaide. Both of these properties were demolished in the 1950s. This photograph shows all three properties: Aaron's shop is on the extreme left hand side.

Photograph courtesy of Terry Clarke

These two undated photographs show Mrs Cooper outside her house and a group of four ladies which includes Maude Hunt.

Both photographs courtesy of Jean Jones (née Hodges)

Close neighbours to the Gilbert family were the Pound family with their children: Harry, Daisy and Albert. Mr Pound's garden was along the west of the house and joined the garden of the small bungalow. Between the garden and the railway line was a large piece of ground that the Gilbert family used as an allotment. A bungalow nearby was rented by the Allchins family.

Louie and her husband, Jack, moved to 84 Ware Street in 1958. The house has Seventeenth century origins and was once very close to a house called Arcady which was pulled down after a fire. Jean Jones recalled that when her family owned 84 Ware Street, the deeds specifically stated that at one time the site had been occupied by a property which had been left to 'the poor of Thurnham parish'[1] but it not certain whether this refers to the current building. It is likely that the original building would have been of a basic construction.

This undated photograph from the early years of the Twentieth century shows the close proximity of the two properties. No. 84, is on the left of the picture and Arcady is the property with black timbers and white decoration. It is not known when Arcady was built:

Photograph courtesy of Terry Clarke

These photographs show the front and side of 84 Ware Street:

This photograph shows that the end of the dwelling is slightly lower is on the left hand side of the property, with a single chimney pot. It is possible that this section may be of a later date and may have once been a separate dwelling as there is a bricked-up doorway. This structure is now incorporated into 84 Ware Street.

Both photographs courtesy of Malcolm Kersey

During recent repair work on the roof, a small cache of papers was discovered underneath the tiles. Although some documents were disintegrating, they were legible. They comprised a series of orders and receipts dated 1915 to 1927 from a wholesale merchants called Midmore and Hall, 24 Stone Street, Maidstone to Mr Frost, who was living at the house.

This is the most complete document:

Reproduced courtesy of Louie Smith

The hole through the middle was probably caused by filing the paid bill on a metal spike. Mr Hickmott is noted as the local carrier, using a Ford car for deliveries. Mr Frost ran a bicycle store and repair shop at 84 Ware Street and also sold small items such as tobacco, matches, shoe polish and pins. Louie was able to confirm that at one time, Mr Frost even had a small steam engine stationed in the garden.

Adequate drainage at the lower end of Ware Street was difficult to achieve for many years. Louie's house has been flooded several times. In 1968, after many days of torrential rain, water poured down Chapel Lane. It accumulated underneath the railway bridge and by the lower properties in Ware Street. This picture shows the flood and two stranded cars in the water on the far side of the bridge. The occupants of the cars managed to escape in time.

Photograph courtesy of Norah Giles (née Pettipiere)

As the bad weather and rain continued, water then poured through Louie's garden as shown in this photograph on the right. Barely a day later, an entire garden from a neighbouring property slid down to 84 Ware Street. After the water had drained away, it was decided to leave the remains of the garden where it had come to rest. There is a step down into Louie's house as the level of the ground outside is now raised.

Photograph courtesy of Norah Giles

Chapel Lane

Chapel Lane was named after Providence Chapel that was built there by the Methodist church. However, the building suffered poor drainage. It was decided to construct a new chapel further up Ware Street which was opened in 1877.

On the right hand side of Chapel Lane there were allotments. One house was set back from the lane called St Anne's. There were also some cottages. One family Tom remembered living there was called Grant and there were six children: Kate, May, Fred, Frank, Bert and George. Chapel Lane Farmhouse at the end of the lane was occupied by the Vidgeon family who had seven children: Rose, Amy, Jack, Bertha, Jean, Ethel and Charlie.

Beyond the farmhouse were other buildings, cow-sheds and fields which were all part of Sandy Mount farm run by the Tolhurst family. The rest of the farm was located between the two lanes leading from the south side of Ware Street up to Roseacre Lane.

The South Side of Ware Street from the Green

A diagram that accompanies these memories from Tom and Louie about Ware Street can be found on the next page.

The left hand side of the hill was a wooded area and part of the Snowfield estate. At one time Snowfield was the home of Baroness Orczy. The first house next to the wooded area was 1 Ware Street, virtually opposite the station. It was occupied by Mrs Hodges who ran a shop from the premises. Next door to the Hodges lived the Watkins family who had children called Alf, Les, Vera and Doris. Doris married Tom Gilbert's brother, Cyril. Mr Watkins was a local shoe repairer.

An interpretation of Tom Gilbert and Louie Smith's memories of the south side of Ware Street: (not to scale)

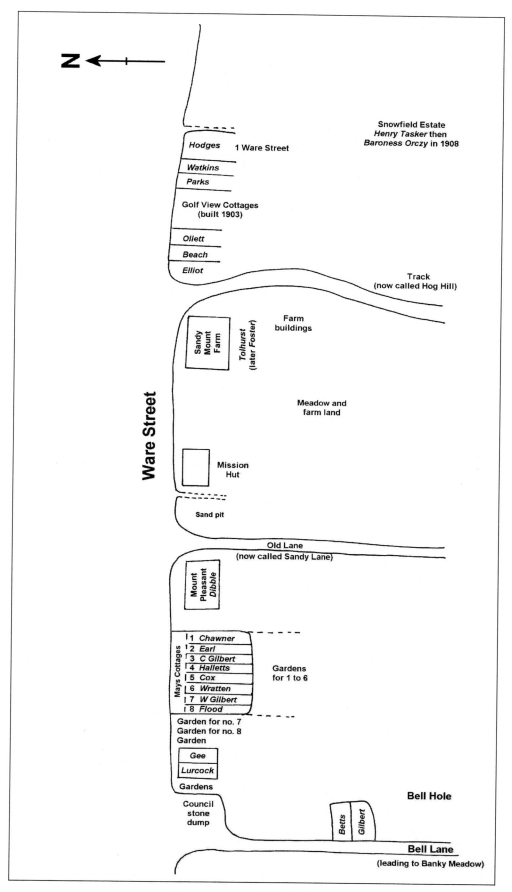

Diagram courtesy of Malcolm Kersey

This undated postcard of Ware Street shows 1 Ware Street on the left hand side and the Methodist Chapel at the top of the incline on the right hand side.

Photograph courtesy of Jean Jones

There were two blocks of cottages a short distance from 1 Ware Street. In the first of these lived Mr and Mrs Parks. Mr Parks was the railway signalman. The second block of cottages was slightly higher up and steps were required to reach them. These were occupied respectively by Mr and Mrs Ollett, Mr and Mrs Beach and their three sons: Percy, Len and Mac, and the Elliott family. Golf View Cottages were built in between these two blocks of cottages in 1903.

Behind the main farmhouse of Mr Tolhurst's farm at Sandy Mount were the farm buildings and yard. A track led to the farmyard which was later developed into a proper road and became called Hog Hill.

A little further down Ware Street was a gate beside the Mission Hut. This gate led to a field by Sandy Mount farm where sand had been dug from the bank. The excavations had formed a cliff and many sand martins nested there. At the end of the field there was a short grassy slope and the lane next to it was known as Old Lane. Today it is called Sandy Lane.

This undated postcard shows the houses in Ware Street opposite the Mission Hut:

Photograph courtesy of Jean Jones

This old, undated postcard shows the view from the field at Sandy Mount farm. Neatherton Cottages are towards the middle of the picture on the opposite side of the road. Behind them is part of the golf course and other parts of Thurnham:

Photograph courtesy of Jean Jones

Beyond Old Lane was a large house called 'Mount Pleasant', where the Dibble family lived. When Louie was fourteen in 1929, she left school. She spent some time at Mount Pleasant, working for Mrs Dibble and her daughters; Grace and Doris. She particularly remembered that there was a massive water pump and very long ceramic sink in the scullery. 'Miss Grace', as Louie called her, was a teacher in Nigeria but came home regularly. During one home visit, she invited a family to tea and then consulted Louie about the menu. This was because she usually employed servants in Nigeria and so had very little practical experience of what to cook for such an occasion. Louie suggested that if a hot meal was required, perhaps a meat pudding would be acceptable but it would need to be boiled in a cloth or a basin. Louie showed Miss Grace what needed to be done. However, to this day, Louie has never found out how the meal was received by the guests.

Mays Cottages

These were situated a little further along Ware Street from Mount Pleasant. The property comprised eight small terraced cottages. They were known as either 'Mays Cottages' or 'The Bank' but were also known for a short time as 'Barracks Row'. Rents were paid weekly and were collected by Mr Brooks who cycled out from Maidstone. At the start of the Twentieth century, the cottage windows were regularly taped up due to outbreaks of Scarlet Fever.

The people who lived in the cottages that Tom particularly remembered were Mr and Mrs Teddy Chawner who lived at the first one with their daughters Emily, Ada and Lily. Louie recalled that their other children were Sid, Nellie and Bob.

Mr and Mrs Earl with their children: Harry, John, Aubrey, George and Winny lived next door. Some other children in this family were called Jim, Charlie, Fanny, Eva, Sid and Clarence. George later changed his name to Horace.

Mr and Mrs Charles Gilbert (Tom's uncle) and their children Minnie, Amy and Arthur lived at No. 3 Arthur was a surviving twin. Their neighbours at No. 4 were Mr and Mrs Halletts, with their children Joe, Bill and Mary. Mr Halletts was a retired railwayman. When Mary became seriously ill, straw was laid on the road outside to deaden the noise of the passing horses and carts.

No. 5 was occupied by Mrs Cox with her children Bobby and Stephen. Their neighbours at No. 6 were Mrs Wratten and one of her sons. No. 7 was home for another branch of the Gilbert family and their neighbours at No. 8 were Mr and Mrs Flood and their children, Caroline and Edward.

There was no running or piped water into the houses at Mays Cottages but one tap was situated half way up the passageway that ran along the back of the properties. This made it quite difficult for the residents to keep things clean. Privies were emptied by buckets and the contents were buried in the small patch of garden as there was nowhere else. The gardens for these houses were not laid out in a straightforward manner as the back gardens situated directly behind the houses stopped at No. 6. The garden for No. 7. was at the side of the house, so the garden for No. 8 was situated next door to the garden of Mr Gee who lived in the last semi-detached house before the railway bridge.

Mr Gee's neighbours were Mr and Mrs Lurcock who had one daughter and a son called Bernard. The council stone dump for the road was situated by the Lurcocks' house. Stones were dumped there and a man would come out and build them into a neat block rather like a dry stone wall. Another man called a 'stone knapper' would then break the rocks into small pieces for road repairs.

This undated photograph from the early years of the Twentieth century shows Ware Street looking up from the railway bridge. Mr and Mrs Gee's house is the property on the right hand side:

Photograph courtesy of Jean Jones

3 The Determination of Henry Hodges

Henry Hodges was a determined man with a burning ambition to run his own farm. He worked as a gardener for Hubert Bensted, an architect living in Thurnham Lane. Mr Bensted was rather taken with Henry and gave him a cow as a present. With this animal Henry started on the road to fulfil his ambition.

Henry's parents, Henry and Mary (née Foster) both came from families that had lived in Bearsted and Thurnham for many generations. This undated photograph shows Henry, as a young man, paused in his work in Mr Bensted's garden:

Photograph courtesy of Jean Jones

Henry started farming with the cow. It was not long before he began to build up a dairy business which he ran from his home although the cattle were pastured on rented land elsewhere in Bearsted and Thurnham. Henry's wife, Ellen, was especially good at making butter and Jean Jones (née Hodges) often used to watch her grandmother shaping the pats of butter with a pair of wooden 'scotch hands'. Both Henry and Ellen longed to have their own farmhouse and dairy.

The family lived at 1 Ware Street. The property was part of the Milgate estate and was owned by Walter Fremlin. Ellen ran part of the premises as a small shop. It was her proud boast that you could buy anything there from a pin to an elephant, but she mainly sold confectionery. At one time a forge had operated at the premises and although it had fallen into disuse, the shop was called Old Forge Stores. Jean still has many screw-top sweet jars and Sharps toffee tins from the shop.

After the Hodges family moved, subsequent occupiers and owners of the property included the Stemp, Marshall and Vidler families. At one time, the District Nurse also rented a room at the premises. There was a separate bell to be rung if the Nurse's services were required. The Foster family, who were farming at Sandy Mount, owned the only telephone in the upper part of Ware Street and passed on messages for the Nurse when necessary.

This picture shows Ellen Hodges outside her shop, accompanied by a member of the Shorter family:

Photograph courtesy of Jean Jones

Henry had two sons: George and Harry. George was the elder. Both went to Thurnham School. Harry left when he was aged 14. He achieved a perfect attendance record whilst at school and was awarded a solid silver medal with seven extra bars: one for each year during 1904-1910. The horse chestnut tree outside the school premises in Thurnham Lane was planted by their father.

On one occasion, when Harry was a boy, he was attracted to exploring other chestnut trees that were in The Spinney in Thurnham Lane. He was wearing a very new tweed suit and as he leapt over the fence, a spar from the fence went up the bottom of the jacket. The material ripped right up his back. He knew that his mother would react badly to the damage and was far too scared to go home; he spent the rest of the day 'over the hills' at Friningham.

As a child, Harry used to toboggan down Sandy Lane in snowy weather. Harry could just remember the remains of a windmill on top of Hog Hill and donkeys that were kept in the next field. They were used to transport goods to and from the station. There was a small sand quarry nearby. All the children in the area knew that Mr Perrin had a store next to his shops at Chestnut Place and another by the golf course in Thurnham Lane. Supplies of fruit and glass jam jars were kept in the stores before use by Mr Perrin's employees who made jam in the factory behind the shops. The stores were sometimes raided by small boys who purloined the jars, washed them and sold them back to Mr Perrin!

Henry was able to run a small dairy business from 1 Ware Street but intended to have proper premises built when he had sufficient capital. The First World War interrupted his business plans as both George and Harry had to serve in the army. Harry was badly wounded during fighting. While a stretcher party recovered him from the battlefield, gas shells landed nearby and he was badly gassed when the bearers dropped him. Harry was rendered unfit to serve. Following his discharge, he returned to Thurnham and rejoined his father.

This undated photograph shows Harry in his uniform:

Photograph courtesy of Jean Jones

Eventually, Henry managed to save £800 in half crown pieces and he bought a plot of land further down Ware Street. The purchase included an acre of ground and an oast house behind two cottages. He built a house which he called Rosemount Farmhouse. The building survives in a somewhat altered form as 66 Ware Street. Henry's ambition to own a dairy had been fulfilled through many years of hard work and dedication.

The farmhouse was constructed with bricks made at the brickfield in Ware Street. They were transported to the building site by cart. Jean recalled that some of the windows came from Hollingbourne workhouse which had just been demolished. The family moved into the house in 1923. A few years later, the area outside the house was landscaped to form a garden. The rose arches came from the Milgate estate.

This undated photograph shows Henry and his wife by the house. Note the thatched hayrick:

Photograph courtesy of Jean Jones

In this undated photograph of the farm in winter, the farmhouse is in the left hand side with the railway line behind it. 64 Ware Street is just visible as a corner of a building, on the right hand side:

Photograph courtesy of Jean Jones

A little further down Ware Street from Rosemount Farm was a Medieval hall house. When Jean was a child, the two ladies that lived there sold beer by the jug and kept a small range of sweets for sale. This photograph shows part of the house before it was demolished:

Photograph courtesy of Jean Jones

Near to the hall house were two further houses, but these were badly damaged by a fire on 16 April 1940. A beam located in the chimney area had smouldered all night before igniting. Audrey Fermor recalled that her great-grandmother Mary Bodiam was living there at the time, together with her widowed son, Frank and his daughter Ellen. Mary was only rescued by being pulled from an upstairs window. Two pets died and they lost everything except the nightclothes they were wearing. The houses were subsequently found to be structurally unsound and demolished. After the fire, Audrey's great-aunt offered accommodation to the family in Tovil until Frank re-married and moved into 1 Triangle Cottages.

Harry married Alice Goodwin from Otham. Alice was born at house called Madam Taylor's, opposite Otham green. She was in service with Elsie White at Barty House, which at that time was owned by the Wallace family.

Alice and Harry's first home was a house called Arcady. It was conveniently close to Rosemount Farm so that Harry could continue to assist his father in his business. This detail, from an undated postcard of Ware Street, shows Arcady. The house has since been demolished.

Photograph courtesy of Jean Jones

On Christmas Day in 1927, the weather was terrible. Thick snow had fallen and all the telephone wires were down. Alice was heavily pregnant and on her way to Rosemount Farm in the snow, when she fell over. They returned to Arcady and for two days Alice was in labour. Help was evidently needed. A neighbour pulled socks over his boots and walked over to Hollingbourne to the doctor, using only a small hurricane lamp to help him find his way. In the event, all was well and Jean safely arrived.

The Hodges and Goodwin families regularly participated in the hop picking at Otham. Despite the hard work, it was a good opportunity to catch up with all the family news. Jean recalled that although Otham was not very far away, it seemed quite distant to Ware Street. This picture shows Jean in 1935, hop picking in Otham with her grandmother Goodwin, Aunt Min and her cousin, Walter Goodwin:

Photograph courtesy of Jean Jones

The family attended church services at the Mission Room in Ware Street. It was rather closer than St Mary's church in Thurnham Lane and it was more convenient to attend services there. The Mission Room was heated by a farrier's stove which still had an opening in which to place irons before applying them to a horse's hoof. Jean was baptised in the Mission Room.

Harry Hodges developed the business further after taking it over from his father. Jean's brother also worked for the dairy. A two-wheeled cart with 'Hodges, Rosemount Dairy' written on the side was used for the milk round. Jean used to jump on the back of it, but was wary of tipping it up. Later the deliveries were conducted in a motorbike and sidecar.

These two pictures show Harry with a cart and a motorbike that were used for deliveries:

Photograph courtesy of Jean Jones

Photograph courtesy of Jean Jones

Jean has always lived in Ware Street but during her lifetime parts of the street have greatly changed. Many properties have been altered or demolished and gardens have been built upon. One major change took place in the late 1960s when main drainage arrived. Before this, there were occasions when waste water ran down Ware Street to Chapel Lane.

This is one of Jean's favourite family photographs. She is the small girl being carefully supervised on one of the farm horses by her grandfather, Henry Hodges:

Photograph courtesy of Jean Jones

4 Sandy Mount farm, Thurnham

There are difficulties in tracing the history of the area that is now known as Sandy Mount in Ware Street as many records have not survived. However, there is some information which confirms that after a lease was granted to William Webb in 1777, a windmill was erected. Later owners were named as James Parton, John Thorpe, Richard Honey. James Colebrook owned it before Elizabeth and Samuel Murton took over the lease in 1830.

At the time of the census in 1841, Thomas and John Tuddingham, aged 30 and 28 respectively, were listed as millers.[1] The tithe map and schedule for Bearsted, which was compiled in 1842, lists the mill as in the ownership of Elizabeth and Samuel Murton but worked by Thomas Bridgland. The property is described as a plot of land measuring two acres and nineteen perches including the windmill and garden.[2]

In 1854 George Baker was living in Ware Street and his occupation was given in a trade directory as a miller, but there are no specific records for a windmill or miller in any census returns after 1841. The mill may have already fallen into disuse or disrepair, but the lease persisted until 1862, when it taken on by Thomas Taylor.[3]

It has been suggested that Sandy Mount might have originally been the mill house, but there are no surviving records to support this proposition.[4] Edward Pretty, who was curator of Maidstone Museum, sketched the area in the 1850s and one of his sketches is shown below:[5]

Reproduced courtesy of Maidstone Museum and Bentlif Art Gallery, Pretty Bequest 1865

Elizabeth Philpott, a sand dealer, was residing at Sandy Mount in 1841.[6] John Apps, an agricultural labourer, was also living there, as were Eliza and John Apps. Although the names are the same, it not clear whether the two Johns were members of the same family. Other households nearby included George Allman, Robert and Emily Bridgland, James and Hannah Waters. Two years later, Thomas Bridgland was living at Sandy Mount.[7]

In 1851 several different families were residing in the Sandy Mount area.[8] These included Edward Habgood, described as a 'Proprietor of houses', and his family; Hannah Hodges, a widow, and her children Edward and Emily; Ann Bolton, a widow, and her family; Edward and Louisa Hobson and their family; and the family of Luke Hepton.

Since 1800, Sandy Mount had been owned by Ann Armstrong. She had inherited it through her connections with Edward Watts of Thurnham. The inheritance also included a butcher's shop in The Street and the Herst Lands in Yeoman Lane adjacent to Snowfield.

Ann Armstrong did not make a will and after her death in 1843, there were at least nine people that could claim a part of her estate. It was agreed that all of the property should be sold at an auction held at The Bell Inn in Maidstone on 29 July 1858.

The documents reproduced below show a section of the auction particulars together with the associated plan for lot ten which was Sandy Mount. At the time of the sale, Sandy Mount comprised two cottages occupied by Messrs Habgood and Bridgland.[9]

LOT 10. THE TRIANGULAR

ENCLOSURE OF MEADOW LAND,

CALLED THE OLD ORCHARD,

IN THE PARISH OF THURNHAM,

Surrounded by Public Roads, in the occupation of Mr. JAMES GIBSON, a Yearly Tenant from Michaelmas, at a Yearly Rent of **£13**, the Landlord paying the Tithes.

TWO COTTAGES, CALLED SANDY MOUNT,

Adjoining the above, built of Brick up to the first Floor, and Tiled above, with a Tiled Roof, each containing

2 UPPER AND 2 LOWER ROOMS, AND AN OVEN, 1 HAVING A CELLAR IN THE BASEMENT,

Pleasantly situate by the side of the Road;

A WELL OF EXCELLENT WATER, ALSO A TIMBER AND TILED BARN, ABOUT 30ft. by 16ft. 10in.,

In the occupation of Messrs. HABGOOD & BRIDGLAND, Weekly Tenants, at Rents amounting to

£13 17s. 4d. per Annum.

A PIECE OF LAND ON THE SOUTH EAST OF THE ABOVE,

In extent 0a. 1r. 10p., unenclosed and in hand, and one other Piece of Land at the North West corner of the Old Meadow, also unenclosed and in hand.

TOTAL RENTAL OF THIS LOT £26 17s. 4d. PER ANNUM.

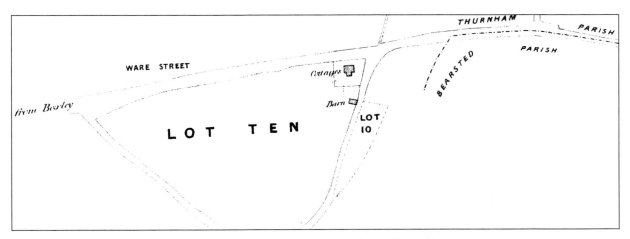

Reproduced courtesy of the Centre for Kentish Studies, Maidstone

James Whatman expressed an interest in the property prior to the sale but it is not known if he actually bought it.[10] Three years later, other families had moved into the area: Thomas and Elizabeth Curtis; Edward and Jane Budden; John and Margaret Flood; and Henry and Elizabeth Slender.[11]

By the 1871 census, Emily Bridgland was widowed but, aged 56, had moved to Sandy Mount and was farming the land assisted by her nephew Walter Turley.[12] Walter was aged 18 and unmarried. Later census returns show Walter married to Harriet and running the farm together with their children.[13] The lease then passed to the Tolhurst family. In 1907 Rose Tolhurst married Charles Foster and they took over the running of the farm.

At some time after the 1858 sale, the two cottages became one dwelling and with the land, it all became consolidated into a small farm. There is no information available about the engraved stone over the front door. The dwelling still had small rooms with low ceilings and very uneven floors. This photograph of the farmhouse is undated but was taken in the early 1900s. Rose Foster is standing by the front door with one of her children.

Photograph courtesy of Barbara Foster (née Westall)

The dairy room was attached to the farmhouse and faced what was called 'Fosters Lane' but which is now known as Hog Hill. To meet hygiene standards, the room was only used for milk processing and cleaning the equipment. A small amount of cheese and butter was made but only for family consumption.

The main entrance to the farm was round the back of the house where vegetables were sold. The cow sheds were at the side of the house by Fosters Lane, as was the heap of manure. A small pig yard with sties, and a chicken shed for the large white cockerels reared for Christmas was located in this area too. There was also a substantial land holding at Chapel Lane farm which was used for arable purposes.

This undated photograph was taken during World War One and shows land girls assisting with threshing at Chapel Lane. Note the thatched hayricks that are just visible behind the corrugated roof on the right hand side of the photograph:

Photograph courtesy of Tony and Sheila Foster

The Fosters rented small pockets of land all over the village for pasture, especially when the cows were not producing milk or 'dry'. At one time there were small pasture areas in the village which were maintained in return for the hay crop, with which to feed the cattle during the winter. This undated photograph shows a hay crop being collected from the Green:

Photograph courtesy of Chris and Sue Hunt

<u>Left to right:</u> Ambrose Croucher, Charles Foster, Neddy Chawner

Some of the usual routes for taking the cows to pasture and to milking involved travelling between Sandy Mount and the rear of Holy Cross church. This photograph from 1925 shows cows in Yeoman Lane:

Photograph courtesy of Chris and Sue Hunt

By the time Ella Cardwell (née Foster) was born, her Tolhurst grandparents shared the accommodation in order to assist her parents in the running of the farm. The largest section was the dairy and cattle stock.

All the Foster children; William, Eric, Dolly, Ivy, Iris and Ella, like many others in the village, began to help their parents as soon as they could walk. They undertook milk deliveries and odd jobs around the farm so they never really had the chance to go hop-picking in the summer holidays. However, there were hop-pickers huts built in Lilk Meadow by the Ashford Road in Bearsted that they used to see as they walked around that area.

The children began working by accompanying their father with the horse and cart on milk deliveries. When they were older, the children went on their own rounds with milk cans, measures and bicycles. Each milk can had a capacity of four to five gallons. They were balanced by hanging two of them, one on each handlebar of a bicycle. Both cans had to be put down on the ground, though, whilst the milk was being measured for sale and dispensed. The weight of the milk cans was distributed by drawing equally on both cans. The milk was poured directly into whatever vessel the house-holder had available - a jug or a basin.

This advertisement, from 1929, appeared in the parish magazine:

Reproduced courtesy of Jenni Hudson

The photograph below shows Charles Foster with some of his children delivering milk around Bearsted and Thurnham using a horse and cart. Note the milk bottles that Charles is holding.

Photograph courtesy of Barbara Foster

Two vans were also used for delivery purposes and this photograph shows one of them parked outside the houses opposite Holy Cross church:

Photograph courtesy of Barbara Foster

When they first left school, the Foster children earned half a crown a week, with 'everything found'.[14] After a year, wages were increased. However, Wellington boots, shoes and overalls then had to be bought. When Ella was growing up, the people that lived in Bearsted were extremely good at looking after each other. Clothes and other items were always passed on to someone else if a use could be found for them. At the time of the Depression in the 1920s and 1930s many families in the village suffered hardship as jobs were particularly difficult to find and wages were low.

Milk deliveries were undertaken twice a day but the Fosters also undertook delivery work for other farmers and smallholders in the area. The farm records show that one regular client was Mr Hodges of Rosemount Dairy, who also grew some fruit. Charles Foster carted sieves of fruit for Mr Hodges to the railway station. 'A sieve' was an old Kent measure for forty eight pounds of fruit. This was not an unusual arrangement as many of the small dairy farmers in the area grew, delivered and sold fruit and vegetables. Some of the land around the Mission Hut and in Chapel Lane was cultivated as a market garden by the Foster family. Rhubarb was regularly sold to the army barracks in Maidstone.

Work on the farm was always physically demanding but it seemed worse in bad weather. Picking sprouts and harvesting swedes just before Christmas in very heavy frost aggravated chilblains. Scratches and nicks to hands and arms were not helped by trimming the very cold vegetables after they were harvested and before they were delivered.

Sandy Mount farm also had a large flock of chickens. Ella quite liked collecting the eggs to sell. On cold mornings the chickens were warm from their roost in the hen house so she ran her hands through their feathers to warm her fingers.

Sometimes bullocks were sent from the farm to market in Maidstone. They went on cattle trucks that were housed in the goods yard at Bearsted station. It was always a treat to see the stationmaster greeting the trains looking smartly turned out. He wore a suit and tie, a white shirt, a hat and carried a rolled umbrella. There were two porters at the station that worked alternate duties. The porters were in charge of the goods yard. The goods train was known as 'the shunter' and moved freight trucks back to the yard.

Before the Second World War a lot of businessmen commuted to London from Bearsted. They made a fine sight as they waited for the London-bound trains with their furled umbrellas, smart suits and copies of The Times newspaper. When war was declared in 1939, the numbers of men that commuted quickly diminished as they either volunteered or were enlisted.

Charles and Rose Foster ran the farm for many years before deciding to reduce some of the holdings. Part of the farm was sold on 24 January 1944. The front page of the sale catalogue is shown below:

SANDY MOUNT. BEARSTED

NEAR MAIDSTONE, CLOSE TO RAILWAY STATION.

CATALOGUE OF THE WHOLE OF THE ALIVE AND DEAD

Dairy Farming Stock

INCLUDING

67 Head of Horned Stock

comprising Valuable Home bred Dairy Herd of 38 Young Cows, 10 In-calf Heifers, 12 Yearling Heifers, 5 Weanyer Calves, and 2 Pedigree Shorthorn Dairy Bulls,

THREE UPSTANDING CART GELDINGS AND A PONY

THE DEAD STOCK includes

Two Motor Delivery Vans, Ton Lorry, Fordson Tractor (October, 1942),

Paraffin and other Tanks and Troughs, Two Waggons, Bavin Tugs, 3 Dung Carts, 3 Spring Vans, Governess Car, TROLLEY ON PNEUMATICS, 6 Quoiler. Chain and Plough Harnesses, Pair Balloon-tyred Wheels for Fordson, Plain & Cambridge Rolls, MASSEY HARRIS 13-SHARE DRILL, a 7-share Drill, 3 Mowing Machines, 2 Horse Rakes, Swathe Turner, 3 Hay Sweeps, Hay Grab, Martin's Cultivator, Harrows, Ploughs, Brakes, Stack and Waggon Cloths, Chaff Cutter, 2 Root Mills, Ladders, Wheelbarrows, Fruit Scales, 55 Cow Chains, STERILISING CHEST, VERTICAL STEAM BOILER, Galvanized Wash-up Bins, the usual Small Tools and Effects ;

WHICH

Messrs

E. J. PARKER & SONS

Are instructed by Mr. Chas. Foster (who is relinquishing business) to Sell by Auction,

On Monday, 24th January, 1944

Commencing at 11 o'clock.

Catalogues Price 2d. each (proceeds to the R.A.F. Pilots' and Crews' Fund)

Auctioneers' Offices : **8 Pudding Lane**, Maidstone Tel. 2264/5

Reproduced courtesy of Barbara Foster

After Charles' death, Rose stayed on at the farm, assisted by Eric and his wife, Barbara. They decided to build the farm and stock up once more from what was left after the 1944 sale. They began with a few house cows and a smallholding and after a great deal of very hard work, expanded the holdings.

Captain Lichfield had a house-cow for Snowfield which he kept in a field at the top of Hog Hill for many years. The Foster family milked the cow for him. Ella remembered that when she was small, she had been told that over fifty years previously, there had once been a windmill at the top of a high field on the Snowfield estate. This area is now called Windmill Heights.

On some of the land at Sandy Mount, a Mission Hut had been erected by the Vicar of Thurnham before the First World War. It was used until just after the Second World War when it was closed because of the amalgamation of Bearsted and Thurnham ecclesiastical parishes. The Foster family used the building as a barn in which to store hay. The Mission Hut still had a bell on the roof but before it could be decided what to do about it, it was stolen. Curiously, a bell that Captain Lichfield owned, and which was mounted on one of the outbuildings at Snowfield, also vanished the same night!

In the mid 1960s Barbara and Eric Foster made the difficult decision to sell the farm and the land for development as housing. There were many matters to be considered. There were diminishing financial returns from the farm but an equally big factor was that the changing nature of the village now made dairy-farming difficult. Many of the small pockets of pasture around the village were now sold and built upon as Bearsted expanded. An increasing volume of traffic made it difficult to walk the cows to milking twice a day. Many commuters were not pleased with manure on the road and delays due to cattle sharing part of their route to the railway station.

As the village changed, it rapidly became uneconomic for a small farm to continue. The land and farmhouse were sold. During the sale negotiations, it was understood that the farmhouse would be demolished and all of the land used for housing. However, once the sale had been completed, the developers decided to retain the farmhouse and this was bought and renovated by the site foreman. His family added the porch at the front of the house that can be seen today. The rest of the land was used for a housing development called 'Sandy Mount'.

This photograph of Ware Street and Sandy Mount was taken around 1967. The white marker posts used by the building company to indicate levels are visible towards the middle of the picture, right hand side:

Photograph courtesy of Norah Giles

5 Home Remedies for Livestock

These remedies were found in a small paper-bound book of receipts once kept at Sandy Mount farm by Charles and Rose Foster. The contents include horse cures, treatments and other information copied from unknown sources, but none of the information is dated. However, it is likely that it was compiled before the First World War. The recipes give an indication of the type of knowledge that was needed by a farmer to treat animals before the advent of effective veterinary medicine.

These are two pages from the book:

Reproduced courtesy of Barbara Foster

The modern reader would have great difficulty in obtaining some of the ingredients but the recipes should not be attempted in any circumstances. All the spelling and grammar is taken from the original recipes.

Cholic or Other pains in horses

½ oz Laudanum
2 oz Anniseed
1 oz Garlick
1 oz Sweet Spirits Nitre

Boiled in a quart of ale and it will in half an hour give relief.

Salve for bite on the eyelid on any other wound in a horse

2 spoonfulls of Honey
4 oz of Mutton Suet
2 teaspoonfulls of Tar
2 oz Frankincense
One pennyworth of Beeswax & Turpentine

Simmer all together to salve. Keep it close and when you use it warm it up. Dress once a day.

Milk Fever in Cows

Mr George Etherington of West Ayrton near Scarborough who cured his cow twice when dangerously ill of milk fever says that any person may avail themsalves of the remedy if they have a cow or cows with the same complaint viz:

7lbs of treacle made into a liquid state by adding a pint of water. Then after giving that, immediately give a gill of brandy best. Five or six hours after repeat the dose. Repeat the dose by giving another dose 7lb mixed with half a gill of brandy. 12 hours after this give ½ lb of yeast if required - that is, if she does not appear better.

For a horse with a bad cold

Take 2 Eggs put into half a pint Vinegar.
Bind them down for 48 hours from the air.

After that, beat the eggs well up with the same vinegar with 2 tablespoonfulls of honey and mix them together. Give each morning fasting an hour, after give him a bran mash and half a pint linseed: boil them in 2 pints of water, mix them well together put in the manger boiling hot.

How to make ointment to cure scab in sheep

4 lbs Hogslard
1 tb Quicksilver
½ pint Oil Turpentine
½ lb Venice Turpentine
2 oz Black Brimstone

Well beat in a mortar, till the quicksilver is quite killed and then it will be fit for use.
N.B. This ointment will keep the fly from sheep.

Foot rot in sheep

1 oz Oil Turpentine
1 oz Spirits of Wine
1 oz Salmoniac
1 oz Tincture of Myrrh
¼ pint best Vinegar

Dress twice a day, omit on the third day, once.

Recipe for weeds in garden walks

1 lb of Arsenic to 5 galls water
Pour on boiling hot.

This undated photograph is of a very fine dairy bull once owned by the Foster family:

Photograph courtesy of Barbara Foster

Purge for Cow

One ounce of Aloes
One ounce of Ginger
12 - 16 ounces of Salts in three pints of warm thin gruel, well shaken

Ewes with staggers have congestion of blood in the brain and should be purged gently and a daily small dose of nitre and salts given. First give a fifth of the above dose for Cow then fifteen grains nitre and one drachm salts for a week

Cow Pox

In a quart bottle mix half a ounce of boracic acid, half a drachm of alum and two ounces of glycerine, filling up with rain water. Warm this on the hob and dip the teats for two or three minutes after milking. Drain but do not wipe dry.

Pigs not Thriving

Give seven grains of santomine, one grain of calomel as a powder Mix with a handful of wet thirds after a part of twenty four hours. An hour later give a mash of their usual meal with half an ounce of castor oil for each.

For the cough

Give five drops of Oil Cloves and five of Turpentine in two teaspoonfuls of Linseed Oil three nights a week. This will have to be drenched if they don't have it in there food.

Milk Making Tonic

2 oz Nitrate of Potash & Ginger,
Fenugreek, Cummin, Anniseed, Fennel, Caraways, of each 1 oz
4 oz Salts

All to be given in warm gruel ale or cider three times a week. Give when milk fails to come or a Cow falls off when she ought not to. Give alternate nights in large doses or daily in half the quantities.

This undated photograph shows Charles Foster, paused in his dairy work, holding a milk can:

Photograph courtesy of Barbara Foster

Rooks in Corn and Seed

For 8 Bushells of Wheat or 6 Bushells of Barley take ½ Pint of gas tar, 2 lbs of Blue Vitrol and 2 Galls of boiling water. The tar should be accurately measured and should be of the consistency of treacle after the tar is put into the pail.

1 gall of water should be poured upon it and well stirred. The black greasy scum which will rise to the surface should be skimmed off with a wisp of straw or a piece of sacking to which it will readily adhere.

While this operation is going on another man should be mixing the vitrol with the other gallon of water. When ready both should be mixed together and poured over the heap of corn previously shot on the floor. The heap should be turned over 2 or 3 times quickly so as to saturate the whole. If any tar or dregs remain at the bottom of the pail they should not be poured on the grain or it will stick together in lumps and be likely to clog the drill cups.

'I have used this dressing for several years with complete success'
James Howard, Bedfords Rise

Selling a Poor one in good Condition

Do not force the pace. Most graziers Profit by a preliminary Ball of Aloes and it pays for itself in getting rid of worms and preparing the digestive organs for better work.

It is a slow and sure road that leads to good muscle and vigorous wind and heart.

Cow Itching Tail

Mix an ounce of sulphur with an ounce of spirit of Tar and 12 oz of lard and dress once a week.

6 Thurnham and Bearsted in the early years
of the Twentieth Century

Through her early years, employment and married life, Winifred Guest has lived in houses situated in Bearsted, Thurnham, Otham and latterly, Willington Street. These are her memories of the area in the early years of the Twentieth century.

Winifred was born in 1912. Her parents were Walter and Rose (née Robinson). Walter's family came from Swanley, Kent. Rose's mother came from Cornwall but Rose was born at Sandway, Lenham. Walter and Rose lived at Thurnham Court Cottages, located near the entrance to Lushington Court.

This photograph of Winifred with her siblings was taken just before the end of the First World War:

Photograph courtesy of Winifred Harris (née Guest)

<u>Left to right</u>: Robert, Winifred, Alfred, Walter and Lucy

Walter Guest worked at Thurnham Court Farm looking after the horses on the estate. The family's cottage was tied to the estate so during the First World War, when he was in the army, they moved to Vicarage Cottages. Rose took part-time jobs to assist the family income. At one time this included helping to clean Thurnham School. Wherever the family lived, they certainly grew enough vegetables for the whole year round.

This photograph was taken of Walter Guest around 1916. Note the spurs that he is wearing. Part of his army duties involved looking after the horses in and around the battlefields in France.

Photograph courtesy of Winifred Harris

Winifred recalled that when the First World War ended, there were no big celebrations. Everyone in her family felt a huge relief that it was all over and that her father would be returning home. The idea of peace just dawned on them gradually. After Walter returned from the war, he was offered his old job back and so the family returned to Thurnham Court Cottages and later moved to Keepers Cottages in Thurnham Lane. Eventually when Walter retired, he moved with Rose to Golf View Cottages in Ware Street.

Rose also worked for the Hampson family and the vicar of Thurnham, Mr Wigan. Both families had a big staff of servants. There many affluent families in Bearsted and Thurnham that needed domestic help. In return, the natural order of things seemed to be that the gentry were, as the local expression said, 'good to other people', in times of illness and bereavement. Mrs Lushington and Mrs Fletcher were regular visitors. Sometimes the assistance included supplementing a limited diet and income with cans of home made soup and other groceries.

Most girls that were old enough to go to school wore white pinafores edged with frills. It was hoped that these would protect the dresses worn underneath. As the pinafores were quite deep the girls used to turn up the lower edge to make 'pockets' for carrying items that they found. Occasionally, Winifred would pick frogs up in her pinafore if she spotted them hopping in the road by her house. The frogs nearly always made marks and a mess on her pinafore: to the marked displeasure of her mother!

Winifred was baptised and confirmed at St Mary's church. The village nurse, Sophia Birch was her godmother as she was a good friend to Walter and Rose. This is Winifred's baptism certificate:

Reproduced courtesy of Winifred Harris

Sundays began by attending the morning service at church dressed in best clothes. Before Sunday lunch, Winifred changed into ordinary clothes for a short while before putting her best clothes back on to attend Sunday School in the afternoon. This was either held in the Vicarage or the Mission Room in Ware Street. If Sunday School was held in the Mission Room the vicar's daughter, Miss Wigan, used to take some of the children in her car which they called 'the Crystal Palace' as it had large windows. After Sunday School there was a short break for afternoon tea before attending Evensong in the church.

All the local girls tried to live what was known as a 'clean life' as they grew up, following exhortations from the Vicar and other people that they respected in the community. As St Faith's Home for Unmarried Mothers was in Bearsted, all the girls were aware of the consequences of straying away from this ideal. Many local girls thought that the 'St Faith's girls', as they were called, always looked rather sad.

Sometimes in the summer, Winifred's family would go out for a walk in the early evening. There seemed so much to see and do in a walk along the Pilgrims Way as there was an abundance of flowers and wildlife. Winifred remembered banks carpeted with primroses in spring. Some of the flowers were picked for posies and distributed at a special Mothering Sunday service in church during Lent.

Like many other children in the village, Winifred spent a great deal of her time helping her mother in the routine of the week. Each day was allotted one particular task. Monday was washday and kept her mother busy all day. Cardboard and paper was used to start the fire to heat the water in the copper. Tuesday was baking day and meals were cooked using a small oven by the side of the fireplace.

Shopping was usually done by Winifred's mother on Saturdays but lots of tradesmen called at the house during the week. All the shops had half-day closing on Wednesdays. The family bought groceries from Holly House Stores in The Street which was run by Mr Bates, and later by Mr Eversden.

Bread came from the bakery by the Green run by Mr Rowland. Winifred particularly remembered that the bakery sold delicious hot cross buns on Good Friday. The shop opened for a couple of hours for this purpose and then closed, like the rest of the shops on this day. Winifred knew, long before the shop was open, that the buns were being cooked as the smell drifted up Thurnham Lane!

Coal was obtained from Marshall and Naylor who were also corn and seed merchants and whose business had an office in The Street. A horse-drawn wagon made the coal delivery before the company had a lorry. Logs for the fires were obtained from the estate and her family regularly went 'wooding' to collect branches and twigs to put on the fire. Mr Moss supplied meat for their family and milk came from Thurnham Court Farm.

One place Winifred loved visiting was Thurnham Mill in Otham Lane to see the wheat being ground into flour. There were usually two or three men assisting the operations at the water mill which was well known for being a dusty place. Winifred used to like listening to the sound of the millstones grinding. The flour was usually bagged up in massive sacks at the mill, so it was bought from Holly House Stores where it was available in smaller packets instead.

In the evening, the family would gather round the dining table. The room was lit by a large oil lamp with a beautiful glass globe. Mending was regularly completed by this illumination and sometimes games of cards such as whist and rummy were played. It was not until the 1920s that some of the village houses had a gas supply. Lighting the gas lamps without singeing the mantle could be a tricky business. Further supplies of mantels were obtained from 'the Gas House' which was situated on the right hand side of Musket Lane where it left the Ashford Road on the left hand side, just before a turning to Hollingbourne. Today this is on the A20 Ashford Road just beyond the Maple Leaf garage.

As Winfred was growing up, walking was the most usual means of travelling. A return journey of six miles was not considered to be a long distance on foot. Walking into Maidstone from Yeoman Lane along the Ashford Road involved passing endless hop gardens and arable fields. Before the 1920s Winifred could not recall passing any houses on the Ashford Road on the way into Maidstone.

Winifred and her friends spent a great deal of their spare time playing out of doors 'on the Downs'. Their activities included small camp fires on which they tried cooking leftovers of food that were not required by the rest of their families. Winifred recalled that her family referred to their house being located 'just up under the hill' in Thurnham Lane. As it was very quiet, with little or no traffic, she could hear her mother call her in for dinner.

This undated postcard from the early years of the Twentieth century shows the view that could be gained from the hill above the Black Horse public house.

Photograph courtesy of Terry Clarke

During every season, there were regular activities that provided a useful supplement to the family's diet. In the spring and summer, watercress was gathered. It grew in the abundant and clear local water supply. Winifred recalled that it was delicious in sandwiches and salads. Wild strawberries were also picked but it needed a great many of the tiny berries to make a decent mouthful! In the autumn blackberrying and nutting were popular pastimes. Near Thurnham Castle was an enormous sweet chestnut tree which grew magnificent nuts.

As a child, Winifred thought that Friningham, one of the most northern parts of Thurnham, was the highest spot on the Downs. It seemed quite distant to Thurnham Lane and on a very clear day Winifred believed that you could almost see over to France.

When snow fell, it was usually in great quantities so there were endless opportunities to play in it. Winifred loved the challenge of tobogganing down as much of Thurnham Hill as was possible. If the toboggan overturned it was usually into a further pile of snow, which always seemed soft and deep.

Winifred left school when she was fourteen and went straight into service. Girls sought employment in a 'situation', a process that was known locally as 'My First Place'. Winifred's 'First Place' involved looking after Mrs Palmer's two children in a house by Bearsted Green called Fairview, near to the White Horse. This was followed by a situation in a household which included looking after the children of Mr and Mrs Batchelor who lived in a house just beyond Fancy Row Cottages in Thurnham Lane. Robert Batchelor was a timber merchant. Winifred later looked after some children for Mrs Hanbury, who lived at Mote House by Holy Cross church.

Winifred's next position was working for Mrs Tasker at Danefield where the family had moved after selling Snowfield to Baroness Orczy. Mrs Tasker was very kind to her. Initially she just did housework and then became a parlour maid. She loved learning how to set a table appropriately and wait on people properly. In the morning, Winifred wore either a blue or grey dress covered by a big white apron that almost enveloped her, with cross-over straps at the back and strings which tied into a big bow. In the afternoon she had to wear a black dress, a white apron and a white frilly cap.

Winifred married her first husband, Alfred Smith, in 1934 and so had to give up work. However, Mrs Tasker lent them her personal chauffeur and car for the wedding at St Mary's church. This picture was taken at the wedding:

Photograph courtesy of Winifred Harris

Mildred Sierakowski

Mildred Sierakowski (née Higgins) recorded her memories in 1989. Many of her recollections were about Bearsted village green and convey a good picture of everyday life in the early 1900s:

When I was a child there seemed very little need to hurry. Wagons and carts went at a leisurely pace up and down the lanes in and around Bearsted and Thurnham which were always thick with mud during the bad weather.

During my lifetime, a great many of the same houses remain in Bearsted, but some in the lower part of The Street have been replaced. I believe the three oldest are the Bell House, the Old Manor House and the one at Roundwell called Wright's Cottage. It was well known that the Old Manor House had about twelve bedrooms, twelve downstairs rooms, but no bathroom or indoor sanitation and only oil or candle lights. Later, it was divided into several smaller houses to make homes for several families.

Sunday was not a 'Day of Rest' for people who looked after farms or horses. The children did not spend much time resting either! We assembled at the school at 10am and went to our individual Sunday School classes. We had to know the Collect for the Day by heart and by the time we arrived at the top class, we had to be able to recite the Gospel. At 10.45am we marched up to the church for Mattins. We sat at the back of the north aisle and were nicely hidden away from the main body of the church. Some of the congregation still paid for the pew in which they regularly sat. It was a long service often including the Litany, which was intoned, and a lengthy sermon. The little ones left before the sermon, but the older children stayed until 12.30. Then we had another service at 3pm. The annual Sunday School treats consisted of a tea with games and races in Church Field in the summer.

We had a very energetic Lay Reader who ran a Guild on Monday evenings and a Band of Hope on Wednesdays. After he had given a talk we used to sing and provide our own entertainment. In later years a group called the Kings Messengers was started which was run by Margaret Blamire Brown. We all made garments, including the boys who knitted items such as socks for poor people. During this part of the meeting a book would be read by the leader, and the meeting finished with prayers and a hymn.

A Bible Class was held for teenage boys at a private house in Church Lane for some years. Confirmations were held every three years in Bearsted, and in alternate years at Thurnham and Boxley.

When King Edward VII was crowned we had a tea on the Green and were given Coronation Mugs as souvenirs. The prizes for the races were 3d, 2d and 1d.

Games for children were according to the season. In winter, we favoured hoops. They were made out of iron for the boys and wooden ones were used by girls. Other pastimes were skipping tops, hop-scotch, tag, and hide and seek. All kinds of ball games and cricket were played by the men and boys in the village. Boxes on four wheels were among the most popular of boys' possessions. They used to sit on the front with a guiding line to the two front wheels. Few people had bicycles, and very few children had such a luxury. 'Marl carts' were used to transport babies in the village rather than prams. Older children sat back to back in the seat part, and the cart had a long handle.

A Nursing Association was formed and a District Nurse was installed. She helped the doctors considerably as people often called in the Nurse for a minor illness. In fact, she became a friend of the whole population, which of course was not very large, and she always seemed available. In the case of an illness or childbirth, there was always someone who had a little knowledge to help out. Few people sent for a doctor and there was not one in the village. However, there was a doctor nearby in Hollingbourne. He sometimes left bottles of medicine in the Post Office for patients to collect. There was also a doctor who came from Maidstone either on horseback or by bicycle.

Mrs Tasker came to the school on Mondays at noon to collect payments for a Coal and Clothing Club which paid out at Christmas. The payments were usually 3d or 6d a time. She also organized a play every year for the children. That was a great event as we all hoped to be picked for a part. It was performed in the White Horse Hall or Men's Institute. Some of the older people ran Penny Readings at the Men's Institute with singing and short plays, and we often had artistes from Maidstone and Hollingbourne. Some of the men in the Church Choir took part. One of our greatest enjoyments was the musical evenings, when friends came to our house and we gathered round the piano to sing and play different instruments, and have light refreshments.

Very few people had holidays, and if they did, they went to relatives who were able to offer hospitality. In the summer, we were lucky enough to go to Hastings each year as an aunt had a boarding house on the sea front. One of our greatest pleasures though was a picnic. We would travel by brake or some other conveyance to Rochester Gardens, Boxley, Kings Wood or up to the hills. Only a few people in the village were sufficiently wealthy to own a Victoria or Landau carriage. The gentlemen were driven to their business in Maidstone, and were fetched at night. Their lady wives used the carriage to pay calls in the afternoon.

As there was no street lighting everyone carried lanterns lit by a candle, and lamps and candles were used in every home. The oil man who came round selling oil and candles every week did a very good trade. The Post Office was in a little front room in one of the cottages opposite the Royal Oak. The front room also functioned as a little shop that sold sundries, and was run by Mrs Potter.

Wages were quite low: a head gardener received about £1 per week, and farm labourers earned twelve to eighteen shillings according to their abilities. The usual clothing for farm workers included a waistcoat and corded trousers tied with string below the knee. Lots of men mended their own boots. No one wore shoes and every pair of boots had one inch soles with hobnails for everyday use as the roads were always dirty. Wellingtons had not been heard of and overcoats had to be worn if it was wet as mackintoshes were not easily available. Mr Bickerfield, who was a tailor, lived in the village street. He made cassocks for the choir and suits for anyone who could afford one. He was a popular little man and his work was marvellous.

A man called Hughie Hopkinson lived in Church Lane. This undated postcard shows some houses in the vicinity of his shop:

Photograph courtesy of Roger Vidler

Violet Hale (née Pollard) recalled that her father's family lived in one of the neighbouring houses, to the right in the picture. These were later demolished. Today, the Dolphin House occupies part of the site. One large stone remains which is now by the front drive.

Hughie Hopkinson was a very small man. He mended bicycles, prams and shoes. He was also interested in photography and took many local pictures. He was a great attraction to the children and his dark little shop was always cluttered with bicycles and spare parts. As some of the parts had to be cleaned with special bicycle oil, there was a quite unique smell in the shop.

One local visitor who employed Hughie to look at his motorcycle was a gentleman who was known only as 'Smiler'. He used to come to the village to sell ice-cream. He had a motorbike with containers on the side which held ice packed around the ice-cream to keep it cool. It tasted rather like thick custard but was very popular with everyone. During the summer, he often visited the village twice a day.

Mildred had one other abiding memory of Bearsted from her childhood: a pile of quarry stones always stood at the corner of the Green at the bottom of Church Lane. A man called 'a stone cracker' used to break up the stones into small pieces. A steam engine operated by another man came round at periods and the small stones were used to mend the roads.

This undated photograph shows a cow being driven up Church Lane. Note the pile of broken stone for road mending and repairs on the left hand side:

Photograph courtesy of Tony and Sheila Foster

7 John Perrin's enterprise: the shops at Chestnut Place

John Perrin's business as a shopkeeper had already been established for some years before he built and opened some shops at Chestnut Place in 1882. He was listed in a trade directory for 1878 as a shopkeeper. Below is an account for mourning clothes. As the bill heading shows, by 1881 John was already advertising his business:

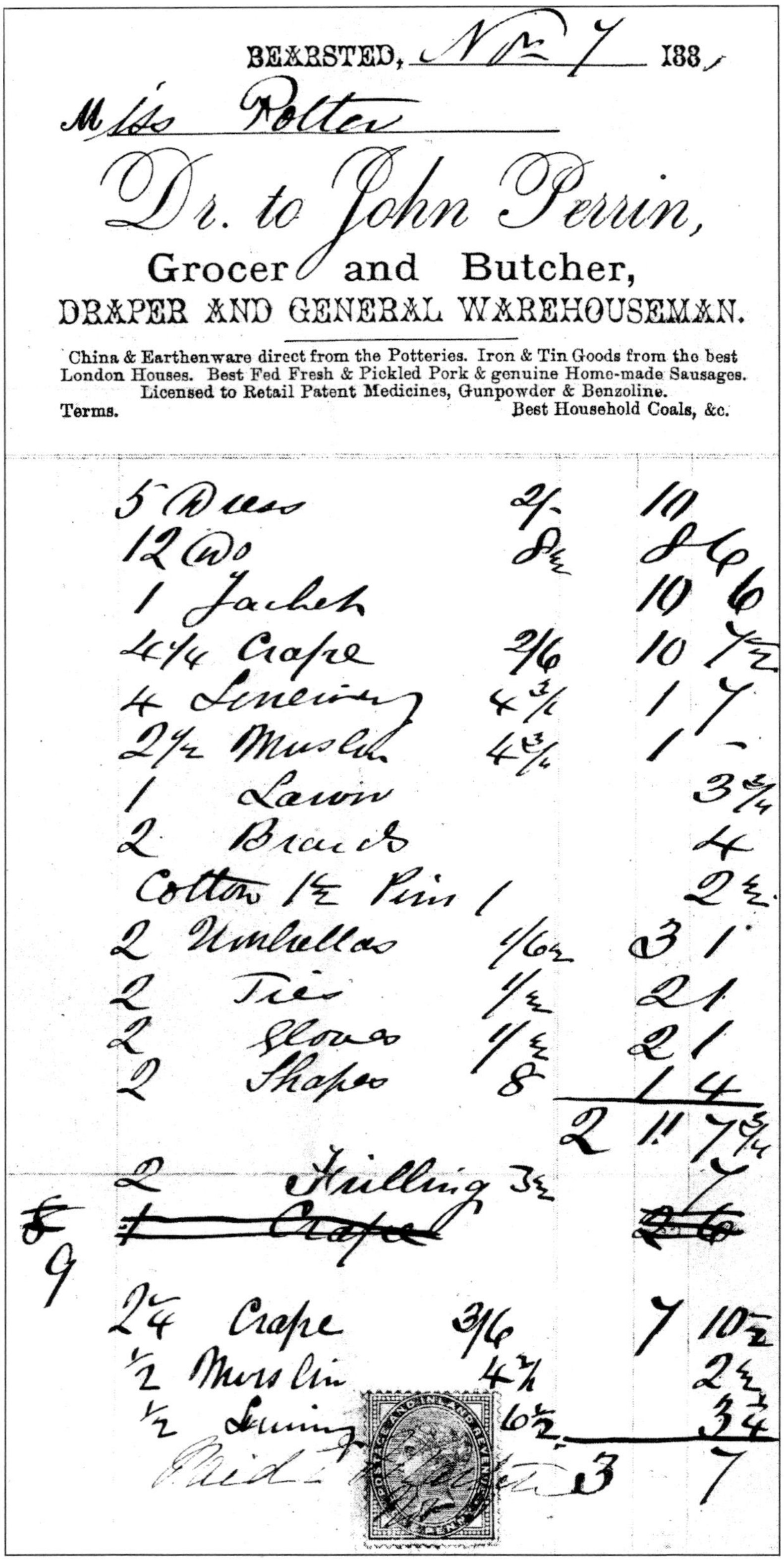

BEARSTED, Nov 7 1881

Miss Potter

Dr. to John Perrin,

Grocer and Butcher,

DRAPER AND GENERAL WAREHOUSEMAN.

China & Earthenware direct from the Potteries. Iron & Tin Goods from the best London Houses. Best Fed Fresh & Pickled Pork & genuine Home-made Sausages. Licensed to Retail Patent Medicines, Gunpowder & Benzoline.

Terms. Best Household Coals, &c.

5 Dress	2/-	10	
12 do	8½	8	6
1 Jacket		10	6
4¼ Crape	2/6	10	7½
4 Lining	4¾	1	7
2½ Muslin	4¾	1	-
1 Lawn			3¾
2 Braids			4
Cotton 1½ Pins 1			2½
2 Umbrellas	1/6½	3	1
2 Ties	1/½	2	1
2 Gloves	1/½	2	1
2 Shapes	8	1	4
	2	11	7¾
2 Frilling	3½		7
~~1 Crape~~			~~2 6~~
2¼ Crape	3/6	7	10½
½ Muslin	4¾		2½
½ Lining	6½		3¼
	3	7	

Paid

Reproduced courtesy of Joy Hope

The shops gained the name Chestnut Place from a very large chestnut tree that stood for many years in the road outside As this undated photograph shows, there was an upper storey to the building in which were accommodated some of the Perrin family and shop staff:

Photograph courtesy of Margaret Morris

For the first time in Bearsted, a butcher, a grocer, a small haberdashery, a Post Office and a general store were in all in one location. Customers were also able to order coal and other fuels. In bad weather, there was the convenience of an external canopy under which customers could shelter.

This undated photograph shows some of the staff outside the shop. Note the large lamp for illumination which was hung on one of the horizontal canopy supports:

Photograph courtesy of Roy Datson

During the first decade of trading, John Perrin developed a jam factory behind the shop. The older children in the village often picked fruit and collected used jam jars to sell to Mr Perrin. Both fruit and jam jars were stored in a separate building alongside the shops. Some residents regarded the processes involved in making the jam as a nuisance. The staff at Bearsted School, which was adjacent to the jam factory premises, regularly wrote entries in the log book which recorded that smoke and pungent odours had intruded into the classrooms and impeded the lessons. It was a common occurrence for some of the jam to run down The Street; small children delighted to dip their fingers into it as they played in the road!

On 13 January 1900, there was an extensive fire at the shops The Kent Fire Office Brigade was summoned at 5.30am and thirty local people assisted them in pumping water whilst they were in attendance. The brigade spent eleven hours at the premises but the house, shop and store were gutted.[1, 2] The lower side of Bearsted School sustained considerable damage as the western window, the roof, the school bell housing and the two front windows were burned. Although the school re-opened as usual on the following Monday, it was closed for a week in February whilst repairs were effected. This is a transcript of the report in *Kent Messenger and Gravesend Telegraph and Dartford News,* 20 January 1900:

DISASTROUS FIRE AT BEARSTED
JAM FACTORY AND SHOPS DESTROYED

Early on Saturday morning a fire occurred at the extensive premises of Mr J Perrin at Bearsted. The establishment, which was well known in the district, consisted of three large shops, with post office, jam factory and store-room, and the whole premises have been burnt to the ground.

It appears that about half-past four a.m. one of the domestic servants in the upper rooms was awakened by a strong smell of smoke, and Mr Perrin and the household being aroused, it was found that the ceiling of the store-room over the drapery department was on fire, and the rafters were extensively burnt. The shop assistants and other helpers used their utmost endeavours to prevent the fire spreading to other parts of the premises, but their efforts proved futile. The flames spread with alarming rapidity, in consequence of the inflammable nature of the stock-in-trade and the large quantity of woodwork used in the construction of the buildings. The boot and provision departments were quickly enveloped in flames, and after the roofs fell with a tremendous crash the central and outer wall gave way. Amid the fierce roar and crackling of the fire, numerous tins of meat etc., in the grocery shop went off with sharp reports resembling small explosions. The cellars contained a large quantity of bacon, lard, etc., and this as well as a big stock of calico, was destroyed. The old jam factory was soon attacked and tons of jam and marmalade in bottles and nearly all of the appliances were utterly destroyed. The residents in the neighbourhood rendered every assistance possible, and a portion of the household furniture, a valuable piano, and the books were saved, although those who rescued the latter did so with hands muffled in towels. Two horses in the stables got out early, without sustaining any injury. As soon as possible too, a messenger was dispatched for the Kent Office Fire Brigade but by the time of their arrival, under Capt. Oates, the fire had obtained such a hold on the main premises that their efforts were largely directed to the saving of adjoining property. In this they were to a large degree successful, the National School escaping with comparatively little damage, while a new building recently erected by Mr Perrin for the requirements of his growing business was also saved, together with boilers, coppers and other machinery. A plentiful supply of water was obtained from the pond on the Green.

So great was the heat from the fire, that the paint on the White Horse Inn, which is on the opposite side of the road, was much blistered. The origin of the fire is unknown. The damage which is estimated at about £5,000 is covered by insurance in the Kent Fire Office. A temporary shop and postal office has been opened in the Village Hall, where Mr Perrin is carrying on his business for the present. It is gratifying to know that the new and commodious buildings at the west end of the scene of the conflagration escaped destruction, as here Mr Perrin will be able to continue the manufacture of Kentish fruit jam, which has secured such a good reputation.

Rarely has the village had such a concourse of visitors as on Sunday. It was a fine day, and all roads leading to Bearsted were crowded, especially during the afternoon with people all going to the scene of the disaster.

Reproduced courtesy of Kent Messenger group

Despite the fire damage, John Perrin and the shop staff were able to salvage some of the stock and with a touch of empire spirit, immediately continued trading from the village hall before later moving to a marquee pitched in the front garden of his house, The Limes, which was by the Green.[3] The shops were rebuilt but the insurance company funds only extended to payment for a single storey building with a flat roof.

This photograph, taken in 1900,[4] shows the temporary shop arrangements:

Photograph courtesy of the Centre for Kentish Studies

John Perrin (senior) had a large family and two of his sons, John and Sydney carried on the business when he retired. John, known to some as 'young John', took over the butchery and grocery shops and Sydney took over the drapery, Post Office and hardware departments.

When the younger John Perrin emigrated to Canada, Sydney took over control of his brother's share of the business. This did not include the butcher's shop which was bought by Mr Ovenden. It was subsequently owned by Mr W J Moss and Mr John Wood. Sydney Perrin did not prosper as a grocer and in 1915 was declared bankrupt. The grocery shop was sold. Nevertheless, some of the Perrin family continued to trade as coal merchants for many years.

John Brook, together with his wife, Lucy, and baby daughter, Jessie, moved into a house by the Green in 1915. John was known as 'Harry'. It was a quiet start to taking over the largest grocery shop in the area as he had just agreed to buy Sidney's Perrin's business. Lucy Brook was in charge of the drapery section. It was the beginning of one family's connection with the community which lasted nearly fifty seven years.

These advertisements, from 1929, appeared in the parish magazine:

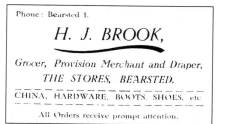

Reproduced courtesy of Jenni Hudson

Residents of Bearsted that used the shop will recall the pervading smell! It included a curious amalgam of varnish from the shop fittings, cheese, bacon, vinegar, tea, coffee and even the odd touch of shoe polish. Rosemary Arbiter (née Brook) recalled that the walls were lined with wooden, glass-fronted, drawers containing supplies of flour, tea, coffee and sugar. These goods were weighed out and measured before being placed into bags made of brown paper or blue sugar paper. Ella Cardwell used to love visiting the shop as a child because the purchasing power of a farthing was quite phenomenal. Huge bags of broken biscuits were always good value. This photograph shows the interior of the shop around 1930. The layout of the shop continued virtually unchanged for many years:

Photograph courtesy of Jessie Page (née Brook)

This undated picture shows the staff outside the grocery shop. Harry is in the middle at the back.

Photograph courtesy of Jessie Page

Harry occasionally kept geese on the Green which were later sold to Mr Moss the butcher. The geese were very clever: at 4pm they always visited the shop. Mrs Dibble did not like them though and used to brandish her umbrella as they hissed at her! This picture, which was taken in April 1933, shows the geese in Thurnham Lane on their journey. Note the charabanc in the background by the White Horse and the adjacent two-storey stable building. There was a riding school behind the White Horse which was owned for a time by Mildred Bennett.

Photograph courtesy of Jessie Page

It was due to Harry's encouragement, that Edward Taylor, usually known as Ted, began a newsagency. Shortly after the First World War, Edward was working as gardener at the vicarage. He had noticed that there were many business men in Bearsted that commuted to London with nothing to read on the trains.

Edward took over a section of the Brooks premises in 1927 to develop his business. He introduced new lines such as photographic postcards of the village and this grew into a stationery department. A small lending library was set up and this was followed by a toy section was very popular with children. Roger Vidler could remember a good stock of Meccano kits which were particularly desirable to small boys at Christmas. This advertisement, which dates from 1929, appeared in the parish magazine:

Reproduced courtesy of Jenni Hudson

At the time of his death in 1935, Harry was assisted in the shop by his wife and Jessie. Jessie married John Page and ran the shop as a joint venture with Lucy before eventually inheriting it.

Jessie and John retired from the business when John became unwell at the beginning of the 1970s. The shop closed in 1972. By this time the property was owned by the Batchelor family. For a brief time, Joan Harden ran an outlet for feather dusters and "floral" decorations made of feathers from a small section of the shop. The grocery premises were then re-modelled as a mini-supermarket which was run by William Dyer. However, less than two months after re-opening, a fire caused extensive damage as the press cutting overleaf shows. Once more the shops were repaired.

Mr Norman Rickwood then traded from the premises and his business included a butchery, delicatessen, a cheesemonger and bakery. The current owners are the family of Mr William Crouch, following his untimely death in February 2005.

This photograph accompanied the fire report in the Gazette newspaper, 2 May 1972. It shows papers being removed from the Post Office during the blaze:

Photograph courtesy of Kent Messenger group

This is a transcript of the newspaper report:

Blaze destroys old shops

A FIREMAN suffered a heart attack whilst trying to save two of Bearsted's oldest shops which were gutted in a £25,000 blaze on Friday morning.

The fire was spotted just before 7am by newsagent Mr Donald Taylor, as he prepared the early morning rounds. He saw smoke coming from the roof over the four single storey shops just off Bearsted Green, known as Chestnut Place. At first he thought it was a chimney, but as smoke began pouring out, he gave the alarm.

Four fire engines from Larkfield and Maidstone were on the scene within minutes. Three hours later, as a crowd of villagers looked on the blackened shells of the shops, things took another dramatic turn as Retained Sub Officer Jim Homewood of Maidstone staggered into the road. He had been in the thick of it, and it was thought he had been overcome by smoke. But as oxygen was given, and his condition worsened, he was taken by ambulance to West Kent Hospital, where it was found that the 46 year old officer had suffered a heart attack. Mr Homewood, who is married and lives at Sutton Road, Maidstone, was said yesterday to be 'satisfactory'. The cause of the fire remained a mystery and the figure of £25,000 is the first unofficial estimate.

Landlords of the shops are Batchelor and Sons of Thurnham Lane, Bearsted. The two shops, gutted were the butchers, Mr John Woods, who had £400 worth of meat roasted to a turn and the grocers run by Mr William Dyer, which had been open for only two months. Bearsted Post Office looked after by Mr and Mrs William Harris and Taylor's, the newsagents, were not destroyed, but there is extensive smoke and water damage.

Chestnut Place was rebuilt in 1901, following a fire one year before. The original shops, which included a butcher and stores, were put up in 1882. Mr Donald Taylor described what had happened: 'It was lucky that I was there, sorting out the newspaper rounds. No-one lives in, and most of the shopkeepers didn't know about the fire until they got here and saw the damage with their own eyes. I saw the smoke coming from the roof some minutes before I realised that it was billowing out too thickly to be a chimney – you just don't think a thing like that could actually happen'. Mr Taylor's mother supplied 26 cups of tea for firemen, when the danger was over, and villagers rallied around to help the shopkeepers out. By yesterday, they were hoping to start trading again on a limited basis, in a few days time.

Reproduced courtesy of Kent Messenger group

Throughout the period of rebuilding after the fire, Edward Taylor was able to continue trading, assisted by his son, Donald. Edward then retired and Donald took over from his father. He retired in 1990 and sold the newsagents to Ronald Fullex who continues to trade from the same premises.

This picture and report appeared in a local newspaper. Donald is on the left, handing over the keys and accounts to Ronald, watched by Edward:

Photograph courtesy of Kent Messenger group

Change in Store

AN ERA came to an end when the Taylor family gave up their newsagency in Bearsted. The shop had been in the family since 1927 when Edward Taylor, now 88, took it over as general store. The newsagent in Bearsted Green was later taken over by his son Donald, 57, but he too has now retired.

Taylor's had to be re-built in 1972, after being badly damaged in a fire.

Donald Taylor said: 'I have been here all my working life, apart from two years' national service, which totals more than 40 years. Obviously a lot has happened in that time. 'It is going to be strange without the shop. I think I will just have a rest for a while and then decide what I want to do from there.'

Reproduced courtesy of Kent Messenger group

Although it is not clear when the Post Office opened at Chestnut Place, this was the location recorded in a trade directory in 1899.[5] The Post Office was certainly included in the sale of the premises to Harry Brook in 1915 following Sydney Perrin's bankruptcy.[6]

George Willson was listed in 1825 as a Receiving Post Master for Bearsted and Thurnham, but there are no further details. The first Post Office for Bearsted and Thurnham was a Penny Post Receiving House which opened in 1837.[7]

A special handstamp was used in Maidstone for the Penny Post and each village had a different numbered mark enclosed in a rectangular frame.[8] These two illustrations show the Maidstone stamp and a village mark, but it is not known if the mark is that for Bearsted:

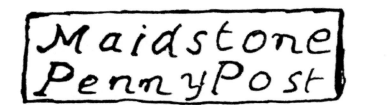 

Reproduced courtesy of The Postal History Society

In 1840 a national Penny Post was introduced. This led to an increased use and range of postal services. As a result, better accommodation and separate counters to transact postal business became essential. In many villages, the shopkeeper who also acted as the Post Master was replaced by a permanent Post Office premises and a full time Post Master.[9]

There have been several locations for the Post Office in Bearsted, including the Royal Oak and Egypt House. John Copping was recorded as Post Master in a trade directory for 1855[10] before the business was classed as a rural sub-office in 1864.[11]

After Harry Brook, people that subsequently ran the Post Office include the Farmer family and the Cook family who were followed by Bill and Joyce Harris. Bill ran the branch for twenty six years. It was then taken over by Bill's family, with John and Marion Thompson succeeding to the business around 1990. The Post Office occupied the back of the premises, whilst the rest of the floor space was used to sell small hardware items.

The Bearsted Green branch, as it became known, continued to trade up until 11 November 2004 when it was closed by the Post Office in a re-organisation of local outlets. This included the closure of other branches at Roseacre Stores and Downswood. A vigorous campaign of widespread opposition was mounted by residents to save all three branches but it was unsuccessful. John and Marion Thompson were the last Post Masters at Bearsted Green and ended a tradition of over 145 years. This photograph of John and Marion was taken inside the premises on the day of closure. They are holding an engraving which was an impression of the original premises.

Photograph courtesy of Roger Vidler

The Post Office continues to trade in the area, but in a new location at Cavendish Way adjacent to the Ashford Road. The branch shares floor space with the Spar Shop premises and Paydens chemists.

8 A Crotal Bell: land holdings and local farming practises

In September 2003, at a meeting of the North Downs Young Archaeologists Club, Sian Jossi showed what she had found on the allotment cultivated by her family in Bearsted: a small metal bell. It is a little larger, but of a similar design and shape, to those worn by cats. It is not known what metal was used to make the bell but there is a small amount of verdigris evident on the surface, so perhaps some copper had been included. The picture below shows the bell with a £2 coin to indicate the scale:

Photograph courtesy of Malcolm Kersey

Andrew Richardson, the Kent County Council Finds Liaison Officer was at the meeting. He recorded and identified the find as a 'crotal' bell. The bell provides valuable evidence and a glimpse into evidence of farming practised around Bearsted and Thurnham.

Crotal bells are believed to have been used between the Fifteenth and Nineteenth centuries in animal husbandry. Each bell had a loop so that a leather thong could be laced through it and tied round the neck of the animal. In England, animals wore bells because livestock was valuable. Before land started to be enclosed, sheep and cattle were mainly kept and grazed on open fields and land that had no fences. If an animal wore a bell around its neck, it could be located from the sound made. It is thought that they could also have been used as good luck charms and to attract attention during activities such as dancing. To this day, Morris dancers sometimes wear a similar sort of bell on their costumes.

The allotment where the bell was found is situated on the north side of The Street, just over a hundred metres from the Royal Oak public house. Although unable to obtain a precise date for the bell, using records held at the Centre for Kentish Studies and the Saddlers Company,[1] it has been possible to assemble the following history of this area of land.

On 20 December 1645, Edward Hill, citizen and saddler of London, made his will.[2] He belonged to the Saddlers Company which was founded around 1362 as a livery company of the City of London. Separate companies regulated trades and crafts in the city. The word 'livery' probably comes from the word 'delivery'. Entrance to the Company was by an apprenticeship during which a trade was learned. At the end of the apprenticeship, freedom of the city of London was claimed, allowing a former apprentice to serve under any master or work on an independent basis.

The Saddlers Company had a governing body called a Court which was run by a Master, Wardens and Assistants. The members of the company included apprentices and journeymen. The latter were craftsmen who had served an apprenticeship but had yet to obtain the freedom of the City of London. Full members of the Company were freemen of the city and liverymen.[3]

Although it is not clear if Edward was a liveryman, he stipulated in his will that his wife, Martha, would hold an interest in some land held in Bearsted and Boxley. After her death, the land should pass to a relative called Stephen Marsh on one condition. Out of the rents and profits of the land, every year at Christmas, Stephen was to give and deliver four gowns to the Master, Wardens and Assistants of the Art or Mystery[4] of the Company of Saddlers. The cloth for the garments was to cost eight shillings a yard. Four pairs of shoes and stockings were also to be purchased, to the value of twenty pence, and presented. These items were to be bestowed upon four poor, decayed men who were free members of the Worshipful Company of Saddlers. Two men were to be saddlers by trade and two to be harness makers.

The will also stated that if Stephen Marsh died before Martha, or if there were no children, the land was to pass to the Company of Saddlers. It was stipulated that the clothing was still to be given to other poor and decayed men that were to attend Saddlers Hall for the bequest. Edward died shortly after making his will as it was proved in the Prerogative Court of Canterbury on 29 October 1646.

The land eventually passed to the Saddlers Company and there are records of leases granted to local people. The first of these names Thomas Burr of Bearsted, cordwainer,[5] who was granted a lease for the house and lands for twenty years from Lady Day 1666 at £10 per annum.

In September the Great Fire of London destroyed the Company's Hall. The Company urgently needed to raise money for rebuilding and so sent two members of their Court to Bearsted to dispose of the estate or at least re-negotiate the terms of the lease for an increased sum.[6] There is no surviving record to indicate whether the Company's men were successful in their endeavours, but it is possible that as the lease had only been signed a few months previously, they did not proceed with a re-negotiation.

Another lease was granted on 12 July 1687 to John Ravell and Alice, his wife, of Maidstone. John Ravell was succeeded by Francis Curtis and John Coveny, although the precise dates are not recorded.

The counterpart of a lease between the Saddlers Company and David Humphreys, citizen and saddler, dated 20 October 1742, gives a very full description of the premises:

> …and all Barns, Stables, Orchards, Gardens &c. with their appurtenances and all those closes, pieces or parcels of land meadow or pasture ground containing together by estimate, 10 acres more or less with the appurts. thereunto belonging situate in the said parish of Bersted.[7]

The lease included a house with two dwellings, hop garden and lodge, stable, barn, and lodge. The boundaries were lands specified as owned by the Widow Mills, Richard Iden, James Houlship, Thomas Simonson and John Allen.

On 7 May 1782, a lease was granted to Clement Taylor for twenty one years. In 1802 he was succeeded by William Richards of Bearsted, who was a blacksmith. One year later, the Company granted:[8]

> Cash allowed to Mr Richards, the Company's tenant at Bearsted, toward repairs: £10 10s.

When the tithe map for Bearsted was compiled in 1842,[9] the land and property was leased from the Saddlers Company by John Jenner, who was also a blacksmith. By this time at least part of the holding was called Banky field but this was some distance from the forge or 'smithy' which was by the house and garden. John's main trade was shoeing horses but he would also have undertaken larger tasks such as repairing ploughshares. John may have used Banky field to pasture a small flock of sheep.

The later history of the forge remains slightly unclear. In 1851 John Jenner was recorded there in the census returns but by 1861 it was held by Charles Burbridge who employed one worker and one boy.[10] Rather confusingly, Thomas Diprose is also listed on the census return as a wheelwright and blacksmith in the same area of The Street. There was some overlapping of the two trades but the majority of Thomas' living would have been earned as a wheelwright.

At Michaelmas in 1862, John Larking commenced a twenty one year lease of the land holdings which included the forge.[11] However, John was a farmer, and so sub-let the forge. In 1871 George Morgan was recorded as a smith and farrier working there.[12] In 1876 the forge passed to John Wood and then to his son, also called John Wood.[13] In 1920 Charles Tester took over the premises.

This photograph shows the forge and farmhouse around 1900. The forge is on the left hand side. The building on the right hand side of the photograph is now Donn's greengrocery and flower shop:[14]

Photograph courtesy of the Centre for Kentish Studies

Although the precise date is not known, at some time after 1900, the forge was re-located from its original site to behind the farmhouse building. The original forge site was then used by Mr Fremlin to establish premises for the Men's Institute, which opened in 1906. At this time the farmhouse was also renovated and became divided into three cottages which are now known as Forge Cottages.[15]

This undated photograph shows the Men's Institute on the left hand side and the cottages fashioned from the renovated farmhouse which are in the middle of the picture:

Photograph courtesy of Jean Jones

The tithe map, and other early maps, show that the surrounding area to Banky field was used for arable farming and included orchards. It was a common local practice for farmers to pasture sheep underneath the trees in the orchards as it meant a greater economic use of the land: two products rather than one. Until the last decade of the Twentieth century, sheep regularly grazed under the apple trees in orchards around Bearsted and Thurnham. It is therefore possible that at one time Banky field was used in this way. In all probability the animals were wearing bells made by a local blacksmith.

There is difficulty in tracing part of the history of the land because some of the Saddlers Company records were destroyed in enemy action during the Second World War. However gaps in the records can be augmented by documents in the Centre for Kentish Studies.

Since 1783, the Watts family of Thurnham had shared an interest in the land near to Mallings Lane. As described in a previous chapter, other areas owned by the family included Sandy Mount, the Herst lands and a butcher's shop in The Street. The land passed to Ann Armstrong. Shortly before her death in 1843, the tithe map and schedule was completed and recorded it as farmed by George Betts.[16] By 1858, the remaining members of Ann's family decided to sell it. The sale particulars describe it as occupied by Mr John Dawson, who was paying an annual rental of £35.[17] The purchaser of the land is not known.

In August 1897, the Finance Estates and General Purposes Committee of the Saddlers Company received an offer for the lease of their remaining property from Henry J Knowles.[18] Henry was the landlord of the White Horse Inn.[19] Whilst Henry's offer was being considered, in September, the Company's surveyors declined another offer of £750 from Mr Brewer of Maidstone. The Company granted the committee authority to negotiate the lease or sale of the estate if the terms were satisfactory and provided not less than £1,000 could be realized from the sale.[20]

By July the following year, terms for sale were agreed: £1,000 for the freehold but complete possession would not to be granted until any growing fruit was cleared and sold. From the specific details concerning fruit, it is evident the land was still being used as an orchard. It is likely that there was a fruit auction. Such auctions were usual farming practice and persisted in the surrounding areas to within the last decade of the Twentieth century. The land was sold on 29 September 1898 to Mr Colgate of Windlesham, Surrey.[21] He probably leased it to a local person.

In 1918 it was recorded in the log book of Bearsted School that the owner of the corner of land by Mallings Lane, had generously allowed boys to start gardening lessons on part of it.[22] This undated photograph was taken during such a lesson in the school plot. The Headmaster, Frank Goodman, is towards the middle of the photograph:

Photograph courtesy of Tony and Sheila Foster

In 1927 a section was sold to Maidstone Rural District Council which built eight semi-detached houses opposite Oliver's Cottages in The Street. The local name for the area became 'Pollards Hill' after a family that lived in one of the new houses. Behind the houses, land was still used for allotment gardens. Lessons for the children were relocated to the garden attached to the school.[23]

In 1929 the remaining corner of the land bordering The Street and Mallings Lane was sold. Valued at £120, the area measured just over three acres.[24]

The sketch below, which is not to scale, shows that the land on the corner of Mallings Lane had been sold. The allotment gardens were now in two separate pieces. The first extended from behind Eden Cottage to South View in The Street. A track which ran between South View and the council houses was the boundary. The second area was behind the council houses and extended up to the railway line and across to Mallings Lane.

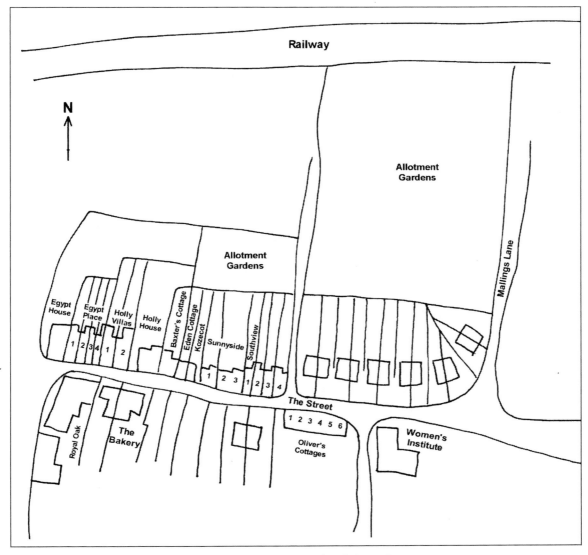

Diagram by Kathryn Kersey based on Ordnance Survey

A further set of records shed some light on the subsequent history of the land. Before 1966, part of the land behind the smaller area of allotment gardens was used to build a bungalow called Paignton. The bungalow was rented by Harry and Eileen Howard. Eileen was Captain of the 1st Bearsted Girl Guide Company and she used the substantial area of land around the bungalow for camping activities.

In July 1966 Bearsted Parish Council wrote to the Kent Association of Parish Councils concerning pressure placed on them from Maidstone Rural District Council to sell land used as parish allotments for housing.[25] The reply has not survived.

Shortly afterwards the parish council decided to sell the land used for allotments behind the council houses, which bordered onto Mallings Lane. However, approval had to be obtained from the Rural District Council and the Ministry of Agriculture, Fisheries and Food, before the sale could go ahead. The Ministry would not give consent until it was proved that an alternative allotment site was available.

By March 1968[26] the parish council was in negotiations with Mrs M Wright, who now owned the land by Paignton to provide the alternative site.[27] Permission was obtained by the parish council for a change of use to allotments, after two hundred and twenty six years as an orchard. On 12 August 1968, the purchase of the land was completed at cost of £2,500 plus surveyor and legal fees.[28]

The parish council experienced some trouble selling the land by Mallings Lane. The value was assessed at £37,500[29] and the Rural District Council expressed an interest. However, shortly before the sale was due to be completed, the purchaser withdrew.[30] Instead, an auction was held on 15 January 1970 at the Royal Star Hotel, Maidstone by Messrs Walter and Forknall. It was purchased by TBC Developments Limited which was part of the Tilbury Construction Group.[31]

In order to allow the allotment holders time to remove crops and equipment, the parish council agreed to clear the land before the purchaser took possession. Messrs Turton and Blackford of Oak Meadow, Hollingbourne, undertook the work and charged £145.[32] A letter to the contractor concerning access, lists some of the last holders of these allotments:[33]

Mrs S Pellett	Mr R Rose
Mr L Dowding	Mr W B Thompson
Mr E M Harden	

Houses were built on the left hand side of Mallings Lane and these were followed by further developments creating Fremlins Road and Mallings Drive.

This sketch below is based on an Ordnance Survey map shows the changed land use, but is not to scale:

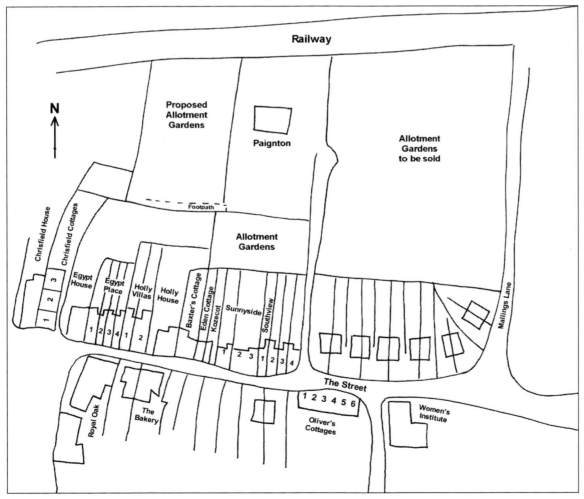

Diagram by Kathryn Kersey based on Ordnance Survey

The parish council arranged to clear the land to provide sixteen allotments. The two allotment pieces were to be linked with a short footpath. J Belsom and Sons, based at Howt Green, Bobbing, near Sittingbourne, supplied chestnut fencing at 12s 6d a yard, and a gate complete with a galvanized locking bar. The final account totalled £63 11s 3d. It was settled on 30 September 1969.[34]

A list of original allotment holders also survives:[35]

Allotment	Name of Holder	Allotment	Name of Holder
42	Mr Fagg	50	Mr Clark
43	Mr Beavis	51	Mr T Smith
44	Mr Selwood	52	Mr Marshall
45	Mr Hathaway	53	Mr Bassett
46	Mrs Behan	54	Mr Richardson
47	Mr Yorke	55	Mr Thomas
48	Mr Fourie	56	Mr Ibbs *(? Name unclear)*
49	Mr Hunt	57	*Name unclear*

The allotments continue to be cultivated and are a valued asset to the parish. In 1645, when Edward Hill signed his will, he could not have foreseen the consequences of his charitable intentions: to this day there is still an area of land in Bearsted used for the benefit of the community.

9   The Village Blacksmiths:
Charles Tester and Eustace Thwaites

As Robin Martin grew up, he often stood at the door of the village forge to watch the sparks that flew as Charlie Tester worked at his anvil. Some thirty years later, Robin became very closely involved with him when he asked for tuition and help in shoeing a horse. By that time Charlie was seventy three years old. Robin later recorded these memories and passed them to his niece, Rosemary Pearce:

It was 1946, and about ten months after the war in Europe had ended. Beer was in very short supply. Across the road from the forge was a club where Charlie liked to have a break from the heat of the forge and a drink. However, he frequently went across the road only to return disappointed that no beer was available. Clement Attlee's Labour government was in power at the time and came in for much criticism from Charlie, who would often mutter, 'Bloody old Labour government. How do they expect hard-working blacksmiths to labour over the hot hearth without any beer to quench their thirsts?' One morning, after looking outside and up and down the village street, he came back into the forge with a smile on his face. He said to me, 'The relief column has arrived. The brewer's dray is up at the White Horse. We shall be all right for a glass of beer today.'

Charlie was a very fine and skilled craftsman, and could tackle any job that came to him. His anvil weighed 364lbs, and it was his proud boast that he could pick up it from its block and place it on the floor unaided. It was no small feat for an elderly man.

On my first day at the forge, I was handed an old leather apron to wear. It was fringed along the edges and split up the centre. In the few weeks I was able to spend with him he taught me many useful things and the proper way to handle tools. He also had a good sense of humour and enjoyed music. Together, we would often sing while we worked away on the anvils: real 'harmonious' smiths. Once while I was tapping away, he said to me, 'You are playing a fine tune on the anvil.'

This is one of Charles' certificates to show that he was a competent blacksmith and farrier:

Reproduced courtesy of Bearsted and District Local History Society

Charlie told me this rhyme:

Up high and down low
Up fast and down slow

It was an easy way of remembering how to achieve the best efficiency from the forge fire. It refers to the handle of the bellows. 'Up high' meant to completely refill the bellows with air, and 'down low' to get the full use of the air contained in the bellows. 'Up fast' because the action had no useful effect on the fire, and 'down slow' to give long and steady blasts of air to blow the fire hot.

He was keen to stress how necessary it is for a smith to be strong and quick. He pointed out that once the hot iron had left the fire, it must be dealt with quickly on the anvil with true and strong blows. It is no use getting the iron onto the anvil and thinking of what to do with it, as it cools quickly. The blacksmith should know exactly what to do with the iron whilst it was still in the fire. Then he went on to say, that it is easy to see why so many of the old prize fighters had been smiths. They were able to move fast and knew how to direct blows with their hands.

This undated photograph shows a working day at the rear of the forge. Charlie Tester is standing next to the horse, wearing a leather apron:

Photograph courtesy of Bearsted and District Local History Society

When Charlie was younger, a journeyman who was really a gypsy came to the back of the forge and started to take some of the old iron scrap lying there. Now, what sometimes looks like rusty old iron is never regarded as rubbish by a blacksmith. Often the exact piece can be found there to complete a job, after fashioning it on the anvil. His boss told him to go and tip the gypsy's bag out. The gypsy struck him, knocking him down. A violent battle then followed which Charlie eventually won. He concluded by saying that he had to be very quick and strong to beat the gypsy as the chap could certainly fight.

Years before, Baroness Orczy, the famous authoress, had lived in the village. In her heyday she had kept a carriage with three horses which she drove abreast. Charlie said her horses were lovely creatures, soft and gentle, and would lick the neck of the farrier while the fore hooves were being clinched[1] and the shoeing finished. However, there was one mare which was so nervous that she had to be roped and thrown and then shod whilst lying on the floor of the forge. This was during the time that Charlie was employed and before he took over the forge.[2]

One day, the Baroness brought the nervous mare to be shod. Charlie asked his boss, John Wood (the younger), if he could try to shoe the mare without throwing her. He said that he had noticed that the trouble all started when the farrier tried to take the mare's hind hooves back behind her. He wanted to try to shoeing with her hoof under her belly. John reluctantly agreed to let him try. So, stooping under the mare's belly with her hind hoof on his lap, Charlie managed to take off the old shoe, prepare the hoof and then nail on the new shoe. It was an awkward task because he had to drive the nails upwards. All the work had to be done more by feel than sight. However, he managed to complete the task and the Baroness was delighted. After the operation was completed, she thanked him and said how pleased she was with Charlie's work. She placed a coin in his hand and when he looked down into his palm, he found that she had given him a golden sovereign.

Another morning, a young farmer came into the forge with a badly-twisted length of steel from a tractor-drawn plough. He said that he had struck a tree root and if he had been using horses, they would have stopped. The tractor had just gone on and caused the damage. He asked if Charlie would do the job quickly, so that he could get back to work. Charlie took on the job and heated up the steel. He eyed it carefully and with a few deft strokes of his hammer, he straightened out the bar and set it aside to cool. After some ten minutes, Charlie told the farmer that he could now take it. The young man picked it up with an old piece of sacking and asked Charlie how much he owed for the job. Charlie replied, 'Seven shillings and sixpence.' The young man objected to the price. He said that it was too expensive as it had not taken Charlie long to do it. Charlie told him then that it had taken him many years to learn his skills. He ended the disagreement by saying, 'Try it for yourself and see how long it takes you.' Even in those days, seven shillings and sixpence was not an exorbitant sum to ask for such a skilled man's work.

On another occasion, a bank manager's wife came in with a garden watering can which had sprung a leak. Such items were in very short supply. Charlie told the lady he would do what he could, and then when she had gone, he turned to me and said, 'What does she think we are? Tinkers?' However, he managed to stop the leak with a tube of cold solder which could be bought in Woolworths, so he kept the lady happy.

This account from 1926 was signed by Charlie's daughter, Blanche. It shows some typical work that was undertaken:

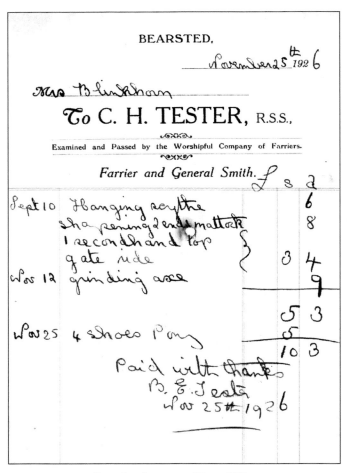

Reproduced courtesy of Roger Vidler

Charlie knew all the horses in the area and at times when work was not pressing we would make up sets of shoes for the various farm and riding horses which were soon to be due for shoeing. There were plough horses, hunters, hacks and vanners[3] as well as children's ponies. In his head, Charlie carried all the knowledge of their sizes and peculiarities of shape that he needed.

I learnt to make a set of shoes, stamp out the nail holes, shape the foreshoes to be quite round and the hind shoes to be more of a diamond shape. The outer branches were always shaped slightly longer than the inner branches in exactly the way that horses' hooves grow. I prided myself, that, under Charlie's guidance and tuition, I could, in a few weeks, knock out a set of hunter shoes in twenty minutes. He once said to me, 'Robin, you would make a capital smith' and I felt quite proud!

All around the village was evidence of Charlie's skill that lives on today. Perhaps his most accomplished work was a beautiful pair of wrought iron gates that he had made and erected at the Crismill estate – about a mile from the village centre. Charlie told me that he quite often went for a walk at weekends when the weather was favourable and he would eye his pair of gates at Crismill and would say to himself, 'You didn't do a bad job when you made those gates, Charlie.'

This photograph, taken around 1925, shows Charles Tester with his wife, Jane and their daughter Blanche:

Photograph courtesy of Norah Giles

One day I had to help him weld two lengths of 1¼ inch round bar together. We carefully prepared each end that was to be welded. First Charlie thickened them and then he shaped them so that each had a small projection which could fit one against the other. Charlie showed me what I had to do with one piece and he marked with chalk just where I had to place it on the anvil. I had to get around the anvil, so my route was cleared of any obstruction. Then both ends were blown hot in the fire until they were white-hot and the temperature needed to fuse both pieces together. Then he shouted, 'Right', and I quickly nipped around the anvil and placed my section the right way up between the chalk marks. At the same time Charlie brought his section on to mine while both pieces were sparkling hot. He struck with his hammer and fused them both together. "Let go," he cried to me, and I stepped back while with several deft strokes with his hammer, and several turns of the bar the two pieces were perfectly welded together. It was now impossible to see the join.

On another occasion, he told me that Mr Betts' horse, Duke, was coming to be shod. Duke had the most perfect hooves and so he would let me drive some nails to fit the new shoes. Where the sensitive and non-sensitive laminae of the horse's hooves meet it forms a white line. The line is known as the 'farrier's guide'. If the nail is driven into the white line, and then outwards, into the hard, horny, non-sensitive part of the hoof, it does not hurt the horse. To do this, one must listen carefully to the sound made by the hammer on the nail. When the nail is first driven into the white line, the sound made is a soft, dull thud. Then as the tip of the nail meets the hard outer hoof, it rings with a metallic sound, pitching even higher until it pierces the outer wall. So long as the hard ringing sound is heard, it is safe to hammer the nails.

Duke arrived at the forge, and it was obvious that the horse was a great favourite of Charlie's, as he welcomed him with a pat on the neck and the words, 'Hallo, Duke, my friend, how are you?' Then we got to work. I was allowed to remove the old shoes and do some of the preparation work with the rasp. At last came the nailing on of the shoes. I was given careful instruction and under the keen scrutiny of my teacher, I nailed on the fore shoe. Duke was a lovely big shire horse and, as Charlie had told me, did have the most perfect hooves. Duke was a perfect gentleman, or as I have recently heard the Irish say of their good horses, 'a real Christian.'

At the back of the forge was a small recess covered by overhanging eaves. Here, Charlie told me, he had done his fire-watching while air-raids took place during the war. He used to stand in the recess and smoke his pipe, which he held upside down in his mouth so that no German airmen would be able to see the glow of the burning tobacco. Shrapnel from the anti-aircraft guns sometimes came down, so the recess gave a slight protection.

One evening, during the war, he was on duty, watching, during a heavy raid. Bombs fell and the anti-aircraft guns were firing. It was very noisy and shrapnel rained down so that it felt like all hell was let loose. He said that then he must have fallen asleep, for some hours later he awoke and found himself lying in beautiful and peaceful calm. All the stars were shining brightly. He felt sure that he must have been killed and was up in heaven. Then as he lay there, he gradually began to recognise the roofs of the surrounding houses and began to realise that he was still on earth. He got up rather stiffly and walked into his house, where he found Jane, his wife, asleep in a chair, and the evacuee child that they had taken in, asleep under the table. They were hard times for people in the war: they had to work all day and then do fire-watching at night. It was everyone's duty in the village to do fire-watching on their own property.

I had intended to pursue a job in schooling and dealing in horses, but it was not to be, and I followed a police career abroad. Charlie retired, sold his business, and settled down to a quiet life of pottering around, giving a hand to the new owner of the forge on odd occasions and tending his fruit and vegetable garden. Years of peering into the flames to observe the degree of heat and the state of any metal in the fire took its toll on Charlie's eyes and steadily his sight began to deteriorate. Now, of course, welders all use dark screens to protect their eyes. In his younger days, no-one had ever advised Charlie of the dangers. It was all taken as part of the hazards of the job that he loved.

Each time I came home on leave, I made a determined effort to visit Charlie. We would retire to the local public house, the Royal Oak, and have a drink or two. We would chat over past and current affairs. He told me how bad his eyesight had become, but never in a self-pitying way, as he treated this loss as an inevitable joke that the Lord had played on him. Telling me of his efforts to plant cabbages he said, 'I am now a useless old fool. I dib a hole for the cabbage plant, pick up a plant, but then cannot find the hole. I have to feel around with my fingers to find the whereabouts of it'. Then he would soundly laugh at what he had become, with never a grumble that his work had caused his loss of sight. He once had said to me while we were working in the forge that he thought perhaps God had made a mistake and we should have been born old and grow young. 'Look at me now,' he would say, 'I've learned a lot of things and am now a really useful chap, but I'm getting ready to die.'

At ninety three years of age, Charlie was not ill but completely worn out. He took to his bed and refused to get up. After a couple of days, he died. He was satisfied that he had spent a useful life, always dealt fairly with people, and had no debts. When I think of Charles Tester, I recall the words from the poem The Village Blacksmith:

> He looked the whole world in the face
> For he owed not any man.

Eustace Thwaites

By the time Mick Patterson began work, Charlie Tester had largely retired and the forge was run by Eustace Thwaites. Eustace had previously worked at Milgate as an electrical engineer. Mick started at the forge during his school holidays and also worked there on most Saturday mornings. He was still sometimes asked to assist his father who worked in Bill Moss's butcher shop when large orders were received. Mick enjoyed making sausages and chipolatas when required, but his friend Trevor Cleggett was the permanent Saturday morning lad.

This account shows work undertaken by Mr Thwaites:

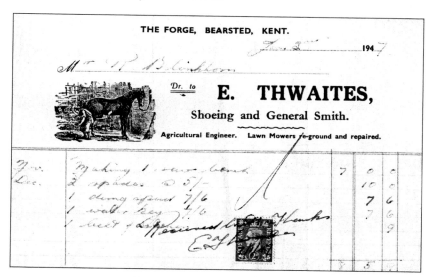

Reproduced courtesy of Roger Vidler

The first item Mick had to make at the forge was a set of tongs. He showed them to Charlie Tester. By this time Charlie was almost completely blind and could only assess the workmanship by touch. However he was quite impressed, saying that Mick had not made a bad job of them and rewarded him with sixpence. Mick's first duties included 'holding the fort' when his boss had a break at eleven o'clock at the nearby Men's Institute and undertaking small jobs on his own, such as drilling holes. One job that Mick did not appreciate was refilling the coal bunkers. This was important to the running of the forge but the coal dust easily spread everywhere and rendered nearby surfaces filthy.

Despite undertaking some very routine tasks, Mick was taught many aspects of the blacksmith trade. He enjoyed learning the craft of wrought iron work. The intricate skill was appreciated by customers who were prepared to pay a good price for hand crafted articles. Mick believes that much of what is called 'wrought iron work' for sale in shops today is factory made and not the first class craftsmanship of a forge.

Mick also met the challenge of learning the skills required for welding with a huge enthusiasm. However, he did not realise that his welding skills would largely provide his living in later life. Eustace normally asked Mick to do any welding jobs that arose and this included working for Lady Baillie at Leeds Castle. Other contracts included sharpening the shears and mowers for local farmers. The Burden family were regular customers. By this time there were four forges in the premises: two of which were back to back.

When Eustace Thwaites decided to give up the forge, he hoped that Mick would be able to take it over. However, Mick was only 19 and he estimated that the immediate costs of continuing the business would be around £1,000. It was a sum which far exceeded his resources. Mr Hooker bought it instead and Mick went to another post in Detling. He went on to work for other engineering companies before establishing his own company in 1981. The majority of his contracts now involve welding repairs to agricultural machinery.

Despite many commercial pressures, Mick's passion for undertaking wrought iron work and welding persist. Perhaps they can be regarded as his legacy from the last generation of blacksmiths at the forge.

Rosemary Pearce

10 Baroness Orczy in Bearsted

Baroness Emmuska Orczy moved to Bearsted around 1908, although her autobiography does not give the specific date. By this time, she had already written The Scarlet Pimpernel; the work for which she is largely remembered. This formal photograph of the Baroness is undated, but was in wide circulation as a picture of a popular author:

Photograph courtesy of Bearsted Scout Group

The inspiration for The Scarlet Pimpernel came in the most unlikely of places: on a platform of Temple underground station. She was waiting for a train on a cold, foggy day when an image was conjured of Sir Percy Blakeney; including his superb attire, monocle and distinctive, drawling speech.[1]

The novel had been rejected by at least twelve publishers before she decided to convert it into a play. It was accepted for production by Fred Terry and Julia Neilson who were renowned performers in sword-and-cloak dramas. Fred, the younger brother of Ellen Terry, produced and directed the play which opened at the Theatre Royal in Nottingham in 1903. Despite scathing comments from critics who intensely disliked the play, the production moved to the New Theatre, London in 1905. The Daily Mail theatre critic wrote:

> The Scarlet Pimpernel is a little flower that blossoms and dies in one day, which is the obvious fate of this play…

However, it had a great popular appeal and achieved phenomenal success. It ran for four years and broke many stage records. The production was revived many times over the next forty years. The story was also adapted into films starring Leslie Howard, David Niven and Anthony Andrews.

This photograph from 1911 shows Fred Terry and Julia Neilson in a scene from a stage version of The Scarlet Pimpernel:

Photograph courtesy of Roger Vidler

Emmuska Orczy was born in 1865 in Toarnoars, Hungary and was the surviving child of Baron Felix Orczy and his wife, Emma. In 1868 her father's attempt to introduce modern farming techniques caused their workers to revolt, burning crops and breaking machines. The Baron, who tended to avoid problems rather than confront them, never fully recovered from this blow and gave up tending the family estates.

The family began a nomadic existence. They first settled in Budapest, where the Baron was appointed Supreme Administrator of the National Theatre. Franz Liszt encouraged him to take up the post. After Budapest the family moved to Brussels, Paris, and then, in 1881, moved to London. While Emmuska did not inherit her father's skill as a musician, she enjoyed music and met a steady flow of artistes who frequented her parents' house.

In 1886 she began to study painting at the South Kensington School of Art. Emmuska developed the ability to see pictorially what she later attempted to describe with her pen. During this period she met, and in 1894 married her husband; Montague Barstow. He was an artist and they worked together on book and magazine illustrations. Their only child, John Montague Orczy Barstow, was born in 1899.

After moving from London in 1908, the Baroness and her husband first set up home at Cleave Court, on the Isle of Thanet. They then moved to Bearsted after buying the Snowfield estate from Henry Tasker, a director of the Kentish bank. He had decided that the estate was now too large for him and had built a new house, Danefield, in Church Lane.

Whilst the Snowfield estate was the size that the Baroness and her husband required, they considered the original house to be quite ugly. She commissioned the architect, Andrew Prentice to re-fashion the property. His efforts, assisted by Emmuska and Montague, resulted in the Queen Anne style façade that now adorns Snowfield.

This undated photograph shows the house before the renovation:[2]

Photograph courtesy of the Centre for Kentish Studies

This undated photograph gives some indication of the changes made by the Baroness:

Photograph courtesy of Roger Vidler

A studio was also built towards the north end of the garden. It is shown on the right of the photograph. The Baroness and her husband worked together there, although it is known that she sometimes also used the studio at Bell House.

The Baroness made a great impression on the local people as she drove about in her carriage. Due to her aristocratic upbringing she felt that she should be treated as the Lady of the Manor. She expected the little girls to curtsey and the small boys to raise or remove their caps as she passed. Ina Chester, whose family lived in White Lodge, recalled that the Orczy coach always had five horses; two 'wheelers' and three 'leaders'. A postillion sat behind the Baroness and sounded a long slender horn as they neared a corner or approached Snowfield. When it was heard, the domestic staff assembled in two lines in the hall, bowing as she entered the house. The horses were bred on a family farm in Hungary: they were supremely beautiful but very difficult to handle.

When Hetty Walkling (née Bromley) was fifteen, she took a serving post in the household. In 1987, she recalled some of her working environment:

> It was a lovely house, and had to be kept perfect. We only had brooms and brushes to work with, and all the polishing had to be done on our knees. When visitors were staying at the house, the coach and horses would be brought to the front door, and the visitors would be taken for a ride along the Pilgrims Way. There were four grey horses and one chestnut, three in front and two at the back You could hear the horn for miles.

An insight into the Baroness' view of her position in society is gained by a note in her autobiography that her nearest neighbours were the Pelham Warners. This referred to Plum Warner, who captained Middlesex and England, and who later became Chairman of Selectors. As he and his wife lived at Caring House, some two miles from Snowfield, it is evident that the Baroness held little regard for people who lived in between.

Ina Chester recalled that when she was aged twelve, she was unwell. During her recovery, the Baroness unexpectedly paid a visit. Although she had brought along an armful of books for Ina to read, they were all written by the Baroness. Later, to Ina's horror, she asked her many questions about the contents to check that she had read them properly!

This next photograph shows Baroness Orczy's coach and pair outside the White Horse in January 1910. The pub is decked out in election bunting in support of the successful Conservative and Unionist candidate, Colonel Warde, who held an election meeting in the village..

Photograph courtesy of Margaret Morris

During 1913 Bearsted was, like many other communities, divided by the increasingly militant campaign for women's suffrage. The Baroness held decided opinions about the Suffrage Movement; she felt she had no place in it, being content to wait until parliament conceded to a popular movement.[3]

However, whilst acknowledging that everyone had a right to free speech in a democratic country, there was one incident of protest which aroused her astonishment. As she recorded in her autobiography,[4] in May a cricket match was held between Bearsted and the Royal Marines depot. The Baroness planned a large tea party at Snowfield to mark the occasion. On the morning of the match the Green was speckled with small flags indicating that if there could be no votes for women, there would be no cricket for the village. Despite this, no further action materialised and the match went ahead as planned. The Baroness made widespread enquiries, but it was some time before she discovered that her secretary was a secret supporter of the suffrage movement and had been behind at least part of the protest.

Cricket was an important part of Emmuska's social calendar and like many others from the social elite, she took a tent at Maidstone Cricket week to entertain friends in 1914. This photograph was published in the Kent Messenger. It is possible that Baroness Orczy is seated by the notice at the front of the picture, but has turned away to speak to a friend:

Photograph courtesy of Kent Messenger group

In 1912 the Baroness became one of the founders of the scout troop in Bearsted. It was one of the earliest in the county and is named after her hero, the Scarlet Pimpernel. Montague Barstow painted the first Troop Flag which bears the device of a scarlet pimpernel flower. The Baroness took an immense interest in the Troop for the rest of her life, regularly communicating with the Secretary, Mr J L Ollett. She thought of herself as the Troop's godmother. Each year, she provided a signed copy of The Scarlet Pimpernel for the winner of a competition chosen by a committee from the Scout Troop.

This photograph shows the Troop displaying their flag and was taken in 1920:

Photograph courtesy of David and Theresa Elliott

This photograph shows an enrolment certificate for James Elliott who joined the Scout Troop on 24 July 1912. James later went on to become the Scout Leader. The certificate is an astonishingly rare survival.

Reproduced courtesy of David and Theresa Elliott

Jessie Page recalled that the troop used one of her father's storerooms for some of the first meetings. In 1953 the Scout Troop took possession of a new hut built on the Snowfield Estate. By this time the estate was owned by Captain John Litchfield, who performed the official opening on 25 July 1953. This photograph shows Captain Litchfield receiving the key from Wolf Cub Robert Whibbley:

Photograph courtesy of Bearsted Scout Group

After a move to The Glebe, and as Ian Lambert recalled, some meetings held in the Memorial Hall, the scouts now have premises in Church Landway. The site on which the Snowfield hut stood later became part of the Windmill Heights housing development. The original troop was later enlarged and Bearsted Scout Group now includes Beavers, Cubs, Scouts and Explorer sections. All members still wear the troop name of the Scarlet Pimpernel on their uniform. This photograph shows the badge that was designed and worn by the Scout Group in 1997 to commemorate its eighty fifth anniversary:

Photograph courtesy of Malcolm Kersey

On the declaration of war on 4 August 1914, life changed for the Baroness. Almost immediately, the horses in her stable were requisitioned by the Kent Yeomanry for use as chargers for the officers. She was glad to make a positive contribution to the war effort but missed her horses. For some months after their departure, she received letters from the officers and men giving her news of Goldie, Netti and Tatiana. The news became more scarce and then ceased.

Anti-German feeling was rife during the war. The local Member of Parliament, Colonel Warde, pressed for all Germans in England to be relocated on the West Coast. He envisaged that they would be detained in guarded localities until 'other arrangements' could be made. The Baroness must have known that she was regarded locally with a degree of suspicion and ambivalence due to her Hungarian ancestry. Ina Chester recalled that there were many rumours about the tennis court at Snowfield: it was viewed as being of an unnecessarily strong construction and suggestions circulated in the village that it may have been prepared as a gun emplacement.

It is rather ironic that Emmuska could hardly have been more patriotic; regarding all things English with a fervent and great reverence. On the outbreak of war she began an active participation in patriotic events and meetings. She later described that she was in constant demand at this time to address conferences, and give lectures. She also held teas for ladies desirous of making a suitable contribution towards the war, but who regarded organised work schemes as inappropriate.[5]

The Baroness is sometimes said to have been one of the founders of The White Feather Campaign. There is no evidence for her support of the Campaign: in a letter published in the Kent Messenger newspaper, she described the Campaign's activities as senseless. However, she used the opportunity to also promote the activities of an organisation she had set up; The Women of England's Active Service League. She went on to outline the aims of the League which included supporting all those men who signed up for service, their mothers and wives:

> …and not to make the life of the 'real shirker' (i.e. the man who is in every way free yet refuses to serve his King and country) any more pleasant for him by going out with him, and giving him the pleasure of their company at cinemas, theatres or other public places.[6]

Towards the end of the war, Emma Orczy, the Baroness' mother, felt that her presence as an 'alien enemy' was causing difficulties for her daughter in Bearsted. By June 1918, the government had begun to repatriate aliens who were not already interned and those who expressed a desire to return to their own country. Emma Orczy discovered that one of her friends was about to leave and after making some arrangements, together they departed to Switzerland.[7]

Following the armistice in November, there were further difficulties for the Baroness and her husband: the Hungarian economy collapsed and she lost her personal fortune. Montague developed health problems which were aggravated by the uncertainties of English weather. She sold Snowfield to Major Clarence Craig in 1919 and after a short stay in Little Snowfield, moved to Monte Carlo. Later she also acquired a villa in Italy, and for several of the inter-war years, she and Montague divided their time between Italy, Monaco and England. Following the outbreak of World War Two, the Baroness and her husband found themselves trapped in Monte Carlo. The state of Montague's health made it impossible for them to attempt one of the escape routes used by some English residents. Montague Barstow eventually died there in 1943.

At the end of the war, the Baroness returned to London where she died on 12 November 1947. She did not leave a will. Her remains were cremated and interred in Putney Vale Cemetery. However, many years before his death, Montague had made rather different arrangements for their last resting place. In 1913 he had reserved space in Holy Cross churchyard for four graves: for Emmuska, himself, and their two executors.[8] As Montague had died overseas, his remains were buried in Monte Carlo. It is not known whether their son, John, was aware of the plots in Bearsted churchyard when he arranged for his mother's ashes to be interred in Putney. It is entirely possible that he felt because many other writers and actors were buried there, Putney was more appropriate for his mother. Perhaps it was simply more convenient to visit her grave from his home in Kensington. John finally surrendered the burial plots in Bearsted in November 1948, nearly a year after his mother died.[9]

Emmuska Orczy's last few years were lonely and involved hardship of a kind she had not previously encountered. But if she had one consolation it was, perhaps, the words Arnold Bennett had spoken to her many years before:

> Don't be afraid about the future of your Scarlet Pimpernel. It will live because of its character long after far finer books have gone the way of oblivion.

Roger Vidler

11 The White and Sent families

The members of the White family can claim many extraordinary statistics. Over 181 years, eight generations led to thirty marriages with fifty nine descendants and eighty nine Christian names between them. Thirty five baptisms of those descendants have taken place in St Mary's church.

Amelia Hodges married Horace White at St Mary's church in October 1864. It was the start of a long connection with the church. Horace was born in 1841 and died in 1908. They lived in Ware Street and he worked as a builder.

One of Horace and Amelia's sons was Frederick. He was born in 1867 and married Emma Coomber at St Mary's church. Frederick followed the same trade as his father. Below is shown an account issued by Frederick for work undertaken on the school house at Thurnham School:

Reproduced courtesy of the Gordon Ward collection, Kent Archaeological Society

In 1890 Frederick was commissioned to build a parish room next door to St Mary's church. He used pitch pine for the main part of the building and oak for the sash windows. However, it was only a parish room for a short time as it was realised that the Mission Hut fulfilled a greater need in Ware Street. The room was closed and although it still belonged to the church, the property was converted to a residence. One of the first people to live there was Miss Howden, who kept bees.

Emma and Frederick had five children including Stanley, Walter and Ernest. Ernest was tragically killed in the final two months of the First World War in 1918 whilst his wife, Agnes, was expecting their second child. The rest of the family took care of his widow and children, who were known as Little Agnes and Little Ernest.

Evelyn Fridd and Margaret Plowright (née White) still possess a small memoir that Stanley wrote about his life and some of the incidents that occurred when he was a boy. Stanley was an observant child. When he attended Thurnham School, he noticed that the building was surrounded by at least twenty apple and damson trees, together with some red-currant and gooseberry bushes. During the summer, when everyone else in the village went hop-picking, Stanley enterprisingly offered to pick the fruit for the Mistress of the school, Miss Rosa Beck. He arranged for the carrier, Mr Hickmott, to take them to Maidstone market in boxes supplied by Perrin's stores at Chestnut Place. Once the expenses had been met, Stanley found that there was a profit of ten shillings on the sale of the fruit. He offered the money to Miss Beck and she returned two shillings for his trouble.

Walter's second name was Victor, commemorating his birth on Queen Victoria's birthday. During the First World War, Walter was part of the Kent Cyclists Battalion. His service saw him travel to India before being demobilised. He had an unusual pastime in the Army: he spent a great deal of time unravelling the tops of worn-out woollen socks to crochet an enormous blanket. It was made up of different shades of grey and khaki wool but was very warm and lasted for years. After Walter returned, he married Elsie Sent in 1924 at Holy Cross church. Her wedding dress was made of silk that he had brought back from India.

This is one of Elsie and Walter's wedding photographs:

Photograph courtesy of Evelyn Fridd and Margaret Plowright (née White)

Elsie was the middle of three children from the Sent family. Her elder sister was Florence and her brother was Arthur, who was known as Jack. The family came from Norfolk where her father, Walter had worked as a nurseryman for a local company called Notcutts. Today, Notcutts is a national chain of gardening stores. Walter married Annie Willgress and they came to Kent when he took a job at Bunyard's Nursery in Giddyhorn Lane, near Queens Road, in Maidstone. Elsie had been born in Maidstone in 1898 but shortly afterwards her family moved to Sutton Street as her father took a job at Crismill Nurseries which is now called The Potted Garden.

Before marriage, Florence Sent worked at Friningham Manor. She married Wilfred Wilkinson on 12 October 1922 at Holy Cross church. Florence and Wilfred later settled in Maidenhead, Berkshire. He worked as a chauffeur for the Eastick family who had a large house fronted onto the Thames and owned another house in Devon.

Jack married Mabel Emma Jones on 7 June 1924 at Holy Cross church. They lived at 2 South View Cottages, The Street for most of their married life. This undated photograph shows 1-4 South View Cottages. No 2 is the second door on the left hand side:

Photograph courtesy of Heather Downer

Jack made a good living a as shoe repairer. This account shows details of Jack's business, although it actually records the sale of a motorbike:

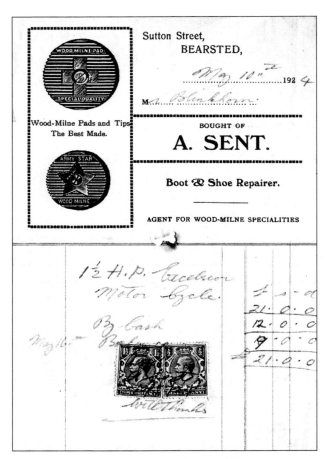

Reproduced courtesy of Roger Vidler

For a time, Jack ran his business from a large hut behind his house. This photograph of the rear of South View Cottages was taken in 1975 and shows Jack's hut on the right hand side directly below the windows:

Photograph courtesy of Heather Downer

Mabel was rather proud of retaining so many of the original features of the house which had been built in 1905. However, this meant that the only washing facilities were in the back scullery, there was an outside toilet and a black lead range was still in the back room. Heather Downer, recalled that in 1975, when she moved in next door, Mabel's house was still lit by gas! The supply was converted to North Sea Gas but there had been concern about the arrangement. Mabel was always very amused during power cuts that her house remained unaffected.

Ultimately, the low level of lighting in the house caused Mabel's demise as she fell badly whilst going upstairs to bed, carrying a torch and hot water bottle.

Walter White carried on the family building business but he sometimes found being self-employed brought difficulties as people were not always prompt in paying their bills for work undertaken. This advertisement is undated, but appeared in the parish magazine:

DECORATING   PLUMBING.

W. WHITE,
BUILDER,
SUTTON STREET,
BEARSTED.

REPAIRS.   ESTIMATES.

Reproduced courtesy of James Moore

Although Walter and Elsie's eldest child, Graham, was born at his Sent grandparents' home, in Sutton Street, the family moved away from Bearsted and Thurnham for a short while. Evelyn was born in Chegworth, Harrietsham. By the time of Margaret's arrival in 1933, the family had moved back to Bearsted and into a house now called Pin Cottage in Sutton Street. Their youngest daughter, Janet, was also born in Bearsted. Pin Cottage was not particularly spacious but it did have a big garage and workshop. The White children used to play in and around the sandy banks in the area.

Walter was thoroughly involved in the life of the village and became a stalwart of the horticultural society and the British Legion. During the Second World War, he was a member of the Home Guard. Meetings were held in the function room of the White Horse. The Fayre was suspended during the war but when it was revived, Walter helped to build the wooden chalets for the side shows and stored them until required. He also erected the swing boats: a task that he was to undertake regularly at the event. For the first Fayre that was held after the war, he managed to obtain some nylon stockings as prizes for the hoop-la stall, which was a great draw that year!

In 1946, Walter was seeking to expand his business premises and so bought the former vicarage in Thurnham Lane, together with the converted parish room and just over four acres of land.

This view was taken for a postcard in the early years of the Twentieth century and shows Thurnham Lane. It has changed very little in recent times:

Photograph courtesy of Terry Clarke

Although the former vicarage was not a very old property, it had been requisitioned during the war and little maintenance had been undertaken. Along with the former parish room, it had been used as accommodation for officers and lady members of the Royal Air Force.

This undated photograph of the former vicarage was taken before the First World War:

Photograph courtesy of Michael Perring

76

At the old vicarage, there had been a bar for the officers. Limited redecoration of the rooms had been undertaken but it was largely in shades of yellow, green and brown. It is believed that during this time, the bar area was decorated by members of an air force regiment with a series of wall paintings executed in aircraft paint. Both buildings were fairly dilapidated but it did not take long to renovate the old parish room. It was then occupied by Mr and Mrs Cowell.

Walter was amused to see that there was a clause in the deeds which stated that the purchaser was not allowed to call the property any name that was vaguely ecclesiastical. It was decided to call the property Little Dane after a field near to their old house in Sutton Street. The four acres of grounds, also bought with the former vicarage, became land that Walter was able to develop as an area which the family could use for future generations.

Some years later a house was built for Margaret on some of the land, whilst the old parish rooms that had been originally built by Horace White for St Mary's church became a home for Evelyn. Eventually, around fifty years after the original purchase from the Church Commissioners, the White family decided to sell Little Dane and it was bought by Mr and Mrs Ashdown.

The new owners undertook further restoration and modernisation of the property and during 1998 they found that some of the wall paintings had survived. Although conservation advice was sought, it was not possible to preserve all of them as they had begun to deteriorate. However, a full record was made.

These photographs show details from two of the wall paintings:

Both photographs courtesy of Downs Mail

12   Bearsted Green Bakery

In the mid-Nineteenth century, most people were able to bake bread at home in their ovens beside the fireplace. A growing number of new houses included an iron range for cooking but the ovens were too small to produce the large amount of bread required to feed the average-sized Victorian family. A new market for professional bakers arose, trading as 'Public and Family Bakers'.[1]

William Tomsett's bakery in Bearsted, was not the first, and certainly not the only one in the village. His bakery was sited facing the Green, a few doors down from the school. It was some distance from John Copping's bakery which was located in the area now occupied by Egypt House.[2]

Both William and John were skilled craftsman and rate-payers, they were married and had children. John was also, at various times, a Post Master and later a sub-postmaster for the village.[3] As the parish vestry records show, along with the status of rate-payer came civic responsibilities. William was a member of the community who was content to fulfil his duties within the parish; he was regularly amongst those selected as an Assessor of the Poor for the parish between 1875 and 1894.[4]

John Copping's bakery eventually closed and William Tomsett continued to run the bakery by the Green until his sudden death in 1898.[5] William's widow, Harriett, continued the business, assisted by her youngest son, Lewis and her son in law, Thomas Hayward, who had married her daughter, Minnie.[6]

The Pye family took over the bakery for a short time before it was bought by William Rowland. Some long-established residents could remember Mrs Pye's popularity with the children in the village because she occasionally took a tray of cakes over to them as they played on the Green at lunchtimes in the summer. It is possible that the cakes were slightly stale, but no-one minded and it was a kind gesture.[7]

Rowland Powell

Rowland Powell's grandfather ran the bakery for many years. These of some of his memories about his family's involvement with the business:[8]

William Rowland, moved with his wife and family from Uttoxeter into the bakery on the Green at the beginning of the Twentieth century. By this time the only remaining aspect of the public bakery facility that had once been offered to the village was the roasting of Sunday joints, while families went off to church. When I first began to take notice of such things, this service had almost ceased except for a few friends and neighbours, but on Christmas Day the oven was still filled almost to capacity with poultry. The ensuing deliveries and collections of orders were more of a social occasion than a chore.

This advertisement, from 1929, appeared in the parish magazine:

Reproduced courtesy of Jenni Hudson

My grandfather had a large family with seven children. To assist the housekeeping, he cultivated a small-holding on a plot of land adjacent to his own property where he also kept a couple of pigs and twenty or thirty laying hens. These all provided a plentiful supply of meat, eggs, vegetables and fruit. He also bred Angora rabbits for show and for eating. He cured the skins for glove-making by my grandmother, my mother and her two sisters. One of his sons, Reginald, emigrated to America to earn his living as a baker.

This photograph of the bakery is from an undated postcard, but was taken around 1930. The bakery is on the left hand side of the picture:

Photograph courtesy of Malcolm Kersey

This undated photograph shows William Rowland standing by his delivery van:

Photograph courtesy of Rowland Powell

At Easter in 1939, I cycled from my home in Deal to Bearsted for a week's holiday with my aunt and uncle at the bakery. I soon found that I had to earn my keep undertaking deliveries each morning on an old trade bicycle. The bicycle had a large front basket which was filled with fresh crusty bread for the customers on one of the more remote stretches of my uncle's normal round. My deliveries round took me out of the village across the main A20 road and into a switch-back of lanes. I passed through the Kent countryside but it was some time before I really appreciated the beauty of it all: for every freewheel down-hill there was a hard slog up the next pushing a well-loaded bike.

My school holidays from 1940 to 1942 were spent the same way. It was during one stay that my grandfather told me thirty years earlier, my mother had also done that round with a pony and vanette because her brothers were too young. She had found the job rather boring, but she enjoyed calling on the hop pickers during their annual paid holiday 'pulling bines'. There was only one hop farm on her round. Apparently she enjoyed the friendliness of the 'hoppers' and their daily exchanges.

When my grandfather retired he moved, with his youngest daughter, into an adjoining cottage called 'Popinjay'. Jack took over the running of the bakery, the smallholding and the chickens. His new wife, Dolly, produced the cakes for the shop and made, iced and decorated all the celebration cakes. Surplus eggs from the hens were stored in isinglass to preserve them for future use in the bakery or sale in the shop. Dolly bottled fruit and vegetables in Kilner jars and made jam which was also sold in the shop. These services proved a boon to their customers throughout the years of the Second World War.

In their spare time Jack and Dolly joined in the social activities of the village. Jack was a leading member of the local Amateur Dramatic Society, sang in the Church choir, and was a bell ringer. During the war, he served in the Observer Corps. Dolly, apart from being active in the Women's Institute, had a lifelong passion for dancing which stayed with her until she was admitted to a Nursing Home in Sussex. Jack died soon after he left the Bakery in 1950.

In this letter head from around 1940, the date of establishment shown refers to the Rowland family business, rather than Bearsted Green Bakery:

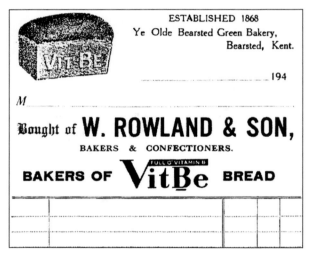

Reproduced courtesy of Rowland Powell

Rowland's Bakery closed after fifty years of trading in Bearsted as there was too much competition through the advent of sliced bread. It was cheap, readily available at every corner shop and village store, and sounded the death knell for many small craftsmen bakery businesses. The name Rowland disappeared from the list of tradesmen in Bearsted. The premises were later used as a chemist shop with a pharmacy run by Mr Wheeler.[9] The shop also sold knitting wool. After this, the premises were used as a boutique and now it is an excellent restaurant called Souffle.

The five tall trees which once stood in front of the shop have long disappeared. The former open space in front of them, where teas were once served in the summer, has been hedged and fenced. There is now a splendid patio overlooking the Green where lunch can be enjoyed in pleasant surroundings. The old oak beams of the former dining room are a valued part of the restaurant's architecture. The bay window of the old shop, with views out over the Green, makes a pleasant place to eat. The bakehouse is now an extension of the restaurant with just one reminder of its past use; the old black iron oven door has been inserted into the back wall.

13   The Bridgland and Moon families

Emily Bridgland was born in Loddington, near Linton but came to Bearsted as a young girl when her father moved to start a new job. He had been a bailiff on the Holmesdale family estates which were later owned by the Cornwallis family. The Bridgland family had a maid and owned several horses. Emily went to school in Linton. Sometimes when her father visited the big house on business, she would accompany him so that she could talk to the cook and watch her making wonderful dishes.

Emily married Edward Moon at Holy Cross church. Edward was the youngest son of the Moon family who were all born in Brenchley. Frederick, William, Alfred, Richard and Emma were his siblings. For a while his parents, Frederick and Sarah, ran the Royal Oak public house.

This photograph of Emily and Edward was taken in 1888:

Photograph courtesy of Norah Giles

Edward and Emily named one of their children Emily, after her mother. She was born at a house called Maybank which is in Church Lane near the Green She attended Bearsted School, then Thurnham School and then returned to Bearsted School as her father changed employment. This pattern of changing school was quite common to families involved in agricultural work.

At one time Edward Moon was a bailiff on the Madginford Farm estate, owned by Mr Leney. The farmhouse for the estate was situated on the right hand corner by the junction of Madginford Road and Willington Street. There was also an oast house and four farm cottages. However, they were all demolished prior to the construction of the Madginford housing estate.

This photograph shows some of the family in 1910 during a short break during the harvest in a hop garden on Madginford Farm.

Photograph courtesy of Norah Giles

<u>Back row, left to right:</u> Jack Bridgland, Emily Moon, Emily Moon
(née Bridgland, bailiff's wife), Tom Bridgland

<u>Front row:</u> Robert and Marchant Bridgland

After she left school, in 1904 Emily was apprenticed to a dress maker in West Malling for three years. Below is shown the letter agreeing to the terms of the indenture:

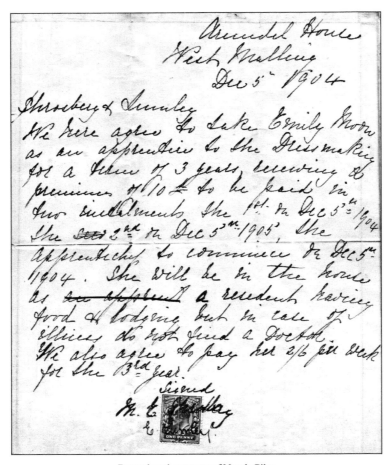

Reproduced courtesy of Norah Giles

The indenture specified that she was to be resident at the dressmaker's premises with food and lodging supplied but fees for a doctor in the event of an illness were not met. She received £10 paid in two instalments and in her final year she was paid two shillings and sixpence a week. When Emily received her first wages, she spent all but a half-shilling on a hat and then had to borrow the bus fare home.

Emily married Edgar Pettipiere at St Mary's church on 30 June 1915. This photograph of the wedding guests was taken at Sandy Mount farm:

Photograph courtesy of Norah Giles

Although the majority of the guests are not identified, many members of the oldest families in Bearsted and Thurnham attended. The two older bridesmaids were Lila Pettipiere and Nell Moon. The two young girls seated at the front are Blanche Tester, sitting on the left hand side, and Dolly Forward.

Emily and Edgar Pettipiere's daughter Norah was born in 1916. On leaving school in 1930 she went straight to work in Mr Taylor's newspaper shop at Chestnut Place. One of the village boys that delivered newspapers was Paul Ashbee. Norah clearly recalled that Paul was viewed by others in the village as rather eccentric, due to his overwhelming interest in archaeology. Paul became well-known locally a few years later with his efficient excavation at Thurnham Court Farm. It was the start of a distinguished career.

Norah married William Giles. He had a business as a builder. Their homes have included 21 Ware Street also known as 'Sandy Mount Cottages', 15 Ware Street also known as Golf View villas because of the view over the golf course from the front door, 54 Ware Street and latterly, in Madginford Road. William was Clerk to Thurnham parish council and served as Chairman between 1964 and 1966.

Edward Moon's elder brother Alfred married Eliza and their youngest child was called Rose. She married Charles Mills who originally came from Boughton Monchelsea but had moved to Ware Street. Charles and Rose's two children, John and Phyllis, are therefore related to Norah Giles. Although John is unsure of the dates, he recalls that Alfred worked at Snowfield for a time.

Charles and Rose lived in the Moon family home, which was two doors down from Frederick Marshall's corn merchant's premises in The Street. They shared their home with Alfred, and with Rose's brothers, Edmund and William. Edmund had served in the Pioneer Corps during the First World War. He lost part of one leg and the heel of the other when a shell had exploded near to him. Despite this disability, he was quite mobile and worked as a road sweeper for the council.

This undated photograph shows part of The Street where the extended Moon family lived. Their house was on the immediate left hand side with a bicycle by the door:

Photograph courtesy of Terry Clarke

This photograph was taken around 1926 and shows Phyllis and John Mills, standing by their front door:

Photograph courtesy of Tony and Sheila Foster

John remembered that parts of the house seemed very old. A wooden shutter went over a window at the front of the property and slid down below it when not required. This is clearly visible in the photograph. The bedrooms were accessed using steps that that creaked heavily. In the back garden, there were some hens kept in a pen. Nearly all the neighbours kept chickens in their gardens.

The property seems rather picturesque today, but in 1931 the house was condemned as unfit for habitation and was demolished. It was the start of a gradual dispersal of sections of the Moon family as they had only rented the house from Frederick Marshall. He lived in The Street too, at a property known as John's Villa, but which is now called Caldicotts.

Despite the short notice, Edmund and William managed to find lodgings elsewhere in the village. Charles Mills took his family to Boughton Monchelsea, where he had worked since he left school. John transferred from Thurnham School to Boughton Monchelsea School. However, the only place that Alfred, who was by now rather elderly and frail, could be accommodated was Coxheath workhouse.

Before the establishment of the Welfare State and sheltered housing schemes, many elderly people found themselves in this position. The workhouse was no longer a feared bleak Victorian institution, but it was still disliked. Although the family was now scattered, they regularly visited Alfred for the rest of his life.

Although Rose spent the rest of her life in Boughton Monchelsea, she was never completely reconciled to living there. She spent many hours talking about Bearsted and the tightly knit community that she deeply missed. After thirty eight years, she finally regained a place in Bearsted. In accordance with her wishes, she was buried in Holy Cross churchyard.

14 Garages and Mechanics

There were several garages in Bearsted and Thurnham during the Twentieth century. The Westwood Motor Company was owned by Mr Waight and was based in Thurnham Lane, adjacent to the shops at Chestnut Place. William Hill was the main mechanic at the garage. This advertisement was placed in the Centenary magazine for Bearsted School in 1939:[1]

Phone Bearsted 6333

The Westwood Motor Co.
(F. C. WAIGHT, A.M.I.A.E.)

Thurnham Lane,
Bearsted

SERVICE & REPAIRS
WOLSELEY HIRE CARS

A.A. Appointed Garage

Reproduced courtesy of Roseacre School

Thorpe's Garage

Thorpe's garage by the Green was originally a wheelwright's premises. Chris Hunt's family could remember that the front of the premises always seemed to be full of logs and other timber that was being seasoned. This picture is a detail from an undated postcard; on the left hand side can be clearly seen several carts and a supply of timber:

Photograph courtesy of Chris and Sue Hunt

At the back of the premises was a saw pit. Carriages were built there and then hoisted up so that they could be painted. This was a very skilled job and the paint was mixed using small paste pots. Some of these were later found under the floorboards when the property was renovated. This photograph shows James Ellis and William Hunt standing in front of the wheelwright's premises which has a pitched roof.

Photograph courtesy of Chris and Sue Hunt

This photograph shows the premises in 1923: Thorpe's garage has opened, and replaced the wheelwright on the same site. On the left hand side of the photograph, there is an advertisement for Dunlop tyres. A sign on a striped pole is an Automobile Association road sign giving the name of the village.

Photograph courtesy of Margaret Morris

These next two photographs show an interesting sequence of development. The first was taken around 1950. The garage has become a white-fronted building with no pitched roof. There is a petrol pump on the right hand side. The second photograph, which is undated, shows that the front elevation had been altered once more:

Photograph courtesy of Terry Clark

Photograph courtesy of Chris and Sue Hunt

During the 1980s, the garage closed and the premises were later converted to a dwelling. The site is now occupied by a house called 'Wheelwrights'. However the property still has extensive garaging, as an allusion to the previous uses for the building.

Yeoman Garage

Yeoman Garage was run by Frederick Grout, known as 'Freddy'. He had served in the Royal Flying Corps during the First World War. Whilst he was recovering from his war wounds he began to repair vehicles to boost his income. He initially undertook repairs at his house, which was adjacent to the entrance for Walter Fremlin's estate at Milgate Park. Freddy's enterprise sometimes caused problems as the road to Milgate House became blocked by vehicles awaiting repair. Mr Fremlin thought that if there was a separate garage on the Ashford Road then access to his property would be improved. He gave Freddy some financial assistance and the new garage began life as a small shed.

Below is shown a typical example of work undertaken by Freddy and a subsequent account:

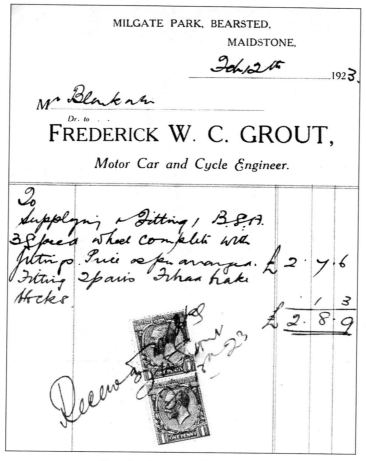

Reproduced courtesy of Roger Vidler

After Walter Fremlin's death in 1925, Freddy was able to buy the garage. This next photograph shows the 'shed' around 1925. Note the lack of traffic and houses along the Ashford Road:

Photograph courtesy of Chris and Sue Hunt

This undated photograph shows another view of the original buildings. Note the large lamps on the forecourt and the recovery vehicle with a crane on the back:

Photograph courtesy of Ted Wingrove

When the road was later widened, the shed was replaced with the building that became widely known as the Yeoman Garage. Margaret Blamire-Brown recalled taking wireless accumulators there to be charged.

A machine shop and panel beating facility were added. There was also a small cottage behind the main premises. The cottage became Audrey and Joseph Fermor's first home after they married. Joseph was usually known as Eddie, from his second name of Edmund. He was one of Mr Grout's mechanics and Audrey also worked at the garage. Barbara Brears (née Grout) recalled that her father was known to be a good employer but kept a tight rein on his staff. He was very keen on cleanliness on the premises and the mechanics often used to say that it was so spotless that meals could be eaten off the floor!

During the Second World War the garage became one of the central collection points for scrap and salvage in the village. The usual business of supplying petrol was limited due to rationing but it was one of the few garages in the area that was allowed to stock and sell petrol. However, this concession brought with it a great amount of administration as the pump had to be read daily to ascertain sales, ration coupons had to be accounted and a daily form returned to the Ministry of Transport.

The garage also took on different contracts which assisted the war effort and employed local people such as Edward Palmer. If he had not been employed by Freddy, he may well have ended up as a Bevin boy. Joyce Bourne (née Palmer), recalled that the garage employees finished aircraft parts. It was known locally that Freddy regarded it as his patriotic duty to undertake this sort of work.

Other aircraft work was completed, particularly for Shorts Brothers of Rochester who made flying boats. Audrey recalled that when a contract for a company called 'Pobjoy' of Biggleswade, Bedfordshire was agreed, no-one had heard of them! About a dozen people worked in the machine shop on this contract, building gear boxes for Hurricane fighter planes. The parts were delivered in packs in a rough state. They were prepared, drilled and tapped, machined and then assembled.

After the war there was continued expansion. Allen Carr's father re-built part of the premises for Mr Grout. He extended a verandah that was on the front of the garage, renovated the paint-shop and erected some lock-up garages. The height of the paint shop was raised and Allen could remember assisting his father to cut down some big window frames to fit the new building. There were now six petrol pumps which supplied different types of fuel.

In 1952, the staff at the garage comprised the owner, Mr Grout; the manager 'Gus Newman; mechanics Cyril and Ronald Bailey, Eddie Fermor and Douglas Turner. The storekeeper was Doris Lower. The machine shop was run by John Croucher. Panel beating was undertaken by Albert Croucher and there was a paint sprayer and an upholsterer. Joyce Bourne also worked there for a short time.

This photograph from the early 1950s was taken on the forecourt of Yeoman garage and shows the view from the garage of the Kentish Yeoman public house with Harnett's rose nursery premises in the background:

Photograph courtesy of Ted Wingrove

This photograph also shows the garage around 1952:

Photograph courtesy of Audrey Fermor

Other Vehicle Businesses

In the 1940s and 1950s, S E Thomas and Sons had a hauliers business at the top of Yeoman Lane. The company had two blue Commer lorries with the company details written on the side. Alf Passmore worked for the company and in cold winters Alf and his colleague spent a long time trying to start the engines using sturdy starting handles.

There were two further vehicles that were available for hire. A small company was run by the Stibey family. Customers could choose between a Lanchester and a Morris vehicle. The company was later taken over by Mr Crump who was known for his smart appearance. He was a familiar sight in a black uniform and cap. In wet weather he wore an immaculate black rain coat.

In the 1950s, a company called Tolhurst Transport was operating from a site where the Esso garage now stands on the Ashford Road. It was a commercial transport company and was run by Iris and 'Tubby' Tolhurst. The business later expanded and became Lenham Haulage.

After serving an apprenticeship, Allen Carr, whose father was the landlord of The Kentish Yeoman public house, opened a car repair workshop at the back of the premises in 1959. The location was not ideal, but no one seemed to mind as it was a further facility for Bearsted and Thurnham. He ran this for around ten years before becoming manager of the Kentish Belle Garage at The Street, Detling. Allen then set up a company called Carr's Coaches which later moved to Pluckley.

15 Thornham Friars

Although sections of Thornham Friars date from the Sixteenth century, for nearly four hundred years it comprised just two small cottages. This photograph, taken in 1903 by Will Stirling, shows the original property. There is no information available about the people pictured in the photograph.

Photograph courtesy of Maidstone Museum

In 1843, the cottages were owned by James Roots, but inhabited by members of the Shorter and Day families.[1] From subsequent census returns, the names of the families living in the cottages cannot be accurately determined as a number of dwellings are recorded in the same area. By 1881, the cottages were known as Eyres Cottages and were occupied by the Whitehead, Smith and Chapman families.[2]

At the beginning of the Twentieth century, the cottages and the forge which stood opposite had passed into the ownership of Percy Wigan of Puckrup Hall, Tewkesbury. In April 1901 he decided to sell them and instructed his land agents and auctioneers, Messrs Seymour and Waring of 46 Earl Street, Maidstone, to make the necessary arrangements. He expressed the view that the combined properties were to be sold for £1,000, although their restoration had involved him in a great deal of expense.[3]

There were two interested parties: James Watkinson of Folkestone and the Hampson family who lived at neighbouring Thurnham Court. Mr Hampson, however, had reservations about the purchase:[4]

> [we have] very considerable drawbacks to letting the principal house as anything more than a cottage, for instance there are no internal sanitary arrangements and the well which presumably supplies the whole block with water is right in front of the windows of the best rooms. There is also the closeness of the Black Horse. Very likely the whole block might eventually be thrown into one house, and sanitary arrangements made, but that would be an expensive matter.

These concerns were reflected in their offer of £500. It was not accepted by Mr Wigan[5] and the properties were put up for auction on 26 September 1901 at the Royal Star Hotel in Maidstone.[6] However, the properties failed to make their reserve of £700. The following day the auctioneers received an offer of £620 from James Watkinson's son, Alfred.[7] Mr Wigan then gave instructions to accept Alfred's offer,[8] but it remains unclear whether the negotiations were concluded to mutual satisfaction.

If Alfred bought the cottages, it is probable that he was the vendor when Mr Beck purchased them prior to the First World War. Mr Beck was the first of three owners who began to create the substantial property that exists today. He had also purchased part of a Tudor house in Sussex that had survived a fire. It was completely dismantled and transported by horse and cart to Thurnham where it was added to the existing cottages. The work was interrupted by the war and so was not completed until the early 1920s.

This photograph, taken from the junction of Pilgrims Way and Castle Hill, shows the finished renovations:

Photograph courtesy of Terry Clarke

The new section of the property completely obscured the original house leaving only its weather-boarded gable end visible from the road. It comprised an oak frame with a brick herring bone design infill. This decorative brickwork reflected the increasing use of brick as a construction material in the Sixteenth century. The second section, known as the barn, was added to the south western corner of the original Kentish house. It projects in the direction of Aldington Lane and is now south of the garages.

This photograph below shows that although traces of the original cottages remain on the extreme left, the property has been greatly altered and extended. The upper floor of the middle section is hung with mathematical tiles. A third wing has been added to the eastern end of the house which is on the right, jutting out slightly from the rest. Inevitably, some of the beams of the Sussex house did not fit and numerous adjustments had to be made to allow windows and doors to be properly aligned.[9]

Photograph courtesy of Geoffrey Fletcher

Mr Beck began terracing the surrounding area to make a garden. During the course of this work some perfect specimens of Saxon beads and spearheads were excavated. He planned the layout of a park to the east of the property with a grand drive from Aldington Lane up to the eastern end of the garden. The brick pillars of that entrance still exist and can be glimpsed through trees mid-way along Aldington Lane.

By 1939, the landscaping carried out at the Friars, together with Thurnham Keep which was constructed in 1910, was very visible and had made a major difference to the appearance of the countryside. However, Mr and Mrs Beck did not live in the house long enough to complete their grand design. It is thought that Mrs Beck did not spend a great deal of time at the house and a decision was made to sell the property.[10]

On 20 July 1926 the house was put up for auction. A transcript of the particulars of sale:[11]

BY DIRECTION OF AC BECK ESQ

ON THE PILGRIMS' WAY, KENT

FOR SALE AT A LOW PRICE

THE FREEHOLD HISTORIC PROPERTY

THORNHAM FRIARS, BEARSTED

About 300ft above sea level and commanding magnificent panoramic views

THE RESIDENCE believed to be a XVIth century 'rest house' has been enlarged and modernised with unusual skill, and contains hall, billiard and four reception rooms, eleven bedrooms, two bathrooms and offices

Company's water and gas. House wired/or electricity. Central heating.

GARAGE FOR THREE CARS.

PLEASURE GROUNDS with old flagged terrace and yew hedges, tennis and croquet lawns, park-like pastureland; in all about

SEVENTEEN ACRES

HUNTING WITH TWO PACKS. GOLF AT BEARSTED

Messrs KNIGHT FRANK & RUTLEY, 20 Hanover Square W 1

Reproduced courtesy of the Gordon Ward collection, Kent Archaeological Society

The property was purchased by Frederick and Ethel Scott. Mr Scott was a merchant who had lived much of his life in China.[12] They commissioned the pair of gates at the entrance to the garden from the Pilgrims Way.[13] Similar gates once adorned the pillars near Aldington Lane but they were removed during the Second World War.[14] During the war, the Scotts moved to Devon to allow The Friars to be used by the RAF officers stationed at Detling.

In 1948 Nellie Kirkham passed by the house and later wrote:

> At Thurnham cross roads is a sudden surprising house of timber and brick, much of it Tudor. Some looks far older, some is newer, a bit added here and there, an example of an old English house, loved and used hard, century after century until, undesigned, it acquires an inherent beauty of design....[15]

She was unaware that the property she described had changed immensely less than fifty years previously.

The Scott family came back to the house and lived there until Mr Scott's death in the mid 1950s. Mrs Scott returned to her family in America and the property once again came to the market. It was advertised in the magazine, Country Life.[16]

When Geoffrey and Judy Fletcher viewed the property, Geoffrey initially thought it far too big for their needs, but his wife saw the possibilities it offered. They decided to buy and then adapt it. Two years later Geoffrey decided to demolish the Sussex house section of the western wing. The remaining accommodation was then re-ordered. Car parking space and a garage were created and the original Kentish house which had been unseen from the road for over thirty years was exposed. At the same time as the Sussex house was removed, a red brick extension was raised in height.

This diagram shows the various stages in the creation and alteration of the property:

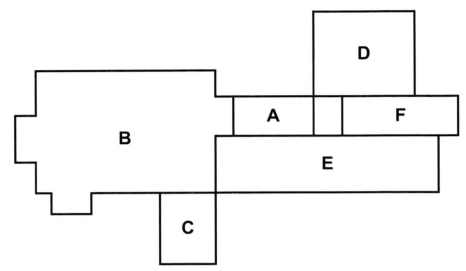

Diagram courtesy of Roger Vidler and Malcolm Kersey

Explanation:

A is the original Sixteenth century property

B shows the eastern wing added by Mr Beck

C is the rear extension raised from single to two storeys in the 1950s

D shows The Barn, also part of Mr Beck's extension

E represents the western wing added by Mr Beck subsequently removed by Geoffrey Fletcher

F shows the garages constructed in the mid 1950s

This photograph shows the house today:

Photograph courtesy of Roger Vidler

When Geoffrey and Judy moved into their new house, the garden was a wilderness. Geoffrey recognised that he would have to learn about gardening if he was to transform the grounds. He was determined to create a low maintenance garden based around shrubs, and eventually found a mentor in Michael Haworth-Booth; a leading expert on designing and planting shrub gardens. Michael's philosophy was that gardening should be fun and not a tedious chore. He felt that a garden should be easier to maintain with every passing year and that there should be a strong sense of constant progress.

This photograph shows part of the house together with a section of the mature garden:

Photograph courtesy of Geoffrey Fletcher

Many years later, the garden is now established and has become an integral part of the estate. It is open to the public once a year under the National Gardens Scheme. One visitor described it as 'a little bit of heaven here on earth'. No one who has seen the house, set in grounds in all their horticultural glory in mid-June could possibly disagree.

Roger Vidler

16   Bearsted in the 1920s

John and Margaret Blamire Brown were both born in Bearsted; their father, the Rev Frederick Blamire Brown, was vicar from 1914 until 1928. These are some of the recollections of their childhood spent in and round in Bearsted.

In a small village, the community was tightly knit. Everyone knew when one of our siblings died, aged four, in an outbreak of diphtheria and the majority of the household was taken off to the Fever Hospital in Loose. The rest of our family survived and we believe that Margaret holds the distinction of the only girl to be born at the Vicarage, which was virtually next door to the church.

Before the village expanded, Holy Cross church was fairly central to community life. A book was kept in the church for cleaning duties and this recorded that over a hundred people were regularly polishing, cleaning or washing linen to keep everything spick and span. They did this in their own time. This meant that the church was visited daily and was never locked except at night. The two banners in church were embroidered by church members.

Father normally worked in his study in the vicarage in the mornings. In the afternoons he put on his black Homberg hat and set off with his walking stick to visit parishioners.

The duties of a vicar included some quite unusual events. When a sewage plant was built on church land, it was thought appropriate that the vicar be asked to perform the official opening. Father was rather surprised to be invited to drink a glass of the purified water afterwards, but did so to encourage others that the plant was working efficiently.

On Rogation Sunday, which was usually the sixth Sunday after Easter, our father, choir and congregation went to various points in the parish to bless the crops. On one occasion we watched with a mixture of horror and anticipation as a goat advanced through the orchard behind the churchwarden, as he, unaware, read the Bible passage! In the event all was well as the goat avoided him.

This photograph was taken of our father with the choir of Holy Cross church in 1913. Ronald Hunt is in the front row, second from left, and Ted Taylor is in the second row.

Photograph courtesy of Chris and Sue Hunt

After the First World War, our father was anxious to do something to encourage the younger people. Some of them used to come to the Vicarage for 'Activities' and from this grew the beginnings of the Bearsted Amateur Dramatic Society which was led by Mr and Mrs Sierakowski. The plays produced were of a high standard and were normally performed in the Women's Institute Hall. Margaret also remembered peeping over the banisters at the Vicarage to watch a group of local people ringing a set of hand bells.

Bearsted was close to the county town, so the village had quite a lot of large houses. Their owners had an important influence upon village life and organisations, in addition to the local economy. At these houses were probably three or four inside and outside domestic staff. There seemed to be a natural, gentle relationship between master and servants.

Just after the First World War, Baroness Orczy moved from the village. Snowfield was bought by Major and Mrs Clarence Craig who had come from Ireland. His brother had been Prime Minister there. Major Craig thought that the row of Smart's Cottages on the Green would benefit from some privacy. He decided to achieve this by planting some trees at the back of the properties. However, the scheme was not a success as the inhabitants of the cottages did not want this intervention and removed them.

Other prominent people that we remember are Lance and May Monckton who came to live at Bell House by the Green. Lance's father, Stephen, was the last part-time Town Clerk of the Borough of Maidstone. Stephen Monckton lived at Woodcut and practised as a solicitor in King Street, Maidstone. Bell House was owned at one time by Mr Sinclair-Lewis, an American author. When he called at the shops, there was always a large carriage waiting outside.

Oswald Jones lived in Snowfield Cottage. Oswald was very keen on the latest inventions and took an interest in radio. At the opening of the British Empire Exhibition in 1924, we were invited to hear the broadcast of the event on his wireless which was set up on a trestle table on the front lawn. There seemed to be a jumble of wires but how we marvelled at the mystery of the wireless!

Sir John Hampson lived at Commonwood which was in Sandy Lane near Roundwell. Sandy Lane led up to the Ashford Road. Brigadier-General Whitacre-Allen lived at Upper Barty. Lieutenant-Colonel Oswald Daniell lived in Yeoman Lane. He commanded the Royal West Kent Regiment at the Barracks in Maidstone. His son, Brigadier A J Daniell, CBE, DSO, had a distinguished military career and was Colonel Commandant in the Royal Artillery from 1956 to 1966.

Walter Fremlin, of the brewing family, lived at Milgate Park. We particularly liked the enormous elephant's foot which was kept on his sideboard. We purchased our butter from the Milgate dairy. During the First World War, a Zeppelin off-loaded a bomb in the park grounds but there was no damage to the house. Following Walter's death, Major H E Chapman bought Milgate Park. He was the Chief Constable of Kent.

Mrs Cloudesley Marsham lived at Bearsted Court and at the lodge lived Mr Camfield, her chauffeur, and Alice, his wife. Their son won a scholarship to Oxford which was a remarkable feat in those days. Bearsted Court later became St Faith's Home.

Several properties in the village changed their names over the years. The most significant of these was Bearsted Cottage which was once known as 'The Firs' as Walter Fremlin who owned it adored fir trees. He planted many trees in the village but particularly near Church Landway. Several properties in Tower Lane were built by Walter Fremlin.

Mr Tasker, who was a banker at the County Bank in Maidstone, lived at Danefield. He was Treasurer of Bearsted School for a time. George Taylor was his coachman and also acted as a Verger and sang in the church choir. He was the father of Edward Taylor who ran the newspaper shop.

At The Mount in Church Lane lived William and Dorothy Whitehead. William was another Maidstone solicitor but he was also Under Sheriff of Kent and knew everyone in the County. He was a past President of the Kent County Cricket Club. He was a wise and stately leader of village life and churchwarden for many years.

The railway station which served Bearsted and Thurnham was halfway up a hill at the start of Ware Street. The lines had to be crossed on foot to get to the down side platform. Steam trains ran to Maidstone East station. We found that the trains were not as convenient as the bus for the shops though, as the stop for the bus was in King Street.

We loved the fresh air on the open top deck bus whilst travelling to school in Maidstone. If it rained, everyone was protected with canvas covers. The adult fare was usually 3d or 2d from the stop by the Yeoman public house on the Ashford Road. A child's fare was 1½d. The tickets were white with a blue stripe. There was a conductor and we had to be careful about sitting down when travelling under the railway bridge as we approached King Street. A bus also ran to Maidstone via Weavering Street and the Chiltern Hundreds public house, but we rarely went that way.

The daily needs of the village were met by the shops and the craftsmen. Mr Wilkinson had his joinery shop behind his house at the entrance to the oast houses and next door to Bearsted House. Occasionally on his work bench would be the makings of a coffin. John estimated that the population of the village was around 600, so funerals were infrequent. One always knew the bereaved family, and to children, the sight of a coffin was a rather awesome. Whenever there was a death, the Tenor bell would be rung. The local phrase for this was 'a tolling bell' but it might have another name in other villages. A series of single rings for a man, a series of two rings for a woman, and a series of three rings for a child – and then the bell would toll the age of the deceased.

In addition to the shops at Chestnut Place, there were some other shops in the village that we recall. Opposite to the Royal Oak but actually situated on the Green, was a grocer's shop run by Mr and Mrs Corps. Nearby were the premises of Mr Sent, who repaired shoes and Mr Raggett, the butcher.

This undated photograph shows Winfred Taylor, a niece of Mrs Corps standing with John Corps outside the shop. Winfred came to Bearsted to help in the shop after Martin Corps was born:

Photograph courtesy of Bearsted and Thurnham Women's Institute

This undated photograph below shows Mr Raggett's shop. Note the open and unglazed front window. The wooden panel on the left hand side is believed to be one of window shutters.

Photograph courtesy of Brenda Donn

On the other side of The Street was a bakery which produced the most delicious bread. The scent of baking regularly wafted over the Green and through part of the village. Mr Rowland was the baker and he married Dolly, who was one of the pretty Irish girls from the gardener's lodge at Snowfield. A little further down was The Forge with Mr Tester and the smell of burning horsehair when horses were shod. Near to this was the Men's Institute with billiard tables and bar.

There was a wheelwright's, run by Mr Ovenden, and a small garage. Such motor cars as there were in Bearsted mostly belonged to the people in the big houses, so we walked to the shops, to visit people, or to post a letter. Some people owned bicycles but otherwise it seemed the most natural thing just to walk to our destination in the village.

Further up The Street and near the shops at Chestnut Place, was the village school under the headmastership of Mr Goodman; Edward Taylor's newspaper shop; the Post Office and Mr Moss the butcher. Edward Taylor was usually known as 'Ted'.

On Mondays at about mid-day, the 'donkey-man' came. His little donkey drew a two wheeled barrel organ. The man set up the organ by the White Horse Inn and played tunes. As children, we would give him a copper or two.

Mr Brook, the grocer, was a big, cheerful and kindly man. He always seemed pleased to see customers in his shop. Mother rarely paid cash in the village shops. Each shop-keeper would record the purchases in a hard-backed cash book which would be handed to mother at the end of the month and she would settle up. The errand boy came to the house on his bicycle to collect the weekly order for groceries and later they would be delivered.

Mr Foster, who farmed in Ware Street, had some cows and a milk round. Deliveries were made on a pony-drawn milk float in churns and ladled out into your own jugs

The road surfaces around the village and to Maidstone varied greatly in quality. Sometimes, when the roads were icy, a horse pulling a cart would slip and fall down. It was a great commotion to get him up on his four legs. The private road leading from Mote House to the Ashford Road was not metalled and the surface largely comprised cinders. At one time there were lots of shirt buttons in the surface that were reputed to have come from the paper mill at Turkey Mill. This was not the only road in the area whose surface was made up from this curious mixture.

The gorgeous smell of hops drying in the oast houses behind Bearsted House was a distinctive odour which permeated the village. The oast houses were owned by the Betts family. The process of drying needed constant supervision, so the men in charge of the kilns sometimes snatched a few hours sleep lying on the hop sacks, or 'pokes'; as they were called.

The 'hoppers' came from the East End of London and treated the occasion as their summer holidays. They lived in huts in the hop gardens on the farms. They had a reputation for being rather light-fingered, so the shop keepers erected grilles on their counters during the picking season. There were no street lights in Bearsted and as the hoppers were used to the lighted streets of London, they were rather scared about going back to their accommodation in the dark after spending the evening at the White Horse or Royal Oak public houses. Sometimes they were fearful of going through the churchyard at night so they used to sing loudly on their way back to their huts.

Bearsted Fayre became a great annual event. We were encouraged to wear Dickens character costumes. Another year it was a Puritan or Cavalier affair. Many of the sideshows were locally made and run by people from the village. A most engaging sideshow involved a mouse selecting a piece of cheese on a lucky number. It was run by Mr Holtum, who was a plumber.

On hot summer evenings we liked to walk to Thurnham Mill, although it no longer ground flour. Behind it there was a dilapidated medieval house called Byfrance. It seemed quite intriguing as no one lived in it. Sometimes on Bank Holiday evenings we used to go down to the Ashford Road near the Kentish Yeoman public house just to watch the volume of traffic returning to London from the coast. There were a good many coaches. The traffic began to pile up as there was always a bottleneck at the river bridge in Maidstone and it was a slow crawl through the town.

17   The Walkling and Bromley families

Graham Walkling's great-grandmother, Grace Golding, was amongst the first children who attended Bearsted School when it opened in 1839. She had to walk from Scragged Oak at Detling Hill every day unless she was able to obtain a lift from a farm cart that was travelling in the same direction: it must have been a bumpy ride at times!

Grace married John Merrall of Farleigh who was a bailiff for Mr Redbourne Clarke at Bell House, the Green. Grace and John had six children: Harry, Thomas, Levi, Grace, Martha and Ada. Grace Merrall first attended Bearsted School in 1886 with her elder siblings. She later married William Walkling of Hollingbourne. Grace and William had at least eight children but three of them died of diphtheria. Their surviving children: Oliver, Frank, Albert, Thomas and Jack, also attended Bearsted School.

Thomas Walkling became a wheelwright and worked at Mr Ovenden's premises which were in The Street opposite the Green. After serving in the army during the First World War, Thomas decided not to return to work in the village. He took a job at the Style and Winch brewery in Maidstone as a company wheelwright. Part of his job included building wagon body sections.

Thomas married Hetty Bromley in 1921. They lived at 2 Egypt Place, The Street, for over sixty years, where they raised their family.

Egypt Place is on the left hand side of the road in this undated postcard:

Photograph courtesy of Terry Clarke

Hetty recorded some of her memories in the later years of her life, around 1987:

Hetty Bromley

I was born into the Bromley family 18 December 1896 at Roseacre in Bearsted. I had two brothers and two sisters. I was baptised at Bearsted church by Canon Scarth.

I'm afraid I cannot remember much until I went to school at the age of five. I went to Bearsted School, and spent most of my school days there. Mr Day was the headmaster and his post was taken by Miss Barclay, who had been a governess. There were two other teachers, Miss Fox and a younger teacher. I cannot remember her name. In those days the older girls used to teach the younger children. Later Miss Fox married Mr Sidney Perrin.

The big stores were at the corner of the Green, and owned by Mr John Perrin and his two sons, Mr John and Mr Sidney. It was a very large shop, and was a walk-through store. You could buy nearly anything there. There was also sleeping quarters above for the staff, but in 1900 it was burnt down. I shall never forget the sight of the fire as my Mother was going shopping. The remains of the building smouldered for a whole week because so little water was available and there was only one fire engine, drawn by two horses. The village pond was pumped dry.

Of course, there was the village pump, near the White Horse, which people had to use for domestic purposes. I remember when I was at school, seeing the poor women going across the Green with the pails for water. They wore very long frocks, and always with a nice clean apron on. We had no water in our house, only the well outside. Also, there was no gas, only a lamp and candles. It was very hard work having to draw the water, and we all had to carry some, especially for the Monday's washing.

On Sunday we went to school for our Scripture lessons, and then we marched across the Green hand in hand. There was a wide cinder path across the Green. Then in the afternoon we had lessons at the room near the Vicarage, which was near the church. By the way, Canon Scarth always took Scripture lessons on Thursdays at Bearsted School, and he was very strict.

We used to go hop-picking, which usually lasted about six to seven weeks, the hops being paid for at the end of the picking: eight bushels for a shilling. When the money was received, it was quite a good day, with lots of fun. Then it was spent on new clothes for the winter and family, and extra fuel. The hops grew in Yeoman Lane, Church Lane, Cross Keys and Mallings Lane, and all along the south side of the Ashford Road. And there were no houses, only one old oast house and four little cottages, on the opposite side of the road to the Yeoman Inn.

By the Green, there was a very large elm tree and a very big pond; during the rainy times it used to stretch across the main road. And in those days, there were of course, only horses and carts, and there was more time. The roads were made out of flint stone, and the footpaths out of earth at the side of the road.

The oilman used to call on Fridays, and deliver the paraffin for the fire, black lead for the fireplaces and blacking for the boots. The baker used to call also daily, and we always had two cottage loaves, and five on Saturday, a gallon of flour and for a very special treat, we used to have 6d worth of buns. They were then sold at seven buns for 3d.

Being no doctor in the village, we had to walk to Hollingbourne. My brother and I often had to walk across after school, if anyone wanted medicine. Sometimes the mailman would bring it for us. The doctor was Dr Whitestone. We used to like to go to the end of the road, at Roseacre, to see the mailman collect the letters from the box in the wall. He had a beautiful black horse, and also a lovely red mail van.

I will tell you that in the summer, the girls always wore such pretty print frocks, and in the winter, very thick wool dresses. There were no knitted garments in those days, but sometimes crocheted ones. We wore tough boots and black stockings.

Now I will miss a few years. When I was fourteen I left school and went to work at several small places, but at fifteen years old, I went to Snowfield to live with the Baroness Orczy and Mr Barstow, being the owners. It was while I was there that I was confirmed at Bearsted church by the Bishop of Croydon. Rev Benton was the vicar at the time, and afterwards joined the Forces and went to France. He was killed in the 1914-18 War. The Baroness was very kind. While I was there, in 1912, the Scarlet Pimpernel Scouts were born. They were presented with a lovely banner, which Mr Barstow had painted and all the boys were presented with a neckerchief with the scarlet pimpernel emblem on and also a knife.

Then I had to leave, owing to illness, (housemaid's knee), and I had to get another job without so much kneeling, so I decided to work in the kitchen. So I took another job elsewhere in a house that had a big staff and went to live in St Lawrence, Ramsgate. While I was at Lady Rose Whyvel's, after eight years I decided to get married, so in 1921 I came home to be married in Bearsted church, nearly 51 years ago, to Mr Alfred Thomas Walkling.

Now here's a few items of what we used to pay in the days when I went to school: we used to get 1lb of pudding beef for 4d, a pennyworth of suet which lasted all the week; treacle which was 2lbs for 4d and also many other items that I cannot remember. The train fare from Maidstone return was 2½d.

Also 2 Egypt Place, next door to where I live now, was once the General Post Office. Old Mr Potter was the postman. Many other things I cannot remember!

Hetty and Thomas' son, Graham, was born at 2 Egypt Place. He was at school during part of the Second World War, but left in 1942 when he was fourteen. He could remember the army undertaking manoeuvres in Mote Park and there were also soldiers from New Zealand billeted in the large houses in Bearsted. Just before D-Day some of the soldiers tried to erect some rugby posts on the Green: they soon realised that Bearsted was known as a cricketing village and the posts were removed. Despite this, the soldiers were popular in the village and keen to participate in village activities, particularly as they could supply enormous tins of corned beef should catering be required!

All the children in the village played tricks on each other. One prank came to light when Police Sergeant Smith visited the school to make enquiries about the culprits who had trimmed the beards of the goats kept by the golf club. No-one owned up to this but there was plenty of speculation about two of Graham's friends!

When he left school, Graham followed the path of many village children and learned a trade. He became an apprentice at the building firm of Charles Walters as a painter/decorator. He was paid ten shillings a week. Graham's apprenticeship included learning coach-painting on wagons that his father had built. After his apprenticeship he then followed the traditional route by moving on to another firm.

The Walkling family have seen many changes to the village and surrounding area. Graham was able to recall that at one time, the left hand side of Roundwell (from Sutton Street) was under the jurisdiction of Hollingbourne Rural Council and the right hand side was Bearsted. This boundary arrangement certainly caused some headaches when it came to dustbin collections and other community services!

Graham's family have been connected with cricket in Bearsted for many years. This photograph of him as an umpire was taken in June 1988:

Photograph courtesy of Pam Gibson

These are some of Graham's general memories about cricket in the village. At one time the area behind Smart's Cottages on the Green was known as 'The Ashes' due to the fact that nearly everyone tipped their coal cinders on it from their fires. This eventually built up into a cinder path and lead across the Green to Yeoman Lane. Graham's mother could remember when this path was stopped up to provide a better playing surface for cricket. The passageway between the two blocks of cottages which comprise Smart's Cottages was once known as Fuller's Passage by some people, as Mr Fuller lived in one of the cottages. He did not like any cricket ball landing in his beautiful garden. There were several occasions when the ball's arrival was swiftly followed by the sound of a hatchet. The ball, either damaged or now chopped in half, was then thrown back!

Before the current cricket pavilion was built on the Green, a wooden building was used which was rather like a summerhouse. It was located just by Bell House. On several occasions during matches, the ball has been knocked high up into the air, striking the bell on the main farmhouse building! This undated postcard shows the pavilion on the left hand side, facing the Green. The reason for the procession is not known, but the photograph was taken after the Scout Troop was founded in 1912 as several boys are wearing Scout uniform:

Photograph courtesy of Roger Vidler

At least four famous cricketers have lived in Bearsted: Alfred Mynn, 'Tich' Freeman, Leslie Ames and Godfrey Evans. Alfred Mynn is depicted on the village sign for Bearsted. A competition was held by the parish council for the design of the sign which was won by Alan Warland. It was erected to commemorate the Festival of Britain and was unveiled in April 1951.

The new pavilion was built on the Green behind Smart's Cottages. Nearby there was a bus stop and small lay-by opposite the Royal Oak. The pavilion was opened by Colin Cowdrey on 26 April 1958 and a celebratory match was played between two elevens captained by Leslie Ames and Colin Cowdrey. At the opening, Lord Cornwallis said:

> Do not forget that this is one of the famous greens in the whole of the cricket world. We hope that
> long after this generation has gone, Bearsted Green will still have cricket played upon it.[1]

18   Snowfield Cottage

Snowfield Cottage is one of the most attractive properties which face the Green opposite the pond. It bears a Grade II listing for architectural significance. The current resident, Thomas Tate, known as Tom, is related to the Jones family, who lived in Bearsted for many years.

Tom does not know the exact age of the current building but there may have been a house on the site since the Sixteenth or Seventeenth century. The dimensions of the current house indicate that the property was once a room and a half deep, with a cat-slide roof at the back. Since then the house has been re-fronted with brick and the sides of the building hung with mathematical tiles. Perhaps the porch was built at the same time as scratched on the lead of the porch is the date 1795.

As part of the Snowfield estate, the house was tenanted. The family of Alfred Mynn, the famous cricketer, was resident there, but Alfred himself was absent when the census was taken in 1841. However, his name was recorded during the compilation of the tithe map and schedule for Bearsted in 1842.[1] By the next census, Alfred and Sarah had moved to Friningham in Thurnham and their former neighbours, William and Ann Streatfield, had moved into Snowfield Cottage. William was land and house agent for Charles Mohun, who owned Snowfield.[2] William and Ann were resident for many years.

One set of Tom's great grandparents were tenants of Snowfield Cottage from the 1890s. Tom's grandfather, Charles Oswald Jones, bought the property in the 1930s for £400. He was called Oswald to distinguish him from other members of the family. Both of his children, Margaret (Tom's mother) and Maurice, have Oswald as their second Christian name.

Eventually, the house became separated from the rest of the Snowfield estate. Documents about the house from around 1870 indicate that it was no longer considered an estate property but was still occupied by an employee of the estate. However there are no further details about the change of ownership.

Like many older properties, the house has been altered many times. Tom has many plans from the 1930s showing schemes for proposed changes. These show the house with extra buildings at the back and roof lines which jut out. Some of the plans depict doors with corners missing to accommodate a cat-slide roof, which no longer exists.

Oswald Jones was one of the first electrical engineers in Bearsted. He also filed many patents for devices which he invented but did not meet with much success. Snowfield Cottage was one of the first houses in the village to have an electricity generator. This was used to good effect in 1924 when Oswald was able to arrange speakers for a wireless in the front garden. The local residents were then able to listen to the official opening speech for the Wembley Exhibition which was made by King George V.

When Tom's parents returned to Snowfield Cottage after the death of his grandmother in the 1960s, the property required substantial renovation. Nearly all the floor boards in the house were removed and re-laid. Full use was made of the opportunity to examine some of the structure of the original house. One unexpected discovery was the mummified remains of a squirrel that had died under the floorboards! It certainly explained Tom's memory of a very nasty smell in the house many years previously. Somehow the episode had been completely forgotten.

It is likely that although much of the property has been altered, the house has always retained its original width, due to the presence of the chimneys at each end. Once the renovations were underway, it was suspected that one of the chimneys was beginning to pull out from the rest of the house. A steel joist was then inserted to correct it. It was also discovered that during the 1920s part of the other chimney had been cut away, so the two chimneys vary in depth. A handsome oak surround had also been added in the 1920s to one of the fireplaces. Other renovations to the house included converting the former boiler house and a further outhouse. Previously the boiler house had also formed part of a wall for the lavatory and bathroom. It seemed rather more logical to make the area into a spacious kitchen.

The room to the right of the front door provided some interesting problems during the alterations. When the wallpaper was removed, it was evident that at some unrecorded point, there had been problems with the plaster. It had been falling away from the wall and so it was bare to a height of about four feet.

Someone had put up a stretcher with canvas pulled tightly over it to replace the plaster. Some of the wall was therefore rather like a drum. The canvas was lined with newspaper using copies of The Times which dated around 1890. Some of the newspapers carried reports about Queen Victoria visiting Scotland and were quite fascinating to read. Part of the canvas covering on an inside wall was retained. Although visually effective, there is little substantial barrier between the house and the outside world on windy days.

The pillars by the front door were also refurbished. During this work it was found that written inside the bottom of one pillar was the information that it had been 'a sunny day' before the pillar was placed into position. When it was repaired, Tom wrote the date and 'pouring with rain' as his contribution.

There is no evidence for a well at the house. However, there had been a well at Snowfield and perhaps this was equally convenient for Snowfield Cottage. For many years Tom has considered that an area in the garden where roses grow with particular abundance may be the former site of a cess-pit that was in use in the 1920s and 1930s. Also in the garden is a sunken brick-lined hole which has concrete slabs laid over it. One explanation for the hole is that it may have been a safe place in which to store glass and silver during the Second World War. Oswald certainly had a collection of very fine Venetian glass that would have required special storage during bombing raids.

Christine and Tom have always been fascinated by other people's recollections of their house. One person who had special memories was Bill Stupple, from Leeds. Bill was a builder and a chimney sweep. As a young man, he had undertaken some of his courting in the attic. It took Tom some time before he realised that Bill's wife, Mary, had been one of the maids when Tom's mother was a little girl. The maids lived on the premises in some small rooms in the attic and always looked smart in their uniforms. Tom liked the idea of getting up early in the morning, and then dressing immaculately to court the local chimney sweep!

This undated photograph shows Margaret (née Jones) and Bob Tate, by the front gate of their well-loved house:

Photograph courtesy of Christine and Tom Tate

Rosemary Pearce

19   From butcher to baker: The Old Bakery

The Old Bakery is a surviving fragment from one of the oldest buildings in The Street comprising an inner living chamber called 'a solar', and a small part of a hall.[1] It is not known how the rest of the property was destroyed but it is possible that it was badly damaged during a fire at the Royal Oak public house around 1880. Disappointingly, very little is recorded about the fire, other than a brief allusion in the autobiography of Helen Thomas.[2] Helen was married to Edward Thomas, the writer and poet. They had stayed in Bearsted for a short time in 1901.

The detail in this sketch below, which was drawn around about 1850,[3] gives some indication of the original appearance of the building:

Reproduced courtesy of Maidstone Museum and Bentlif Art Gallery,
Pretty Bequest 1865

The property attracted the attention of Helen Allingham, an artist who specialised in drawings and watercolours of old buildings. Her picture, described as 'A Village Street, Kent' was first shown in London during an exhibition of the Royal Society of Painters in Water Colours in 1895.[4] This photograph shows the property today:

Photograph courtesy of Malcolm Kersey

Part of the property's history can be reconstructed through surviving records. These show that in 1800 Ann Armstrong had inherited the property through her connections with Edward Watts of Thurnham.[5] George Betts was listed in 1826 at the address as a butcher for Bearsted[6] and in 1839 Thomas Betts was similarly described. It is possible that Thomas was George's son, although this remains unconfirmed. In the 1841 census George was described as being born in Bearsted, but then aged sixty eight and a butcher. Living in the same household was his son, William who was also a butcher and was aged twenty five.[7]

In 1842, the property was again recorded as occupied by George Betts. It was described as a house and garden, yard and premises. There was an associated piece of land called Five Acres.[8]

The property was then occupied for a time by Thomas Burwash, but in the 1851 census William Simons was recorded as trading as a butcher from the premises. He was aged thirty three and single. Peter Elliott, aged sixteen, was working as a servant for him and acted as a 'butcher's boy'.[9] Three years later, the business had changed hands once more and several subsequent trade directories list members of the Dawson family working there as butchers.[10]

As described in a previous chapter, after Ann Armstrong's death, it was decided to sell the property along with Sandy Mount and the Herst Lands which she had also owned. Part of the property description and the plan that was used in the sale particulars are shown below:[11]

LOT 6.

A COMFORTABLE DWELLING HOUSE,

A BUTCHER'S SHOP,

A well Built Barn, Stable and Premises,

ADJOINING THE ROYAL OAK INN BEARSTED,

Well situated, and conveniently arranged for Business, with a good Garden adjoining.   The

House contains an Entrance Passage, 2 Parlours, a Butcher's Shop, Kitchen, Washhouse, Pantry, and 3 Bed Rooms, and a Well of Water.

THE

OUT-BUILDINGS CONSIST OF A SLAUGHTER HOUSE, SHED, STABLE FOR TWO HORSES,

Harness Place, a Barn, Built of Timber and Tiled, in excellent repair.

THERE IS A GOOD GARDEN AND TWO ENTRANCE GATEWAYS.

The whole has a Frontage of 142 ft. 6 in. to the Street.

This Lot is in the occupation of Mr. JOHN DAWSON, a Yearly Tenant from Michaelmas, and is held with Lot Seven, at a Rental of £35 per Annum.

Apportioned Rent of this Lot, £18 per annum.

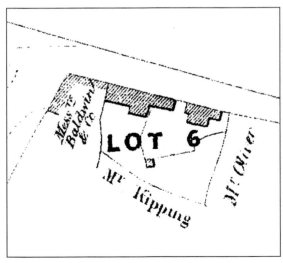

Reproduced courtesy of the Centre for Kentish Studies

Although James Whatman had expressed an interest in the property, it is not clear whether he bought it.[12] The premises continued to be used as a butcher's shop and James Gibson was listed as trading there in 1859.[13] The names of other butchers at the address include James Bridgland, William Cutbath, Alfred Brown and James Streeter.[14] None of these people are recorded as born in Bearsted. James Streeter, an under tenant of George Smith,[15] was the last butcher to use the shop as a business premises.

In 1901, John Datson opened the shop as a bakery. In addition to supplying bread, there was a small confectionery department. He was assisted by Rebecca, his wife, and several of his family.[16] The following year, the property was sold to Frederick Marshall by Mary Ann Dawson and Elizabeth Critall, who were described as spinsters from the nearby village of Detling.[17]

After the First World War, many men returned to the village following their discharge from the armed forces. Life began to return to normal and families worked extremely hard to build their businesses up again. Charles Datson succeeded his brother in the business.

The Datson family often worked eighteen hours a day. Deliveries were made using a horse and cart. Christmas was always a busy time. The bakery oven was never wholly extinguished so people in the village used to bring along geese and turkeys to be cooked for their Christmas dinners. Although there was a small charge for this facility, Mr Datson passed the money on to charity.

This advertisement, from 1929, appeared in the parish magazine:

| Awarded Diplomas, 1927-1928
Our Motto:
Cleanliness and Courtesy." | For Pure Home-Made Bread, try
DATSON'S | The Name which has stood the
test for nearly thirty years. |

Reproduced courtesy of Jenni Hudson

This detail from an undated photograph shows the bakery on the left hand side: the golden letters advertising Hovis bread can just be seen.

Photograph courtesy of Tony and Sheila Foster

After Charles retired in 1934, his son Laurence took over the running of the bakery. In 1935 he married Ethel Green. This photograph shows their wedding cake which was displayed for a short time in the shop window. It was made, but not decorated, by Laurence:

Photograph courtesy of Lesley Reynolds (née Datson)

Laurence and Ethel had two children: Roy and his sister, Lesley. They both contracted scarlet fever when Lesley was aged around seven. Lesley recalled that they were taken to an isolation hospital at Pembury. All their clothes had to be sterilised and no personal toys were allowed. It seemed harsh that their parents could only pay one visit a week due to petrol rationing. Even then, their parents had to keep their distance during visits because of the risk of infection. Lesley and Roy find it hard to imagine how their parents managed to cope at this time. They had two seriously ill children, an enforced lack of contact with them and they were also running a business severely restricted by wartime conditions.

This undated photograph shows Lesley and Roy with their mother during the Second World War. Note the camouflage markings on the roof behind Mrs Datson:

Photograph courtesy of Lesley Reynolds

112

Lesley and Roy particularly recalled one incident towards the end of the Second World War when many doodlebugs were passing over Bearsted. Harry Smith, who lived in the council houses in The Street, was assisting Laurence in the bakery. Baking was begun every evening by putting flour and water and yeast into a mixer. The temperature of the flour and water was assessed using a thermometer before the yeast was added. If it was too hot or too cold, the yeast would not start to work and the bread would not rise. Harry put the thermometer into the mixture but then forgot to remove it. He switched on the machine and promptly smashed the thermometer.

Harry and Laurence were concerned about the situation as there was strict food rationing and regulations controlling the waste of food. They decided to bury the dough in a piece of ground adjacent to the Royal Oak public house. Leslie distinctly remembered both men struggling with a huge armful of dough mixture. Next morning a small crater had appeared in the ground. For a few moments, Laurence thought a bomb had dropped but was baffled by the lack of damage to other nearby buildings. Then he realised that the depression was the result of the yeast continuing to work until it was spent. The dough had then sunk and left a crater. The area of ground became known as the Bearsted Volcano.

Lesley remembered the joy and sense of happiness in the village on V E Day and the celebrations. The bells of Holy Cross church were rung for a long time. Ethel, in her excitement, broke a pane of glass in a window that overlooked the pavement by trying to put her head out. Many flags were hung out in the village. Leslie was very pleased to see the Union flag proudly being displayed. There was also an American flag and even one bearing a hammer and sickle appeared from somewhere!

Part of the letter heading used by the bakery:

BROUGHT OF   Established 1901

L. L. DATSON

TOBACCO & CONFECTIONERY

Specialist in Birds Eye Frozen Foods

BEARSTED

Telephone: Maidstone 37167   ....19......

M ....

Reproduced courtesy of Roy Datson

Laurence was eventually able to purchase the property in 1954.[18] The bakery continued to supply bread and cakes for many years, until the arrival of pre-sliced and wrapped bread, although baking on the premises ceased during the late 1950s.[19] Eventually the bakery could no longer compete and closed shortly after Rowland's bakery by the Green also ceased trading. The property is now a private residence called The Old Bakery in recognition of the building's previous history.

Kathryn Kersey and Rosemary Pearce

20   Over a Century of Travellers Tales

Life in Bearsted for the Hunt family began around 1890 when William and Rose Hunt (née Springett) moved into the village. William had a brief apprenticeship at Button and Collins, grocers in The Broadway, Maidstone but then followed his father, Alfred into commercial travelling. He spent fifty years travelling all over Kent and Sussex. Amongst the companies William represented were Dadswell Brothers of Paddock Wood, Alf Cook of Leeds, Yorkshire, Alfred Couldery and Thomas Poulter both of London.

William's mother was Emma Hunt (née Smith). She moved to Bearsted to live with William and Rose in 1914 having previously run a newsagents in Sandgate. Emma is believed to be the first woman in Bearsted to be involved in a fatal road traffic accident involving a motor car. She sustained a fractured skull on 27 October 1925 near the dip well at Roundwell. She had drawn water there, when Captain Blogg came along in his car and lost control of the steering.

Earlier in 1925, Walter Fremlin died. Some of his estate at Milgate and other land holdings were put up for sale. William attended the sale at the Royal Star Hotel, Maidstone. He bought Ivy House which, in 1903, had briefly been the home of the poet Edward Thomas, Helen his wife, and their family. Edward wrote to a friend that they had moved from Rose Cottage at Rose Acre Farm into:

> The pretty old house on the village green, with a pair of lime trees on the two strips of lawn in front of the house…it is full of old woodwork, which gives the entrance to the staircase quite a monastic look. I expect I shall be able to write there…[1]

However, the move was not a happy time: Helen and Bronwen, their eldest daughter, succumbed to health problems which took some time to resolve. Edward then suffered severe fatigue and depression. The doctor condemned the house and they moved to Weald, near Sevenoaks.[2] By the time William moved to Ivy House, the property was in a far better condition!

This undated photograph shows the house:

Photograph courtesy of Chris and Sue Hunt

At the same sale, William also bought some other land as an investment. Some years later it became developed for housing and was incorporated into Mallings Drive. This undated photograph shows the land, bordered by a railway bridge:

Photograph courtesy of Chris and Sue Hunt

William married Rose Mears Isabel Springett from Maidstone. These photographs show William and Rose:

Photographs courtesy of Chris and Sue Hunt

They had a large family including Alfred, who became the taxi driver for the village, operating from Thorpe's Garage by the Green, and William, who became the head buyer for Selfridges later in his career.

Another son, George, broke horses on the Green before the First World War. He used the stables at the Royal Oak and the White Horse. When war was declared in 1914 he joined the army with William Hodges who came from The Old Plantation public house. It was not long before the army discovered George's exceptional skill with horses. He was removed from hostilities and sent to look after two stallions that were on a stud circuit in Kent, Essex and Sussex. The aim was to cover brood mares in order to produce a bloodline of horses that were suitable for the war effort. George often used to relate that there were occasions he was offered a financial consideration by the local farmers in order to quietly divert the stallions to cover their mares too.

After the war, as a small investment, William bought his son George a package of property that included Egypt House and the abattoir behind the Men's Institute. During the renovation work undertaken there some floorboards were lifted to reveal a large volume of sawdust. It is possible, given the close proximity of Egypt House to the abattoir, that at one time it had been used as a butcher's premises, although there is no record of this. George followed his grandfather and father's footsteps and also became a commercial traveller.

One of George's brothers was Sidney Hamilton Hunt. He trained as a carpenter and worked for a carpentry firm called Hubble and Newsom which was sited next to a garage at Weavering Street facing Ashford Road. Sidney Hunt married Grace Baker at Holy Cross church in 1934. The Baker family lived in Bell Farmhouse in Bell Lane and also owned a wood yard.

This photograph shows Grace and Sidney during their wedding reception at the farmhouse:

Photograph courtesy of Chris and Sue Hunt

In the Second World War, Sidney worked at Rootes in Mill Street, Maidstone, helping to build amphibious craft. Outside the factory was the pond for a mill which had been demolished in 1903.[3] With this convenient area of water to hand, the craft were swung out over the river and tested.

Sidney had a number of escapades in and around Bearsted. For a time, he lodged at the White Horse. He was happy to assist Mrs Brook, the landlady, with laying fires and some of the cellar work if extra help was required. Also lodging there was a gentleman known to all as 'Harry the tramp'. Harry lodged above the stable block which was located behind the back of the White Horse and which was reached by a substantial wooden staircase. Sidney used a car to travel to work and this was usually parked at the back of the White Horse by the stables.

One night Sidney lost control of his car and crashed into the stables staircase. He was able to extract the vehicle despite it being badly damaged. In the dark, Sidney did not realise that he had also completely destroyed the staircase. Next morning, when Harry awoke, he had to call for help as there was no means to get out of his lodgings. Luckily, someone found a ladder so that Harry could escape.

Sidney's younger brother, Hubert was born in 1908. He farmed at Hollingbourne and ran Old England Dairies with Bob Leggett who lived near the Great Danes hotel. Hubert's first married home in Bearsted was at The Limes. However, the house was not as picturesque as it might seem today. Some of the walls were made of hessian sacking which had been tightly stretched over a wooden framework. Initially this arrangement worked well, but with time and damp, some of the sacking had sagged. The local rat population found the walls irresistible as it was easy to climb inside the framework. Traps were routinely used around the property.

Hubert met his wife, Sophia Alice, (usually called Alice), at Lushington Court where she was working as a lady's maid. They had seven children. Five of them were boys: Keith, Peter, Richard, Gerald and Christopher. After a short spell at Tower Cottage, this branch of the Hunt family moved to Cross Keys in March 1951. They were one of the first families to move into the estate. In addition to the farm holding, Hubert had three allotments and kept pigs and a goose. He also raised a flock of chickens to sell at Christmas.

Richard and Christopher (usually known as Chris) have inherited many family memories of Bearsted. During Hubert's lifetime, Walter Fremlin had been a major figure in Bearsted. Walter had many idiosyncrasies. It was well known that he was fond of trees. There was a tree nursery on the Ashford Road where the Potted Garden Nursery stands today. The owner did not succeed in business and a bankruptcy sale was held. Walter bought the premises and used the stock to plant trees, in groups of five, all over Bearsted. It was the start of many such plantings.

After the bankruptcy sale, Mr Goddard ran the nursery for many years. He grew and sold plants and vegetables. The premises were quite extensive so he devised a unique means of rapid service for his customers. It was quite usual for him to fulfil orders by means of travelling to the lettuce beds, cutting the order and returning to the customer, all completed whilst riding his bicycle.

Hubert could recall that Mr Fremlin had once kept a small collection of exotic animals at Milgate. The animals included an emu, an ostrich, a zebra and several Shetland ponies. It was sometimes referred to as the Bearsted Zoo.

In the years after the Second World War, everyone was aware that there were many people in the area that did not have much money. Most were paid their wages in cash. Few had a bank account. Most families in the village managed their finances by holding accounts or 'books' at the local shops. On pay day, which was usually a Friday, bills or accounts were paid promptly and a new account was started.

Despite a lack of finance, there always seemed to be plenty of activities in the village to keep everyone occupied. Pigeon-racing was very popular. Bill Giles, Alan Cecil, Bill Thompson and Reg Jones held races with eight to ten pigeons which were collected from The Green in baskets stacked ready for the conveyor to take them to the race point. Pigeons were also exhibited in a Fur and Feather tent at Bearsted Fayre. This picture shows Chris proudly holding his two best pigeons:

Photograph courtesy of Sue Hunt

Many people kept and raised a few chickens and geese. Richard once encouraged a goose to lay an egg by tickling it with a spoon lashed to a length of stick. He retrieved the egg and persuaded a chicken to sit on it until it hatched. The goose, known either as 'Goosey' or 'Fred', then adopted Richard as its mother and would follow him around the village. Richard kept Fred for a few years and was able to summon it to be fed by whistling to it. The goose would then take off from the allotment where it was kept and fly onto the front lawn of his parents' house.

William Hunt and Norman Ollett were amongst the original members of the Bearsted and Thurnham Rifle Club which was founded in 1903. It is thought to be one of the oldest, continually licensed ranges in the country as the club still meets behind the White Horse. A number of people in the village were extremely good shots. The Home Guard practised on the range during the Second World War.

For many years Arthur Maxted shot at the range. He lived at Crismill Lane and ran a wood yard there. Arthur never married but was always keen to help the younger generation in the village. He regularly took groups of children for outings in the summer which included trips on the Romney, Hythe and Dymchurch railway.

In addition to cricket and football on the Green there were other avenues to expend sporting energies. Quite a few men raced small terrier dogs. Many shopkeepers set traps overnight in their shops. Any rats or mice caught were released on the Green the following morning for the attention of the terriers. Les Simpson's dogs were regular participants. Les lived at Invicta Villas and had once been a jockey. He was a bookies runner and a groom to the Monckton family when they lived at Woodcut House on the Ashford Road. After they moved to Bell House by the Green, the family gave up their horses, so Les undertook gardening for them instead.

There were opportunities for children to earn small amounts of money in the village. Chris assisted both his father and Arthur Adams to deliver milk. Chris used to meet Arthur at Bearsted station by 6am and together they would undertake the delivery round for Ware Street and Cross Keys. Chris would then run home and change into his school uniform prior to catching the school bus at 8.30am from the Royal Oak. On Saturdays and Sundays Chris undertook the whole delivery round. His work on Saturdays finished around 3pm as he collected payments so the round took rather longer. Chris recalled that Mrs White from Little Dane in Thurnham Lane always paid with a £5 note, which seemed a rather large piece of paper! The Sunday delivery was completed by 10am.

One close friend to Chris was Trevor Cleggett. Like many children, Trevor delivered papers for Taylor's newsagents. His round included Hill House and Doctor Ledward's house, which was near Maiford's woodyard at the bottom of Ware Street, near the railway bridge. On a Saturday morning, Mrs Ledward always left a slice of cake and a sixpence out for him on a small plate covered by a basin to protect it against the birds. One Christmas was particularly profitable for Trevor as Mr Taylor gave him a half crown 'Christmas Box' at the start of the round and then another at the end; he had completely forgotten that Trevor had already been paid.

Trevor then gave up his paper round to work for Mr Moss the butcher at his shop in Chestnut Place. This undated advertisement appeared in the parish magazine:

Reproduced courtesy of James Moore

Trevor recalled that being a delivery boy was considered a good job for a young lad in the village. He rode a big black shop bicycle with an enormous wicker basket on the front. The joints of meat were delivered with the account details and bill secured to the top of each one with a metal pin. The top of the bill bore a design that included a picture of a cow's head. It was quite a responsible job as payment for the orders was made at the time of delivery. Trevor estimated that most joints of meat cost around four shillings, so it did not take long to accumulate £10 to £12 on an average delivery round. Most people paid promptly but there was one lady who once tried to pay Trevor in postage stamps.

Trevor did not normally have mishaps when he was working, but there was one occasion when he dropped the meat that he was delivering and so rushed home to wash the dirt off it. This was not appreciated by the customer who complained that it looked very pale!

In addition to Mr Moss, there was another butcher's shop which was the end premises of a row of properties on the Green. Previous owners had been the Raggett family, Mr Chambers, and Cyril Simmons before Mr Exeter took it over. This undated advertisement appeared in the parish magazine in 1929:

Phone Bearsted 6382 for
Prime HOME-KILLED MEAT
A. V. CHAMBERS,
FAMILY BUTCHER,
THE GREEN,   BEARSTED.

PORK SAUSAGES A SPECIALITY.

Reproduced courtesy of James Moore

This photograph, taken in 1965, shows Mr Exeter's shop:

Photograph courtesy of Bearsted and Thurnham Women's Institute

The first property in the row on the Green was the grocer's shop which was run by Mr Marsh. There were also several cottages known as Smart's Cottages. In the same location were the premises of Jack Sent, who was the 'village snob' or shoe repairer and Mr Harden, who repaired watches and clocks. John Hardy could recall that during trading hours, Jack Sent's door was usually open. The shop atmosphere was a heady mix of the scent of leather, shoe polish and gas from a small burner. The latter was used for melting wax to seal the welts on shoes. Customers could take Jack a pair of shoes and they would be repaired and returned, highly polished, within two days. Mr Harden sold Chris his first watch. Small children tended to avoid Mrs Fraser who sat outside her back door smoking a clay pipe. She had a reputation for being very fierce! When the cottages were put up for auction in the 1960s, Chris recalled that Alan Cox paid £4,000 for all of them. Since that time, the cottages have changed hands many times and increasing sums have been paid.

Gerald Hunt, an elder brother to Chris and Richard, became something of an entrepreneur when he was growing up. He paid other children in the village sixpence to collect waste paper for him. When Gerald had a sufficient quantity, he sold it on for £15 a load. With the money he bought other items that he felt could be of use. One of these was an inflatable rubber dinghy.

Micky Simmons worked as a gardener on the Milgate estate. The land holdings of the estate still extended down to Lilk Meadow and up to the Street and included the field next to the Cross Keys estate. It was very low-lying and did not drain particularly well. Sometimes the boys in the village persuaded Mr Simmons to lend them the key to the sluice gate for a few hours. Quickly, they built a dam, altered the sluice gate and created an artificial lake. Gerald's rubber dinghy was used in prolonged games involving the Bearsted version of Swallows and Amazons.

The field next to Cross Keys was used as an extended playground by the children from the estate. One of Chris' friends, Roy, looked after two ponies in the field. One day, Roy, possibly inspired by the film Ben Hur, harnessed the horses and attached an old coach-built pram carriage to them. It was not long before Roy was hurtling all around the field playing 'Chariots'. The horses started galloping as they approached the sheep dip area. Suddenly, the ropes snapped, the horses broke free and the pram went into the sheep dip and promptly sank. Fortunately, Roy clambered out, unscathed, but never played chariots again.

There were further opportunities in the area for young people who wanted to earn some money, particularly at Bradley's farm which is now part of The Landway estate. In the middle of one of the fields, possibly where Birling Avenue and Mynn Crescent now meet, was a big shed-like building. This was used to make and mend the wooden boxes and crates in which crops were stored and transported. Chris' brother, Peter, did this work occasionally. The sides of the boxes were stencilled with Mr Bradley's name. Chris helped with the stencilling.

Also on Mr Bradley's land, fairly near Bell Lane, there was an enormous hole from where a doodlebug had landed. This was used as an unofficial compost heap and tip by local people. The hole was well known to be crawling with rats as a result. One favourite occupation by the boys from the village was to try and shoot the rats with air rifles. There was an alternative pastime. Tins of carbide gas crystals could easily be bought because many people still used carbide bicycle lamps. The crystals were a grey powder. The boys used to add water to the crystals through a hole made in the tin and then throw it in to the rubbish. There was nearly always a most satisfying explosion.

It was quite usual for boys in the village to own at least one go-cart. Once in possession of a wooden crate or soap box and a few pieces of timber, it was quite easy to build one. Wheels were obtained from St Faith's Home where a ready supply of old prams was usually available. Steering required a nut and bolt to connect the front axle to the cart and a loop of rope or string.

Richard and Chris recalled Daphne Clement once asked them to bring her some sawdust from the timber yard in Bell Lane. It was required either for a Brownie meeting or for the guinea pigs kept at the school. The return journey involved pushing the cart with the heavy load on it all the way up Ware Street. It was hard work, so they decided that when they reached the Methodist Chapel, they would free-wheel down to the school. Half-way down the hill, Paul Kirk unexpectedly drove a van out from the railway station and collided with the go-cart. There was no damage, but saw dust was widely scattered.

There were many diversions available for boys who were not interested in school. At Crismill, there was a wooded area that was in the process of being cleared. Much of the timber was either hand-felled or taken down by small charges of dynamite. Mark Baker had several pole barns set up in his wood yard nearby. He was very skilled and often had an audience of young boys watching him using a draw-knife to clean the bark off the logs. There was also a pond, which was commonly known as a 'mattress pond' as the reeds rotted down every year to form a thick layer which could be walked upon to gain access to moorhen nests. The moorhens were the target of many depredations by small boys who raided their nests, took their eggs and upon occasion, the birds too. It was generally acknowledged that moorhen made a good filling for pies as the small carcasses yielded a surprising amount of meat.

The railway ganger huts were another attraction. There were several in the area before the line was electrified. Richard recalled a small patch of gravel at the front of them, under which was hidden a small tobacco tin which held the key to the hut. The workmen thought that no one knew it was there. Once the boys had got into a hut, the first priority was to make a cup of tea using the supplies kept inside which included tins of condensed milk. After this, they used a paint tin to boil up the moorhen eggs that they had collected. Despite care being taken on the mattress pond some of their clothes were wet, so it was also a useful place to dry them.

Fog detonator caps were also kept in the hut. They were circular with lead strips on either side to hold them in place on the rail. If a train ran over one of the caps, workmen on the line would hear the detonation and move away from danger. Some of the boys would clip around a hundred of them in a row onto the rail and then run off into the woods to see what would happen. Often the train would stop, but no culprits were ever found.

On one occasion Chris and his friends attempted to discharge a cap by using it as a target on the rifle range. The resulting explosion slightly lifted the range roof and incurred the wrath of Arthur Maxted, who was supervising them. Trevor threw his supply of caps away when he made a frightening discovery: he found his small brother holding one of the caps over a gas cooker flame. He was trying to melt the lead strips off the cap to make some soldiers. As Trevor commented, it could so easily have ended in a tragedy.

Another favourite occupation for the boys in the village was exploring the local area. 'Bearsted Caves' were a particular haunt. Details of the location have varied but they are best described as a rock formation in a field that faces the Ashford Road, in the angle between the A20 and the Bearsted turning for Roundwell and The Street. The Kent Messenger published this intriguing report on 2 May 1936:

BEARSTED LINK WITH HUGENOT GLASS WORKERS

Underground Passages Discovered in Sand Pits

A link with the time when Bearsted was a centre of glass workers' industry was revealed on Tuesday, when large underground workings were found by men quarrying at the sand pits of Mr J P Weston, of Weavering Street, near Bearsted.

The discovery was made by two workmen, Mr E Hunt and Mr J W Earl, who cut into the side of a circular cavern about 156 feet across, with smaller passages leading out from it.

The average height of the cave was five feet, although there was a considerable quantity of loose sand on the floor. Some of the passages were only a few feet in length, but others were found to penetrate 50 yards. On the walls were marks caused apparently by small picks or digging implements.

At Maidstone Museum, the 'Kent Messenger' was informed that the caves were probably excavated by Hugenot glass workers, who settled in the district about 200 years ago.

It was their custom to dig a shaft and from that work the surrounding sand until the required white sand was found. This method was adopted instead of the present-day method one of open quarrying and many examples of it are to be found in Kent. Among these, Hollingbourne caves are a fine example.

Air shafts, dug to ventilate the underground workings have been discovered in large numbers in parts of Kent where the soil is sandy, especially in the vicinity of Manston, Thanet.

Reproduced courtesy of Kent Messenger group

Today, there seems to be nothing resembling caverns in the area, but all the local children thought that the caves had been there for many years. Chris was able to recall that they comprised a series of distinctly hollowed-out chambers rather than natural caves so it is possible that perhaps they were used as some sort of shelter centuries ago. He had been shown the location by his father.

For a time, groups of boys set off for the caves on a Saturday morning, having previously bought a box of household candles and visited Mr Datson's bakery to obtain a cottage loaf for some food. The candles were used to illuminate the caves and the soot was useful to write messages on the cave walls. Perhaps the caves still exist but they are now on private property.

There were many characters in the village that Richard and Chris could recall. One such person was Bob Sceal. He moved onto a smallholding in Thurnham from Bromley in 1948 following a separation from his wife. He was a builder by trade but he was extremely good at bartering and made most of his living by this means. He discovered that if he bought land at £25 an acre, the government would give him £25 an acre to clear it. This arrangement appealed to him so he bought ten acres of ground in Thurnham Lane, close to Clayswood, for very little outlay. Although the soil was rather poor clay, he managed to find a living as a market gardener and supplied local greengrocers such as Mr Kingsland. Bob built two greenhouses and kept a small orchard with chickens running beneath the trees.

In the course of obtaining planning permission for a dwelling, Bob put the foundations in for a bungalow but the work was abandoned as permission was refused. For many years his dwelling was a caravan but in 1968 he moved into a little hut which he had put up. There was just room for a bed, table, sideboard and a sink. There was a chimney but he cooked meals over an open fire. Lighting was by a paraffin lamp. Bob lived on the rabbits he caught and the surplus of the vegetables he grew. Although his lifestyle would have been regarded as sparse by some people, Bob considered it to be sufficient for his needs.

This undated photograph of Bob Sceal was taken at the golf course, Bearsted:

Photograph courtesy of Chris and Sue Hunt

Unexpectedly, one day a letter arrived to advise Bob that his wife had died, and so he returned to Bromley, living there until his death in 1986. No one in Bearsted or Thurnham knew if he had any other family but he requested to be buried in St Mary's churchyard. His land was later bought by Mr Allan who lived at Clayswood. The abandoned smallholding and the remains of the greenhouses can still be seen today in the vicinity of the motorway bridge in Thurnham Lane.

The White Horse was one of the centres for many village activities. Mr and Mrs Brook ran the establishment for forty two years. Mrs Brook was American and gained the nickname 'Aunty Ben' from her husband Benjamin. Before she married, she had been an opera singer and still sang at the garden parties held at the big houses in Bearsted and Thurnham. Aunty Ben was known for her love of finery. She regularly wore heavy jewellery and big hats. Mrs White from Sutton Street made hats for her using squirrel tails and rabbit furs that had been supplied by Chris and Trevor. Aunty Ben paid them two shillings for each tail.

Beer was usually delivered to the pub from the Fremlin brewery using a team of shire horses. Sometimes the draymen paid local boys sixpence to hold the horses during the delivery. They were occasions when the school bell would ring during the delivery. However, the financial lure was greater than attending school and so many 'assistants' would run into school late, but paid.

Hubert could recall that before the corner door opposite the Green was blocked up, a charcoal burner sometimes visited the White Horse. His donkey would place his hooves on the door step and refuse to budge until his master had poured a pint of beer down its throat.

In addition to the three bars in the public house, there was also a small coffee room. William Hunt used to meet John Buck there to drink coffee and debate politics. John Buck was a Conservative who ran a builders yard in The Street. The yard was later taken over by Mr Tong. William was a staunch Liberal and there were many heated arguments between them over the policies pursued by the governments.

In the 1960s, there were further ways of obtaining goods in Bearsted and Thurnham. A local unofficial 'barter' economy operated on a mutually beneficial basis at the White Horse. Chris and Trevor regularly used to spend a few hours shooting or ferreting on a Sunday morning. If they managed to kill more rabbits than they required, they would take them to the White Horse where they could be exchanged for surplus vegetables that other customers had brought in from their allotments. As they grew older, sometimes the price of the goods was converted into the purchase of a pint. These arrangements persisted until the early 1970s when the village began to change and expand once more.

This postcard shows the White Horse in the 1960s before Auntie Ben gave up the licence. It then became part of the Beefeater chain of restaurants:

Photograph courtesy of Terry Clarke

21 Caring for the community: doctors, nurses and nursing homes

Before the Twentieth century, provision of medical care for people living in Bearsted and Thurnham was largely based at Hollingbourne. The current Yeoman surgery covers a wide area including Leeds, Broomfield, Otham, and part of Grove Green. It was only relatively recently that the separate consulting rooms in Hollingbourne were closed.

One of the earliest records for local medical care shows Thomas Weekes running a practice in 1750. Thomas was an apothecary and was based at Eyhorne House, Hollingbourne. He also instructed apprentice apothecaries. Thomas ran the practice for just over twenty nine years. He was succeeded by John Gurney White, who served until his death in 1790.[1]

Below is shown what is believed to be the first record of a surgeon offering professional services for local people. It is an advertisement for the services of William James Jeudwine, which appeared in the Maidstone Journal, 23 November 1790.

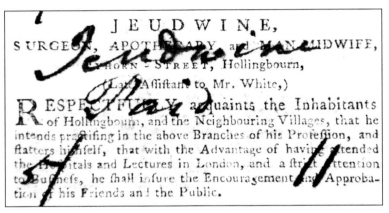

Reproduced courtesy of Martin Moss and Kent Messenger group

Benjamin Wood ran the surgery from 1801 to around 1815 and he, too, placed an advertisement in the Maidstone Journal in 1801:

HOLLINGBOURN.

B. WOOD, Surgeon, Apothecary, and Man-Midwife, informs the inhabitants of Hollingbourn and its neighbourhood, that he has settled at the above place, for the purpose of exercising his profession; hopes by his attention to merit the favour of all those who may honour him with their notice.

Reproduced courtesy of Martin Moss and Kent Messenger group

Thomas Allen succeeded Benjamin Wood, but his career came to an unhappy end as he found it difficult to cope with the constant demands of serving the community. On 21 December 1833 he was committed to Barming Asylum. He was only forty six years old. Thomas was certified by the next doctor to hold the practice, Charles Sedgwick. Charles and his son, also called Charles, looked after their patients for a total of sixty years.[3]

In 1894, Augustus Mayberry Whitestone began work as a doctor in Hollingbourne. His duties included acting as the medical officer for the Hollingbourne Union workhouse. Augustus, or 'Gussie', as he was known, was very keen on rugby. Many long established families of Bearsted, Thurnham and Hollingbourne have fond memories of his kindness and professional manner.[4]

This photograph shows members of the Whitestone family around 1898. Dr Whitestone is holding his son, Berkeley. Mrs Whitestone is seated on the far right.

Photograph courtesy of Martin Moss

Margaret Blamire Brown recalled that in the early years of the Twentieth century, her mother collected payments for a monthly subscription scheme that enabled Bearsted to have a District Nurse through the Queen's District Nursing Association. She recalled that Nurse was regarded as the guardian of the good health of the village. There were very few telephones, so if Nurse was required, a message was sent to her house. The sight of her bicycle outside a house aroused curiosity – perhaps there had been a new arrival! Home delivery for all babies was the usual arrangement.

This photograph shows Sophia Caroline Birch who was the first district nurse for Bearsted, Thurnham and Hollingbourne from 1909 to 1920. Her salary was approximately £90 per annum. She died in 1944 and is buried in St Mary's churchyard.

Photograph courtesy of Norah Giles

After Dr Whitestone retired, in 1923 he was replaced by Francis Cooke Alton who ran the practice for three years before Herbert Stratford Collins arrived. Dr Collins had served as an army Captain during the First World War and had been mentioned in despatches.[5]

Marion Beeton Pull was appointed District Nurse in 1929 and retired in 1961. Her lively personality will be remembered by many older residents as she was thoroughly involved in the community. Her first lodgings were shared with the Stemp family at 1 Ware Street. Nurse Pull's duties included regular visits to a nursing home run at a house called Rose Mount, at the corner of Plantation Lane and Roseacre Lane. Occasionally Nurse had to keep a close eye on the post-operative progress of the patients. In 1934, Miss Clara Sayers, a state registered nurse, was the matron of the home.[6]

This is an undated picture of Rose Mount. Note the pram parked just outside the conservatory:

Photograph courtesy of Malcolm Kersey

Below is an undated list of items required for maternity patients:[7]

Telephone:—Bearsted 6327.

Rose Mount Nursing Home,
BEARSTED,
MAIDSTONE.

BABY.

2 doz. Napkins, Turkish Towelling, ¾ yard square

2 doz. ditto, Harrington's or similar

3 Face Towels

3 Vests

3 Woollen Coats

3 pairs Woollen Boots

½ yard Flannel for Binders

3 Long Flannels

6 Baby Gowns of one thickness

1 Tablet of Toilet Soap

Baby Powder

1 Small Sponge

1 Tube Vaseline

1 Tube Lanoline

1 Large Hot Water Bottle and Cover

1 Box Safety Pins (assorted)

1 Feeding Bottle

2 Teats and Valves

ALL LINEN TO BE MARKED.

Reproduced courtesy of Maidstone Reference Library

This photograph was taken outside 1 Ware Street in 1929 and shows Nurse Pull by her official transport, which was known as 'Bongo, the District car'. Note the stork and baby mascot just visible on the radiator!

Photograph courtesy of Jean Jones and Martin Moss

During the Second World War, Nurse Pull's duties included visiting Bearsted House. Mr and Mrs Stanley Johnson most generously agreed that in addition to becoming the local centre for the Red Cross, a further part of the house could be converted to a small hospital with a ward. Nurse Pull had sometimes to adapt her nursing duties to cope with wartime conditions. She wrote about the air raids on Detling aerodrome:[8]

> I asked my friend if she would like a ride to the aerodrome as my pass had to be endorsed. This was needed to get to patients in farm cottages, who could not be evacuated…we went up and the guard let us through. However, coming back the guard had been changed and it was a long time before he would let us through. [My friend] was annoyed as she would have preferred to have gone the next day, but I had insisted that it was urgent.
>
> The next day, at about the same time, I heard the drone of a plane and looking up I said, "I'm sure that that is a Junker." I then realised that there were hundreds of them and they were going to bomb the aerodrome. I gazed in horror as hordes of planes swept down divided into four columns and dive-bombed the aerodrome. It was a bad raid and we never knew how many casualties there were. The son of one of my patients was beheaded as he tried to run to a haystack in a nearby field. It was the exact time that I would have been at the aerodrome if I had done as my friend had wished.
>
> My patient was expecting her first baby, so I had to go up there the next day. I went in the afternoon and the wail of 'Moaning Minnie' turned my stomach over. The cottage was a very isolated one, and when I got there no one was in sight. Guns and bombs were very noisy and placing my tin hat on my head, I was looking wildly around when I heard a voice say "Nurse, quick, come in here" and found that they were all in a dug-out in the ground. Their spaniel dog was tied up, howling with fright. There was a loud 'ping-ping' of shrapnel which riddled a line of washing and a piece hit me on the head, knocking my helmet onto to my nose. I fell into the dug-out saying "I have been hit", but I felt my nose and it was quite all right.
>
> A few days later I was again at the cottage as my patient was in labour. She shouted down to the grandfather "Don't keep banging the doors, bits of ceiling keep falling on the bed". He shouted back "I ain't a-banging them doors, that's old Jerry a-dropping of 'is bombs". There was a groan and a voice from the bed: "Coo, I wish I could drop this bomb…"

The centre of the practice moved to Bearsted around the middle years of the Twentieth century.[9] A surgery initially held at Forge Cottages was succeeded by one established at The Limes. Marjorie Cork could recall that patients queued outside the door if the rather small waiting room was full. Older residents will recall prescriptions could be collected from a metal box which was located by the main door.

Dr Ledward joined Dr Collins in the practice as a partner in 1948. Dr Ledward was known as 'Tommie' and lived at Bell Farm House before later moving to Little Snowfield. This photograph of Dr Collins was taken in his consulting room at The Limes in 1959. His dog, Jan, is seated next to him.

Photograph courtesy of Martin Moss

Photograph courtesy of Kent Messenger group

In 1973 the surgery moved to Yeoman Lane. It was built to accommodate three members of staff which included Dr Ledward. He continued at Yeoman Surgery until 1982. This photograph of Dr Ledward, and his wife, Peggy, was taken during his retirement presentation.

The surgery building was extended in 1982 and again in 1989 as the number of patients and doctors increased. A range of new treatments was developed together with other medical services which became available and were offered to the local population.

This photograph of the surgery was taken in 1986:

Photograph courtesy of Bearsted and District Local History Society

A replacement surgery costing £1.1 million was constructed and came in to use during April 2005, prior to the official opening when the building was complete. This photograph was taken in Yeoman Lane, November 2004, and shows part of the new surgery under construction:

Photograph courtesy of Roger Vidler

The old premises were demolished and the area is now part of the treatment rooms and a car park for the surgery, which is now called the Bearsted Medical Practice. It was officially opened by Dr Hugh Vaux in September 2005. Before this, the staff and doctors, including Dr Bonds, Dr Dolman, Dr Godsmark and the Practice Manager, Jane Jarrett, buried a time capsule under the ambulance bay section of the premises, as this transcript from the August 2005 edition of the Downs Mail reveals:

> A time capsule has been buried under the new Bearsted Medical Practice at Yeoman Lane. Inside the capsule, the staff included memories of family/surgery life, the cover of one patient's medical records who was born in 1913, photographs of the old and new surgery, a practice leaflet, lottery ticket and set of accounts.

Reproduced courtesy of Downs Mail

Kathryn Kersey and Rosemary Pearce

22   Growing up in Bearsted in the 1930s and 1940s

After eight years in inner-city Liverpool, village life was a revelation for Doris Britcher (née Bentley) when she moved to Bearsted in 1935. Her early life had been very hard as there was widespread poverty and little employment. If there was no work available, her father would receive around twenty three shillings a week from the labour exchange with which to support his family. Although this sum seemed meagre, the Bentley family were luckier than some. As the children were members of the Sunday school at St Clement's church in Dove Street, they also qualified for parish relief of four shillings a week.

George Bentley, Doris's uncle, set up a horse racing business that was based in Gabriel's Hill, Maidstone. In 1933, George offered her father a job as a clerk. He moved to Maidstone and sent his wages back to his family. Then George bought 9 Roseacre Lane and offered to rent it to his brother and family. The house had been built in 1928 and was first sold for £500. As prices had fallen steeply due to the Depression, in 1935 the property cost George £350.

Doris could not believe the contrast with Liverpool. Just over a thousand people lived around Bearsted and Thurnham and she was entranced by all the green fields and the abundance of flowers everywhere. There were many activities and clubs for children. They were regarded as an important part of the community. Both Doris and her brother, Stanley, appreciated what the village and countryside had to offer. Stanley very quickly joined the Boy Scouts and was thoroughly involved in both the Scout movement and athletics for many years. The Scouts were run by Mr Smith and Mr Elliott and their activities included camping and long hikes.

Shortly after the family arrived, Mrs Bentley went in search of the local school. They had no idea where to go, so walked along the Ashford Road until they got to the Otham turning. Her mother disliked walking and after inner-city life, was not used to long distances. Eventually, they turned round and walked back to Yeoman Lane where they finally asked for directions. They were advised to keep walking up Yeoman Lane until they reached the Green. When they arrived at Bearsted School, Stanley was immediately accepted as he was eleven years old but Doris was too young to be admitted so she went to Thurnham School for a year where she was taught by Miss Sage and Mrs Hutt.

One of Doris' earliest memories of Thurnham School was Miss Sage telling the children that if they brought an egg, she could boil it for them on the school stove. They could eat it with some bread and butter at lunch time instead of going home. Doris appreciated this as it seemed quite a long walk back to her house for lunch. Doris settled very quickly at Thurnham School and nobody commented on her Liverpool accent.

It did not take long for the neighbours to introduce themselves. Peggy Goodhew, who lived in one of the houses opposite, called and asked Doris if she would like to go 'chest-nutting.' Doris did not quite know what this meant but decided to go anyway. It did not take her long to learn that 'chest-nutting' involved collecting nuts from the sweet chestnut trees at the top of the track by Sandy Mount farm (now Hog Hill) on the outer edges of the Snowfield estate. The Lichfield family were happy for people to do this as it stopped the nuts being wasted. Doris can also remember a friend telling her that some years earlier, she had walked through the orchard on the Snowfield estate. She came across Baroness Orczy's sledge: it was still draped and lined with furs, and seemed abandoned there.

Doris was very impressed with the many community events that involved everyone and which were regularly organised in the village. The more wealthy families were benevolent to those less fortunate but unlike her previous experience in urban Liverpool, generosity was given in a way that preserved respect on both sides. One example of this was the annual jumble sale that Mrs Sierakowski ran for many years. The profits went to the Missions to Seamen charity. It was the only jumble sale in Bearsted. People flocked to it and it was very profitable. Mrs Sierakowski asked many children to help and they appreciated the responsibility. She was quite concerned that her assistants were properly sustained for the task and gave them each 6d so that they could buy one of the 'teas' that were for sale in the back room at the Memorial Hall. They consisted of sandwiches, cake and some scones and for some children whose families could only supply a basic diet, it was an extra meal that was greatly appreciated.

Doris belonged to many clubs which seemed to operate as an informal framework for the younger members of the village to mix socially. There was always an activity going on somewhere. In 1936, Doris was asked if she would consider joining Brownies as Pamela Thorpe was interested in re-starting the pack. Pamela was a popular leader and as Brown Owl, would invite the Brownies to tea once a year during the summer. She lived in one of the big houses by the Otham turning on the Ashford Road. The garden was enormous and had a miniature playhouse. During the war, Pamela joined the Royal Air Force and married Flight Officer George Lawrence from the Canadian Air Force.[1]

Although there are not many photographs of the Bearsted Brownies in the 1930s, this photograph was taken around 1925:

Photograph courtesy of Jenni Hudson

<u>Back Row, left to right</u>: Eileen Blandford, Margaret Oswald Jones
Dolly Foster, Jean Wilkinson, Kath Playfoot

<u>Front Row, left to right</u>: -----, Norah Pettipiere, Dorothy Frost

Doris progressed to the Girl Guides when she was ten years old. She hugely enjoyed the activities and the joint meetings with Companies from Leeds, Harrietsham and Hollingbourne. There were two Captains that Doris particularly remembered: Eileen Blandford and Joyce Hunt. Eileen lived in a cottage opposite the pond on the Green called The Retreat. Eileen had been one of the first Brownies in Bearsted. Both Eileen and Joyce were to run the Guides for many years.

Many people offered help in running activities for the Guides. Doris particularly remembered that Mrs Grout, allowed her house, Rusaker, to be used to work for badges that had a practical element to them. In this way, many Guides earned their Homemaking badges. Eileen had no favourites in the company, but Doris was made to feel that her presence mattered. She received very little attention at home as her other siblings competed for her parents' attention, so Guides became a special place.

Doris was disappointed that she had to forego a place at a Guide camp that was due to take place at Maidenhead in July 1939 as it coincided with the arrival of her sister, Rita. During the camping trip, there was a visit to Windsor Castle.

This photograph was taken in the grounds of Windsor Castle:

Photograph courtesy of Jenni Hudson

<u>Back row</u> includes Joyce Eversden and Pamela Matthews

<u>Front row</u> includes Margery Green, Kathleen Harnett and Evelyn White

The company ran many activities for the girls in the village. Camps were held locally and in other places such as on the Brabourne estate in Mersham and the grounds of Homewood School, Tenterden.

One regular event was church parade. This first undated photograph shows the company leaving Holy Cross church after a service and the second shows the 1st Bearsted Guide Company forming a guard of honour outside the church when Eileen married Harry Howard in 1944:

Both photographs courtesy of Jenni Hudson

The Brownies and Guides regularly held shows and other entertainments. This photograph of the Guide Company was taken after an entertainment held in the Women's Institute Hall on 22 May 1943:

Photograph courtesy of Jenni Hudson

<u>Back row</u> includes Captain Eileen Blandford, Audrey Lee, Christine Lee, Marion Smith, Betty Vane, Betty Baisley, Joyce Hunt, Evelyn White, Barbara Spendley, Pam Batkin, Betty Gibbons, Ann Cheshire Martin, Muriel Tutt, June Monckton, Pat Batkin, Lieutenant Joyce Eversden

<u>Centre Row</u> includes Marian Shales, Peggy Ann Jessel, Pam Sendles, Barbara Cox, Audrey Humphrey, Ann Coveney

<u>Front Row</u> includes Celia Pantin, Dorothy Green, Margery Green, Margery Avery, Eileen Chittenden

The Brownies and Guides also held joint meetings with the Scout Group; they were known as Great Camp Fire evenings and were greatly enjoyed. This undated, but slightly later, photograph shows a joint Christmas party in the Scout Hut, bordering Roseacre Lane, in the 1950s. Leaders included in the photograph are Joyce Dobson, James Elliott, Jimmy Peate and Eileen Howard:

Photograph courtesy of Doris Britcher

There were two other organisations for girls in the village when they were aged ten or eleven: The Girls' Club and the Girls' Friendly Society. The Girls Club meetings were held in the Women's Institute hall from 6pm to 8pm. Doris could not remember any formal structure to the meetings which were run by the ladies of the village. However, most members were more than happy to bring along a piece of sewing or knitting, arrange the chairs in a semi-circle around a radiator to keep warm and then spend the evening in a companionable way, chatting or discussing recent events or local topics.

A branch of the Girls Friendly Society was run by Mrs Bungay who lived in Tower Lane. When Doris was eleven, she was allowed to join. Meetings were held once a week, loosely based on a religious theme, but which were rather more structured than the Club. The society was able to encourage Doris in exploring her love of music and singing. Previously, there had not been much opportunity to explore the subject other than music lessons at school with Mr Skinner. Doris was physically quite slight and so did not have a loud voice but she felt that it had a good tone. Mrs Bungay learned that the society was holding a competition for music which Doris might be persuaded to enter. She arranged for Doris to have some lessons from Miss Robertson who lived nearby in The Grove. She learned to sing a piece called 'Where the Bee Sucks' and came second in the competition. This experience encouraged Doris to take some piano lessons and develop her life-long interest in music.

Mrs Lichfield later ran the society and she was assisted by Mrs Monckton as her daughter, June, was now a member. June was educated at home by a tutor but had the confidence to be very sociable. She always wanted to talk to everyone in the village. Mrs Monckton held little concerts in her studio at Bell House, providing the piano accompaniment. They were always well attended.

One concert that Doris particularly remembered included both June and her mother singing 'When the Red, Red Robin Comes Bob, Bob, Bobbing Along' Doris's party pieces now included 'The Little Grey Home in the West' and 'Bless this House'. On one occasion, she was inspired by the film, 'Meet Me in St Louis' which had just been released. She encouraged all the girls to learn the words to the title song and devised a small dance to the tune. It was enthusiastically received.

The society was later run by Mrs Yeo and then Mrs Kemp before closure in the 1950s.

When Doris was thirteen, she was confirmed by the Bishop of Dover. Confirmation classes were held in the church room which was adjacent to the Old Vicarage. Despite the wartime shortages, all the girls wore white long-sleeved dresses with white gloves, white shoes and socks. They also wore veils which were supplied by the parish. Her parents did not regard her confirmation as very important but the day was made special by two presents. Mrs Sierakowski gave Doris a small gold cross and Mrs Haggar gave her a pair of lisle stockings. Once Doris had been confirmed, she was invited to join The Guild of the Holy Cross, usually referred to as The Guild. This organisation was run by the church and catered for girls that were slightly older in the village. Members had to be confirmed, and below eighteen years of age. The Guild held social events and games.

A year later, Doris was permitted to attend dances which ran from 7 to 10.30pm. Music was provided from a wind-up gramophone. They were held in the Memorial Hall, in the room at the White Horse and in the Women's Institute hall. These dances were the only ones that the Armed Forces that were billeted in the area could not attend. Evelyn White taught Doris the quickstep to the tune of 'Huts Up, Roll Some'. Doris could also dance the Quick Step and Waltz. She particularly loved participating in the Palais Glide to the tune of 'Ten Pretty Girls on the Village Green'. Another favourite was the St Bernard Waltz. At Christmas two dances were held: the Christmas Dance and one on New Year's Eve. Both these occasions were allowed to continue to 12.15am.

Now many years later, Doris regards growing up in Bearsted with great fondness. Like others girls in the area, she left school when she was fourteen. Shortly after this her mother became seriously ill. Doris grew up fairly rapidly as she became responsible for her younger siblings. There were many people in Bearsted and Thurnham of a similar age that had left school and were employed, but still had to reach maturity. The local clubs provided the opportunity for young people to mature in a safe environment. As the club members grew into confidence and experience, they were then able to take over as leaders and various officers in the societies. The responsibilities that were involved in these voluntary posts came to be regarded as ideal training for later employment or settling down into marriage and family life.

23 'Artily': A smallholding on Spot Farm Estate

On the south side of the Ashford Road, three parishes meet due to the juxtaposition of outlying sections of Bearsted, Thurnham and Otham. Arthur Robbins lived on the south side of the Ashford road for much of his life. He recorded some information about it whilst undertaking family history research. Patricia (usually called Pat), Arthur's daughter, recently heard a local estate agent refer to the locality as 'the poor side of the Ashford Road with small houses and gardens'. With one disparaging phrase, the Milgate Estate; Tudor Park; the large houses with equally large gardens; and the history of this area, was dismissed!

Arthur married Lily in 1935 in London and they began married life in Abbey Wood, SE2. As Arthur later commented, in those days few people had Hire Purchase agreements and credit cards were a financial device of the future. Instead, they went to the Ideal Homes Exhibition and paid cash for virtually all of their home furnishings. In the early years of their marriage they made many friends and thoroughly cultivated an allotment. They also bought a Super Eight car which they called 'Aggie'.

There were many financial schemes in the 1920s and the 1930s which used the idea of living in the countryside as a selling point to urban dwellers. Schemes such as developing smallholdings; chicken, mushroom, and fur farms using animals such as foxes and rabbits, were proposed as ideal investments. Many of the schemes quickly failed due to the changing economic climate, but the Robbins family were able to succeed through a combination of hard work and very careful financial planning.

Some friends asked Lily and Arthur to consider sharing an investment in a smallholding located on land at Bearsted where part of Spot Farm was being sold for development. The land area was insufficient to support two families, so instead Arthur decided to buy two and half acres of land opposite. It did not include a house, so he arranged to have a bungalow built on the land at 17 Spot Farm Estate. It was called 'Artily': derived from their names. In 1938, Arthur and Lily moved into their new home with their two children, Pat and Brian.

Later, when the road was re-named, the postal address became Yeoman Way. Arthur and Lily's land extended to where Greystones Road now stands. Some of the land which was not immediately required was sub-let to a Mr Staker. To help finances along, Arthur bought an insurance round with the Royal Liver Company to generate an immediate income whilst the smallholding was developed.

When Pat and her parents arrived in Bearsted, Royston Road and Winifred Road had been recently constructed. Madginford estate had not been built. One of their neighbours in Yeoman Way was Mr Key. He was a Health Officer for Maidstone who also kept pigs in his garden, which was of a considerable size. Where Copsewood Way was later developed, there was a fine stand of sweet chestnut trees. Pat collected nuts there in the autumn.

Mr Rayner-Sharp lived at Greystones House, named after the big stone wall which marked the boundary of his property in Spot Lane. He came from the family who owned the Trebor-Sharp sweet manufacturers in Maidstone. He had a model railway which ran around nearly all the garden. Mr Morrison, the under gardener, had a reputation for being affable, but rather eccentric.

Pat remembered that Mr Rayner-Sharp had a brightly coloured parrot that used to fly up and perch in conifers in the grounds of the house. The parrot was featured on the box lids for Sharps 'Kreemy Toffees'. Betty Mills (née Pearson) assisted Mrs Rayner-Sharp to look after their two children. She recalled that on sunny days, the butler's duties included taking the parrot out in its cage to be aired in the garden. However, if it came on to rain, the parrot used to shriek 'Help, Help' as it disliked getting wet. It was also rather a menace to anyone playing tennis on the court in the garden of the neighbouring house as the parrot used to shriek erratically, disconcerting the players.

At Artily, there was a spacious vegetable garden, a greenhouse and an extensive orchard. Some grapes were grown in the greenhouses. Apple varieties grown included Bramley, Derby and Newton. A hay crop was regularly taken. The orchard was also used for Scout Camps by Bearsted Scout Group.

This photograph shows Arthur in army uniform by his first greenhouse.

Photograph courtesy of Pat Grimes (née Robbins)

In the photographs below can be seen the orchards which extended to Spot Lane, and some later greenhouses. The abundance of blossom in spring was a typical scene in the Kent countryside before the Great Storm of 1987 obliterated many orchards.

Both photographs courtesy of Pat Grimes

The family kept chickens and geese. Once a goose called Crooked Beak deserted two of her goslings. Pat and her brothers rescued them and called them Pipsqueak and Wilfred after two cartoon characters. Pipsqueak and Wilfred regularly came into the house and were very nosy!

The only disturbance to life on the smallholding was the noise of the ragstone quarrying further down in Spot Lane. The sound of the detonations used to travel up to their bungalow, frighten the animals and shake the local houses. The quarries were backfilled and developed into the Downswood estate in the early 1980s.

During Pat's childhood the winters were quite severe. There were substantial snowfalls. This meant that proper snowballs fights could take place and big snowmen could be built. Mr Baker, who lived nearby, organised sledging and tobogganing in the winter. Pat recalled that a terrific speed could be achieved by sledging down Yeoman Way! During one winter the Robbins family had an entire flock of chickens stolen. They were able to follow some tracks to Royston Road but there, the snow had been cleared from the path, so the trail went cold.

This next photograph shows Pat and her family in the orchard playing in deep snow:

Photograph courtesy of Pat Grimes

Pat had a very free childhood as there was so much land to explore, but there was always work to be done on the smallholding. Work came before playing with friends as a living had to be earned. Pat's mother, Lily, had a difficult time during the Second World War as Arthur was drafted into the army, so she had to run the smallholding and look after the children. Lily walked the children to Thurnham and Bearsted Schools; a journey of around a mile each way, pushing a pram. Air raids often took place during the journey. Pat's youngest brother, Colin was born in the middle of a heavy raid and the midwife subsequently called him 'Bomber Robbins' for many years.

Arthur concluded his career in the Army with the rank of Captain General Staff Officer which he retained until 1959, when he was finally released from active reserve. Upon his return to Bearsted, life was difficult. Most of Arthur's insurance business had disappeared and the economic conditions offered little scope for rapid development as the country began to recover after the war. One of Arthur's friends managed to get him a job as an Insurance Inspector with Midland Assurance. The job offered good pay with a pension and car. The firm was eventually taken over by the Eagle Star Company, and Arthur continued to work for them until his retirement.

Arthur received £50 compensation for war wounds and he used this to buy more chickens, three geese and a goat called Celeste. She yielded at least six pints of milk a day and had quite a luxurious home as the Anderson shelter was re-cycled for this purpose after the war. When Arthur bought her, she was collected in Aggie. On the way home, they stopped outside a pub. A man came out and saw her head poking out of the rear window, so he went back into the pub and several other people then came out to look at the novel sight of a goat in a car. In the meantime, Celeste had turned round and was showing her rear end. Before Arthur could move off promptly, she deposited some manure!

Lily adored flowers and became a Class A1 horticulturist, flower arranger, demonstrator and lecturer. On one occasion she won every Floral Art class at the Kent County Show. This has never been equalled and now cannot be beaten as the organisation of the classes was later changed. She won a special award for the achievement. Arthur was Chairman of Maidstone Horticultural Society for twenty one years and then became President. Lily was Secretary for nineteen years and later Chairman of the Floral Art Group. Together, they continued to win many trophies and prizes in National Area and Local Shows.

For years, the Robbins family were virtually self-sufficient but they still used the shops and facilities in the area. Groceries were obtained from Kingsnorth Stores in Langley. Milk was delivered by the Primrose and Len Dairy. By the Rose public house was a Post Office and small grocery shop called Roseacre Stores. The Post Office which had opened in 1939[1] traded for many years before closure in November 2004 due to a re-organisation of local branches. The building now houses The Bearsted Therapy Centre. The last post mistress was Joan Hills. This photograph of the post office and stores was taken in 1986:

Photograph courtesy of Bearsted and District Local History Society

Although the Robbins family were able to develop the land, building further greenhouses and planting new varieties of trees in the orchards, Bearsted began to change. Life on a smallholding became difficult to sustain in the later years of the 1950s and early 1960s. Many areas of land were sold for housing in the village. An offer was made and Arthur took an immensely difficult decision. He later wrote:

> Our orchard looked lovely after all the years of hard work but we sold it…it was heartbreaking to see the bulldozers in one day clear everything off the ground and burn all our work and hopes in a huge bonfire.

Wimpey Homes bought the land for housing. Part of the Spot Lane development was named Greystones Road after Mr Rayner-Sharp's house which had been demolished as the land was cleared.

24 Bearsted in the Second World War

A few years before the outbreak of the Second World War, part of the south side of the Ashford Road was developed by a Croydon builder called Mr Royston Phillips.[1] Some of the roads: Royston Road, Winifred Road and Rosemary Road, were named after members of his family.

Most of the area still remained as farmland worked by the Edmond family. The land was used to grow strawberries and cobnuts up until the 1960s when construction started on the Madginford housing estate. George White had been the tenant of Madginford Farm in the 1930s. The farm was a fruit tree nursery. The site of the farm is now the location of the Madginford schools.

Christine Hughes recalled that the houses in Royston, Winifred and Rosemary Roads all bore high numbers for many years, despite the small scale of development. This is believed to be because the houses had not long been completed when war was declared. The Post Office decided to use the original plot numbers for the duration of the war and re-numbering took place after the war ended.

Miriam Stevens

Miriam Stevens (née Gardener) was nine years old when her parents moved to Bearsted from Wye. It was September 1939, immediately after the outbreak of war. These are some of her memories of wartime:

As a family, we were fortunate in that neither my father nor my brother were 'called up'. My father was over forty and my brother was then twelve, so neither was liable for conscription into the armed forces. My father went to work for Shorts Brothers of Rochester to help the company build airplanes.

My father had become a fundamentalist Christian during the First World War and my mother, although rather sceptic, went along with him to his various churches. This meant that he considered his family had no such need of things such as air raid shelters. While everyone else was frantically digging enormous holes in their gardens to accommodate air raid shelters, my father was certain 'that God would look after us'. During night time raids we all used to gather in a bedroom.

Bearsted School was less than three miles from home so I walked every day and that included a journey home for lunch, or 'dinner', as we called it in those days, and another journey back again to school until 3.30pm. I had three friends: Peter, Pat, and Monica, who lived on or near the Ashford Road. Miles of walking and larking about on the way to school seemed no hardship and kept us reasonably healthy, and always hungry! We received a third of a pint of milk during our mid-morning break, which was supplied free of charge by the local education authority. This helped to assuage hunger until dinner time.

Although there were few pavements all the way from the school up Roseacre Lane and down Yeoman Lane as far as The Yeoman public house, there was little danger from traffic. Only people with essential needs such as doctors had a petrol ration. The few people in Bearsted that owned cars before the war had to put them away in a garage 'for the duration'.

We used to collect frogspawn from the village pond, in a jam jar with a piece of string round its neck with which to carry it. The raised lip round the top of the jar made this easy. Surrounding the village were places and things to discover by adventurous young children. We took picnics with us and picked blackberries up on the North Downs beyond Thurnham where we discovered some old ruins. One of our finds was the Wishing Well near the Willington Street entrance to Mote Park. Watercress grew in the clear water stream leading to the well and we used to pick a bunch to take home for Sunday afternoon tea for Marmite and watercress sandwiches.

On misty September Sunday mornings, very early, we would pick field mushrooms and carry them home in big baskets. We learned from experience where to find the good ones, generally in fields where horses, or sometimes cows, had been grazing. The big white mushroom caps showing through the grass seemed like the manna we had been reading about in the Bible at school, or perhaps Sunday school. When we arrived home absolutely ravenous, my mother treated us to a big breakfast of mushrooms and fried bread cooked in bacon fat. Many country families used to do this to supplement their food supplies.

Perhaps it was because food was generally in short supply due to rationing, but our meals always seemed delicious! My mother would always cook a batch of buns when she had the gas oven lit for the Sunday roast. The government encouraged householders to contribute to 'the war effort' by using fuel economically. Sometimes we were allowed to eat a bun, hot, straight from the oven, or dip a 'knobbler' which was a piece of the crust of a loaf of bread into the hot dripping when the meat was taken out. To us this was sheer heaven. We did not realise, until we had children of our own, that mother knew a thing or two in preventing the squabbling of hungry children waiting for a meal to be served.

When we moved into our semi-detached house, it had three bedrooms and a bathroom. We all thought it was the height of luxury as there had been no bathroom in our previous home in Wye. My mother used to heat water in the wood-fired copper in the washhouse, where the clothes washing was done, next to the kitchen. We took turns to sit in the copper and bathe ourselves!

The kitchen had a coke-fuelled black-leaded range for cooking. There were open, coal or wood fires in the rooms for heating. In 1939 most people were unfamiliar with the idea of central heating. I recall vividly coming home from school one day in the winter to find water running everywhere throughout the house and my mother in tears, mopping up as best she could. The pipes had burst, as they had not been well insulated against the frost. When the thaw came many people were made to realise just how cheaply the houses had been built.

One lovely summer day in 1940 my mother took several of us into Mote Park for a picnic. I saw what appeared at first to be a flock of lapwings dipping and swerving, glinting in the sunshine further over towards Maidstone. It soon became clear that they were not lapwings at all, but planes fighting for supremacy of the sky. Every now and again one would slide down towards the earth with flames and smoke billowing out behind. Then we would look up with bated breath for one of the others to perform what we called a 'victory roll' across the sky - another German plane had been destroyed. We cheered them on as the boys showed off their knowledge of Spitfires and Hurricanes. We did not comprehend at the time that what we were observing was The Battle of Britain: an important part of the hostilities.

This undated photograph is a rarity. It shows the airplane trails formed in the sky over The Street, during the dogfights which took place in the Battle of Britain:

Photograph courtesy of Leslie Reynolds

My family included four children and as soon as food rationing started my mother had quite a problem keeping us all well fed on the meagre amounts allowed. In 1940 the rations for a week for one person included 4 oz bacon, 12 oz sugar and 4 oz butter/margarine. Meat was rationed by price at the rate of one shilling and ten pence a week. Spam was a wartime alternative to fresh meat as was snoek (this was a name used to disguise that it was actually whale meat).

The government persuaded women to 'help the war effort' by doing essential war work or caring for evacuees. As my mother already had four children she decided two evacuees would not be a hardship and the extra rations would help make the food go further. We had quite a large garden containing a Worcester Pearmain apple tree, so when the government encouraged everyone to 'dig for victory' she decided to live up to the name she had married into and become a gardener in her own right!

Throughout the war, and for the rest of her life, my mother's main interests were in the garden. She produced all our vegetables and some of the fruit to feed us all during the war. This made a tremendous addition to the meagre rations. We took it for granted that we should eat fresh food every day but at that time there was nothing much in the way of imported food due to the German U-boats menacing the shipping convoys.

It was sometime before we had a 'points' system for some things like jams and preserves, tinned fruit, biscuits and dried fruit. There were limited supplies of sweets and chocolates which were also available on a separate 'points' system.

Later in the war, eggs could be bought in powder form. In my family, each child had their own pot of jam which was named and there was trouble if anyone else used it!

Rowland Fairbrass

Rowland Fairbrass's family lived in Hickmott Cottages in The Street. These have now been demolished but they were near to Rowland's Bakery. When Rowland was small the family moved to a semi-detached house in Spot Lane. Greensand Road is now opposite the house where he used to live.

Some of Rowland's friends that lived locally included Patricia Robbins, Peter Stevenson and Donald Taylor. Norman Pilbeam lived in a terraced cottage that although it was just round the corner, was still classified by the Post Office as Spot Lane. Raymond Walkling and some of the Palmer girls: Anne and Joan, also went to school with him.

Rowland's father, Bill, worked at Roseacre Laundry. The laundry staff used to collect big household linen items from the local area and wash them. For many people, if the weather was bad, it was impossible to dry heavy and large items like sheets as they did not have the room indoors.

Next door to the laundry in Roseacre Lane, on the corner of Tower Lane was a shoe repair shop owned by Mr Jack Sunnucks.

Bill Fairbrass began working for the laundry as a driver. He wore a white boiler suit for deliveries which he undertook for the owner, Miss Wade. Her nephew, Rowland Gregory inherited the business. Bill eventually became a director of the laundry. Just before the Second World War, the laundry took delivery of a beautiful, brand-new Commer van. He was very proud of the vehicle as it had big mudguards, lovely swooping mouldings and calligraphy across the sides of it. However, the local police thought it might be used if the village was invaded and so took it away to be destroyed. He was not impressed.

Opposite to Rowland's house in Spot Lane, were orchards full of Worcester and Cox apple trees. Bramley apples were grown a little further down the road. This area has been developed for housing and is now called Greensand Road, Ragstone Road and Gault Close. The land around the Orchard Spot public house was then part of a farm run by Mr Winch. Rowland learned to swim in the River Len near to the Orchard Spot. It was a popular haunt for the local boys but all Rowland's friends used to run off if they thought Mr Winch was coming!

This photograph shows the corner of Spot Lane where it joined the Ashford Road around 1930:

Photograph courtesy of Chris and Sue Hunt

During the war, the Fairbrass family took in one of the boys that had been evacuated to Bearsted. There were particular problems over his meals as all he wanted to eat was crisps and lemonade. It did not take the Fairbrass family long to realise that these items comprised a regular diet for the lad. Previously there had been no other option for him than to wait for endless hours outside public houses whilst his father drank inside. He found the relative peace and quiet of Bearsted and Thurnham difficult to cope with too. Things were so very different in Bearsted that he only stayed for a short while before returning to Plumstead. This is a rare example of an evacuee failing to settle in the area. It was later estimated that by early 1940, over eighty two percent of the evacuees were still in Bearsted. This number stands in direct contrast to the national figure of twenty five percent of evacuees that had remained at their billets.[2]

This photograph shows the bus containing the evacuees arriving at Bearsted. They were initially taken to the local Red Cross Centre at Bearsted House:

Photograph courtesy of Jessie Page

When the raid began on Detling airfield in 1940, Rowland was walking down Spot Lane. The only place to shelter was by the huge ragstone wall of Greystones House. He seemed to spend a long time there before running home.

Rowland took an active part in the government salvage schemes. In addition to collecting paper and metal, such was the enthusiasm of the children at Bearsted School that 147 pounds of rose hips and 212 pounds of horse chestnuts were also collected.[3]

Rowland recalled that Derek Finnis made a marvellous model of a Lancaster airplane, which won first prize in three categories for model aircraft at the Horticultural Show in 1942 held at the Men's Institute. At the end of the show the model was auctioned, reaching over £3 with the proceeds passed to the Red Cross. This photograph shows Derek with the model by the school air raid shelter:

Photograph courtesy of Roseacre School

<u>Left to right</u>
Derek Finnis and Keith Vane

In 1944, there was a big army encampment in Mote Park. Some American soldiers were stationed there and local children visited them, asking "Got any gum, chum?" They were normally very generous with their rations, which seemed very ample in comparison to the size of British rations. American chocolate tasted different, but was still very satisfying to eat. The soldiers took the children for rides on pontoons across Mote Park lake. One day Rowland and his friends went to visit them and were rather bewildered to find that the men and their camp had all vanished. It was only much later that Rowland realised that they had embarked on the D-Day landings.

Rowland particularly recalled details of the air-raid provisions at Bearsted School. The headmaster, Mr Skinner, set up a system for doodle-bug watching: two chairs were placed on the top of the air-raid shelters to sit upon. Children that Mr Skinner regarded as responsible kept watch and if they spotted a doodle-bug, a whistle was blown. At this signal, the entire school piled into the air-raid shelters until the all-clear siren. The main air-raid siren for the village was on the top of Roseacre laundry.

When a doodle-bug fell in Caring Lane, the shock wave from the explosion travelled a long way, it uprooted several trees on Madginford Farm and also slammed a door shut in their house. Other houses were damaged in Sutton Street. The nearest anti-aircraft gun to Rowland's house was mounted near Otham church. When the first doodle-bug came over, the family took shelter in the larder cupboard under the stairs. Rowland recalled the weird noise as the gun shot at the doodle-bug while it came down.

In 1945 there were huge celebrations for Victory in Europe Day. Enormous bonfires were built around the village. Where Shirley Way now stands was open land, and so a large bonfire was built there.

Rowland's uncle who was in the army, was home on leave at the time so the celebrations were assisted by the generous donation and detonation of some army thunder flashes!

Doris and Rowland recalled that Mr Grout arranged a marvellous sports day to celebrate the ending of the war. Land at Cavendish Way was used as the sports ground and a starting pistol was unearthed so that the events could be started correctly. Hilda, Muriel and Rita, sisters to Doris, all participated in the races. Hilda was a gifted athlete and won so many of the races that Mr Grout asked her to stand down from some of the events in order to give the other children a chance! The prizes were books of savings stamps.

This photograph was taken in Shirley Way in front of the unlit bonfire. From the left hand side, the photograph includes Len Mercer, Mr Bill Fairbrass, Herbert Coales, Mr Ron Fairbrass (Rowland's uncle), Henry Hadley, Mr Benger, and James Strettle. The front row includes Mr Passmore and John Coales in RAF uniform, as he was home on leave at the time.

Photograph courtesy of Edith Coales

The following two photographs were also taken at the VE day celebrations in Shirley Way. Included in this photograph are Mollie Carr, Pat Liverton, Peter Trott, John Munn, Nurse Beeton Pull and Jean Harvey:

Photograph courtesy of Allen Carr

This photograph includes Nurse Beeton Pull in the centre of the back row, Raymond 'Bubbles' Feakins and Trevor Osborne:

Photograph courtesy of Tony and Sheila Foster

25 Binbury, Thurnham and Detling during the Second World War

These memories of the Second World War, recalled by Trudy Johnson (née Penney), are particularly valuable. They cover part of Thurnham parish that is fairly remote and consequently least well known. There are very few first-hand accounts of the air raids and wartime conditions of the area due to the disruption that local residents suffered before, during, and after the war.

When I was young, my family lived at Maple Bar Gate, in one of the most northern parts of Thurnham parish. Our bungalow was situated at the top of Thurnham Hill, opposite some meadows known as the Race Course because they had been used for this purpose. It was in this area that Sir Alan Cobham, whose air displays did so much to popularise flying in the 1930's, crashed and was killed. The Empire Air Day Display, held on 20 May 1939 was attended by over fourteen thousand people. The boys from Bearsted School voted to attend it instead of a County Sports day at Tenterden!

I remember that around fifty to a hundred houses were being built in this area. The houses were demolished around 1939, presumably to make room for the enlarged airfield at Detling. The airfield station had been originally opened and used in the First World War but was closed around 1919. In 1938 it was re-opened and became part of Coastal Command. Lower down the hill were the ruins of Thurnham Castle on which, as children, we used to play.

My parents were Thomas and Frances Ellen Penney. They had seven children which were all boys except for myself. Two, however, died in infancy. We were all educated at Detling School. On Sundays we attended St Mary's church, Thurnham, for morning service and Detling Church in the evening. The Rev Arthur Scutt was vicar of Thurnham from 1927 until 1942. He was a small, sociable man and used to visit our house every week to have a cup of tea with us.

My mother had many stories about the First World War that she told me when I was growing up. Near Binbury Manor had been sited a Prisoners of War camp. Each day the prisoners were marched to the woods near our home to spend the day making pit props. In the evening, when they finished work and were making their way home, they were allowed to stop at my mother's shop to purchase chocolates and cigarettes.

One of my treasured possessions is a certificate my father received from the Parish of Thurnham when he returned home from the First World War. I also treasure a certificate my late husband received at the end of the Second World War.

When the Second World War broke out, an Auxiliary Squadron moved into the airfield and brought with them some Avro Anson aircraft. The flying duties were said to involve reconnaissance operations, but everyone who lived nearby was aware of security and seldom spoke directly about the activities at the airfield.

My mother opened a cafe in which I helped. It was a very rough time as we had many air raids and had to be escorted to the shelters. Unhappily the German planes soon discovered where our shelters were and tried to machine-gun us as we ran for cover. So we had to take to the woods along Castle Hill until it was safe to emerge. As a precaution against spying we were given a new pass word every day.

On 30 May 1940, an Anson aircraft crash-landed on the airfield at night. It soon became known what had happened: the aircraft had developed problems and tried to return. Near the airfield, an engine burst into flames as it came into land, still loaded with bombs. Many of the local people were very impressed with the bravery shown by Corporal Daphne Pearson, who ran over from her accommodation and rescued several of the aircrew from the vicinity of the burning fuselage. As she moved the pilot away from the wreckage, she became aware that the bombs were still on the aircraft. Daphne managed to protect the pilot from the subsequent devastating explosion. For her bravery, she was awarded the Empire Gallantry Medal which she was later able to exchange for a George Cross. She was the first woman to receive a gallantry award in the Second World War and her medals are now in the Imperial War Museum in London.[1]

On 13 August, 1940, we were subjected to a massive raid by Stuka planes in which many service men and women were killed. During the raid, the German pilots used their machine guns. The Anson airplanes, which were dispersed round the airfield, were laden with two bombs each on board. They were sitting targets: as the planes were set on fire, tremendous explosions took place. All the hangers were burned too. Afterwards, there were so many people that had been killed that we witnessed the dead being taken away on lorries. The Commander of the Station, Group Captain Davis, was killed. Over ninety people were badly injured.

Whilst the raid was going on, my mother, myself and a baker, who was delivering supplies to us, took refuge under our big table. Our house caught the blast; and ceilings, doors and windows were blown in upon us. The table was two hundred years old and very sturdy: it saved our lives as the roof, windows and doors of our house, all came crashing in. Luck was with us, and we managed to escape without much injury apart from a few cuts.

One of our jobs at this time was to supply the Anson crews with flasks of coffee, rolls, chocolates and fruit before they set out on bombing missions. After we lost our house we went to live with relatives for a few weeks in the Weald of Kent but it was not long before we were back in our 'homeland', as we moved into a house on the Friningham Manor Estate. The air raid shelter and cookhouse for the air men were in our garden

There were two more raids on the airfield on 31 August and 1 September 1940. Messerschmitt airplanes caused enormous damage and dropped high explosive bombs but there were far fewer casualties. When the time came for my son to be born, the air raids were so intense that the nurse from Bearsted, Marion Beeton Pull, had to sleep in our house for two nights. I had to spend long periods on the floor under the bed for some shelter.

A radar station was built at the top of Cold Blow Hill and a Land Army Hostel was built and opened where there was once a fox farm. In 1942, the Duke of Kent visited Detling. This was shortly before his plane crashed in Scotland while he was on a flight to inspect the British forces in Iceland.

In 1946 my mother moved away from Friningham Manor and went to live in Elm Tree Cottage at the top of Detling Hill. Alas, it is no more, having been demolished to make room for the dual carriageway which runs through this part of the countryside.

This photograph, taken in 2005, shows one of the surviving aircraft hangars at Detling airfield viewed from Binbury Lane:

Photograph courtesy of Malcolm Kersey

26   St Faith's Home

St Faith's Home came to be built on an area of Bearsted previously called 'the Herst Land' that was left in a will made around 1750 by Catherine Watts, a widow, to her children Edward and Ann:[1]

> All those pieces of land called Herst Land lying and being in Bearsted...

Tenants that leased the land from the Watts family included William Dawes, Edward Godfrey and Thomas Burwash.[2] By 1800, Ann Armstrong had inherited it from Edward Watts.[3] She was married to Francis Armstrong, a surgeon of Gravesend. Following her death, her remaining family sold the land in the same auction in 1858 as Sandy Mount and the butcher's shop in The Street.[4,5]

From the sale particulars:[6]

LOT 5.   THAT VALUABLE

ENCLOSURE OF FREEHOLD LAND,

In Extent, 8A. 2R. 14P.,

Situate on the North-west side of the Road that leads from the Ashford Turnpike Road to Bearsted Green, known as

THE HURST LANDS, IN THE PARISH OF BEARSTED.

A.	R.	P.	
5	3	34	Called Mill Hill Field, Arable, is let to Mr. JESSE BETTSWORTH, a Yearly Tenant, at £9 12s. per annum.
1	2	20	A Nursery Ground, is let to Sir GEORGE HAMPSON, a Yearly Tenant from 11th Oct., at £3 per year.
1	0	0	Cottagers' Allotments, is let to Miss F. SMITH, at £2 8s. per annum.
8	2	14	Total.

The total Rental of this Lot is £15 per annum.

The Great and Small Tithes have been commuted at £3 14s.

THE EXCEEDINGLY FINE VIEWS FROM EVERY PORTION OF THIS LAND,

Render it a most valuable site for a Gentleman's Residence.

IT

ADJOINS SNOWFIELD HOUSE & GROUNDS, & IS UNRIVALLED FOR POSITION IN THIS DISTRICT.

Reproduced courtesy of the Centre for Kentish Studies, Maidstone

The field called Mill Hill was near to the windmill referred to in an earlier chapter, however Ann had not owned the mill. The land was purchased by Sir George Hampson of Thurnham. It was then conveyed to his mother, Dame Mary Foreman Hampson and leased to James Whatman.[7]

Around 1870, Dr Matthew Algernon Adams, the Medical Officer of Health for Maidstone, bought the land and built a house. He called the house The Kulm, after a German phrase for summit, indicating that it stood on some of the highest ground in Bearsted.[8]

By 1930, the name of the property had changed: it was called Bearsted Court and was the home of Mrs Cloudesley Marsham, widow of a former rector of Harrietsham. Mrs Marsham's daughter, Jessie, was the secretary and treasurer of a charity called St Faith's Home. The charity was looking for new premises and purchased the house for £2,400. Shortly after this, the charity became the responsibility of the Canterbury Diocesan Board of Finance. Five years later, the freehold of the private road leading to the property from Tower Lane was also conveyed.[9]

St Faith's Home was a charity founded in 1898 by a group of ladies which included Evelyn, Countess Stanhope; Mrs Frederick Temple, wife of the Archbishop of Canterbury; Adeline, Duchess of Bedford; Mrs William Moore; and Mrs Spooner, whose husband became Archdeacon of Maidstone. Their collective sense of practical Christian compassion led them to consider providing care for single girls who had become pregnant. Eventually their charity became one of five maternity and children's home establishments supported by the Dioceses of Canterbury and Rochester.

In the 1890s, pregnancy of single girls was regarded as a social disgrace. Many girls found themselves forced into the Workhouse, where the policy was to find a situation for the mother, and to place the child with a foster parent. Often this did not work out satisfactorily. The charity aimed to open a special home, where mothers and babies could be together in a Christian atmosphere, whilst the mothers learned skills to earn their living. It was named after St Faith; a virgin martyr who remained faithful to the Lord until death, though subjected to temptation and tortures.[10]

Two adjoining houses on Hythe Road in Willesborough were bought as premises for the charity but there were difficulties laying on a water supply, so they were closed in July 1899. By December a new location had been found in Wilton Place on Lower Fant Road, Maidstone. As it was quite expensive to run, washing was taken in to defray expenses. This work was useful in training the girls. It brought in sufficient funds for one of them to be paid a shilling per week as an inducement to stay on at the Home in order to provide a steadying influence for the others.[11] The Vicar of St Peter's church, Maidstone, was appointed Chaplain and he requested that one room be set aside as a chapel.

In June 1900, the management committee agreed that the girls were to be allowed 6d per month as pocket money. In 1901 there was a charge of five shillings a week to keep each girl but it is not clear who paid the fees or how far the money went to support the Home and girls.[12]

By 1902 a decision was taken that all the girls should be vaccinated, as much of the laundry came from doctors' families. One girl objected, and as she was soon to leave to be married, the committee refused to give her the now customary outfit of clothing upon leaving. Later, it was decided that the Superintendent should have the opportunity to provide other sorts of training, and that washing for twelve babies and their mothers was quite sufficient to keep the laundry occupied.[13]

Three years later, in 1905 the following rules were agreed:

> Girls placed in the Home are not allowed to go out alone.
>
> Girls in the Home are required to take whatever share in the laundry house or needlework the Matron shall appoint.
>
> Girls in the Home are not permitted to enter each other bedrooms.
>
> Any girl who proves to be subordinate or whose influence is found to be detrimental to the others will be dismissed after due notice has been sent to the lady who has placed her in the Home.
>
> Every Girl is expected to obey the Superintendent and Matron all things.

Reproduced courtesy of Holy Cross church

Demand for places always outstripped availability. In 1914 there were seventy six applications for just ten places and the number grew steadily each year. A year later an epidemic of measles was followed by a case of diphtheria. There is evidence to show that very few babies were lost to illness and this was attributed to the fine nursing skills available at the time.

By 1916 the Home described itself:

> ...receiving fallen girls of previously respectable character after confinement...[14]

The charity moved into Bearsted Court at the end of July 1930. It took two days to move all the property and equipment along Yeoman Lane and into the house. It was officially opened and dedicated on 31 October 1930 by the Assistant Bishop of Rochester, Right Rev G L King.

This undated photograph of the Home was taken sometime after it opened, but gives a good indication of the front of the building:

Photograph courtesy of Holy Cross church

By 1932 the nature of St Faith's had changed. Previously, it had been a place to which girls had gone after their confinement, but now it was decided that there was a greater need for a maternity home. Girls could have pre-natal attention, care during the actual delivery, and post-natal treatment and training in mothercraft; all from the same nurses. Part of the house was adapted to create a maternity wing, which was dedicated by the vicar of Bearsted, Rev Griffiths. The first baby born there on 6 March 1932, was given the name Faith.[15]

Following a generous donation of £100 towards a new chapel in 1932, construction began the following year. The cost of £333 was largely raised by donations but fund-raising schemes included the staff and girls knitting Shetland shawls. Many of the fixtures and fittings were donated, including the statue of Our Lady and the Holy Child, which was bought as a parting gift to the Superintendent, Miss Tope, in 1942. She was entering a convent and so could not accept any personal presents. The statue was thought to be a fitting reminder of her work at St Faith's.[16]

All the Annual Reports show the huge amount of hard work that was involved in sustaining the Home. Over many years the Home was regarded as an excellent establishment, with strong community connections. Hundreds of people visited to witness the work undertaken which was considered to be at the forefront of its kind. One report highlights how the staff gave many lectures about the Home and attended influential forums to promote their work. In one year, visitors arrived by the busload to view it.[17]

Despite this success, adequate funding was always a tremendous struggle and many basic repairs were delayed. For most of the time, the Annual Reports detail the constant state of anxiety and mindfulness about managing on inadequate finances. Such establishments would not face this today as they would have an annual budget.[18]

This undated photograph of a baptism, which seems to have part of a sequence taken as publicity shots, was almost certainly deliberately posed,[19] but gives an indication of the interior of the chapel:

Photograph courtesy of Kay Carlton Hill Film Studio and Holy Cross church

In 1938 a new lying-in ward which connected to the labour ward was arranged. This opened on to the verandah in order that mothers and babies could receive a maximum amount of light and sunshine. A legacy from Marguerita Ashley Dodd was used to install electric lighting. This undated photograph, also taken for publicity, shows the verandah and main part of the building. Note the prams in the foreground:

Photograph courtesy of Kay Carlton Hill Film Studio and Holy Cross church

In 1945, another room was made into an isolation ward, and fully equipped. This was achieved through the generosity of Mr and Mrs Youngman, who gave a substantial donation as 'a thank offering to God for fifty years of married happiness'. Around this time, a bungalow in the grounds was also brought into use as extra staff accommodation.

During 1948, the vicar of Bearsted, Rev Harold Yeandle wrote a booklet celebrating the Home's Golden Jubilee.[20] He commented that there was a very sad increase in the number of girls aged thirteen and fourteen who were admitted. About a third of babies were placed for adoption, and about half of those remaining were able to stay with their mothers. Care continued after the girls left the home as they received letters and visits, and there were also birthday cards for the babies. Reunions at the Home were held, especially on Mothering Sunday and St Faith's Day, which was celebrated on 6 October.

As befits a booklet written to highlight the work of the charity and possibly attract further funding, it concentrates on the positive side of the Home, giving an excellent description of the routines. These revolved around nursery duties and household chores but were varied by classes such as singing and appreciation of music; English speaking and play-acting; cooking and 'keep fit', together with games, dancing and walks. This undated photograph, gives an indication of laundry duties:

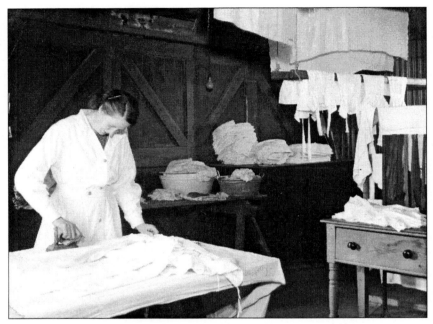

Photograph courtesy of Kay Carlton Hill Film Studio and Holy Cross church

These next two photographs were taken around 1948 and show the nursery and a sitting room:

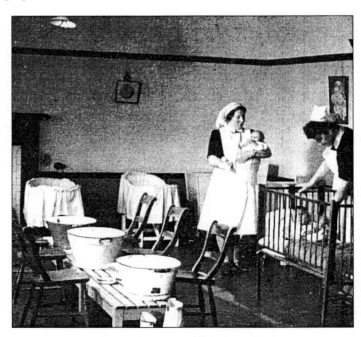

Photograph courtesy of Holy Cross church

Photograph courtesy of Holy Cross church

This photograph shows some of the staff. Their identities are unknown:

Photograph courtesy of Holy Cross church

For a short while, in the late 1950s, the chapel was used as a venue for confirmation classes in Bearsted. Rosemary Pearce recalled that access was by way of a footpath from Yeoman Lane and through a rather steep but quite lovely garden.

No money was ever wasted on luxuries and every penny was used to see the Home properly run. In 1954 a scheme called the 'Half Crown League' was operating, in which those who were unable to make regular donations would send in half a crown when available. Those half crowns were truly appreciated: by 1957 the Home cost £5,443 a year to run with fees for each girl amounting to £4 14s 6d a week.[21]

Today some of the routine would seem very regimented but it reflected the contemporary attitude of many similar institutions. However some of the girls found it difficult to adjust as their backgrounds were so different. Everyone had allotted tasks such as washing floors, ironing and washing the numerous towelling nappies. Girls helped with the work until their babies arrived and they resumed their duties almost immediately afterwards. They slept in dormitories and were responsible for their babies: feeding, changing and bathing them. The food was always good and meals were freshly prepared, using produce from the extensive vegetable plot. However there were always thin lines between the principle of hard work for pregnant young girls, instilling a strong work ethic in them and this ethic being essential to the Home's survival.

Lawrence Allen was born at St Faith's in 1957. His mother has commented that as a young girl, aged sixteen, she found it difficult to scrub wooden floors daily late into her pregnancy and at the time failed to see the value of such a task in instilling the work ethic. Perhaps the secret of the Home's success was that each girl took something different from the regime. The staff tried to be non-judgmental in their approach but did believe that the girls needed to accept responsibility for their dilemma, learn to manage it and prepare themselves for a future life. The rules were in keeping with the prevalent atmosphere which was one of hope and faith that the girls could make something of themselves and go on to have a meaningful and useful life.[22] This philosophy is certainly borne out in the Annual Reports, detailing how many girls returned each year accompanied by their new husbands to meet old friends, and making real progress in the outside world.

In the 1950s, Moral Welfare Workers referred most of the girls, but it is not known to which organisation these workers were connected. Probation Officers also referred some of the girls. Lawrence's mother has no recollection of her referral, only that it happened very quickly and without her involvement. She was trying to cope with the fact that her baby's father did not want to support her, preferring, albeit sadly, to adhere to pressure from his family to follow a career that they considered to be more appropriate to his own young years. It remains unclear how the family received information about the Home and how Lawrence's grandfather met payment of the fees.

During 1952, fifty two girls were reported as passing the through the Home with the adoption of twelve babies but it was not recorded how many babies were fostered or stayed with relatives.[23] Lawrence recalled that his mother was under strong pressure to give him up for adoption but his family stood their ground. Once this had been agreed, further organisations continued to be involved as when his mother returned home with her baby, the family benefited from continued support from Dr Barnado's.

Nora Tolhurst was a part-time midwife at the Home between 1961 and 1963. Other staff during this time included Sister Holbrook, who was another midwife, Miss Amies who was the secretary, and Mrs Green who lived in Forge Cottages. Mrs Green taught some of the girls who were below school leaving age or still at college.

Nora usually worked a set number of hours each day. If a girl went into labour, and it was straightforward, the baby was delivered at St Faith's and Nora stayed on duty until the baby safely arrived. If complications arose, then the girl was admitted to West Kent General Hospital which was located in Marsham Street, Maidstone.

Nora was not involved with the adoptions that took place, but she was aware that part of the procedure involved the mother physically handing over her baby to the representative of the adoption agency. It is possible that this may have been a legal requirement. Adoptions were always a very sad time. Nora recalled that it was not always easy to deal with a distressed girl who had gone through the adoption formalities and given up her baby.

Visitors were made welcome. Boyfriends and family members were permitted and there was ample visiting time. The girls were always encouraged to talk freely to the staff and share their problems. Some of the girls visited Nora's elderly mother at her home in Roundwell for a cup of tea and further conversation. This was not officially encouraged, but the staff were well aware that it occurred.

Mr Tolhurst, Nora's father, undertook gardening at the Home and in addition to tending the vegetables, looked after the rest of the grounds and over two hundred rose bushes! The gardens were well known to be quite beautiful and the view from them across to the Downs was spectacular.

This undated photograph shows the view from the garden, looking south east over the village and Green:

Photograph courtesy of Holy Cross church

Pam Skinner worked at the home from 1966 to 1968 as an assistant to Margaret Miller, who was then Superintendent. Babies were no longer delivered at St Faith's, though Sister Coyle was resident there. The girls went to the West Kent General Hospital to give birth, but stayed at the Home until they were fit to leave. Many girls chose to be churched,[24] and it was not unknown for a girl to be married in Holy Cross church with a midwife in attendance at the vestry.

Matters had changed a little in that girls who decided to give their baby for adoption never saw the child. Adoption formalities were later completed in the staff bungalow. The girls were given some education, depending on who was available to provide it. There were some girls that tried to run away, but the majority were very happy with their life whilst in Bearsted.

Barbara Wraight was a night orderly in the 1960s, and she also undertook some of the cooking. She recalled that the girls largely came from London and the south of the country. They were a very mixed group of mostly young teenagers, although a few were only twelve. Some were very bold and confident, while others were rape victims. Other girls had been involved in incestuous and inappropriate relationships. They seemed to be separate from the rest of the local community. There was little social interaction within the village, although the congregation of Holy Cross church supported them.

In 1976 Alan Duke became the vicar of Bearsted. His wife, Mary, became full-time tutor to the girls at St Faith's so that their education could be organised in a co-ordinated and systematic way. Mary remembered that most girls referred by social workers were part-way through their school public examination courses. The Home liaised with schools so that the girls could still sit their examinations. The cost of tuition was claimed back from the Education Department of the appropriate Local Authority. Margery Gibson and Jo Tuck assisted the teaching at the Home and Jo taught some of the girls shorthand.

As society changed once more, this was reflected in the mixture of girls that came to St Faith's. Many of the girls were of Afro-Caribbean origin, often from an evangelical or Pentecostal family, while others came from unstable social backgrounds. Although it had previously been regarded as shameful to be an unmarried mother, the girls now at the Home were those who had nowhere else to go. Few families ever came to visit them, although there was now open access. Visitors were always made welcome.

Vera Banner was cook at St Faith's from 1975 until it closed in 1981. She recalled that at that time, the girls all had regular lessons, especially before the birth of their baby. These lessons on Tuesdays included cookery, when the girls made African and Asian ethnic dishes. Vera's duties included the provision of good wholesome plain food such as meat and potato pie, steak and kidney puddings, and casseroles. Vera never cooked a roast dinner but she always provided a pudding, and often made cakes for the girls at tea-time. Menus were worked out with the house-keeper, Mrs Bath. At weekends, volunteers did the cooking, and Jean Corps took her baby daughter along when it was her turn.

By 1981, social attitudes changed again and few girls were referred to St Faith's. The Home closed at very short notice. The property was bought by the Angevin Foundation, to provide a facility for mentally and physically handicapped teenagers. The house needed to be adapted and during the course of renovations, the chapel was de-consecrated. Many of its contents, including the communion vessels, went to Holy Cross church.

Vera continued to cook there but her day now began at 8.30am with coffee for the other staff. In the middle of the morning there would be a staff meeting which Vera was expected to attend. Due to the time, Vera's mind was often on the contents of the oven, rather than the subject under discussion!

After a few years, the building was deemed too small for the purposes of the Angevin Foundation. Danefield in Church Lane, was in the process of closing as an old people's home and the premises were taken over for the young people. St Faith's was abandoned.

In 2004 plans were put forward to demolish the building in order to build houses on the site. The future of the site has yet to be decided and various plans are under consideration. Demolition was completed in September 2005.

As Lawrence has commented, it is evident that St Faith's was a huge influence for over eighty years in Maidstone, supporting young girls from all over the world. Each mother or child has their own memories and conclusions about it, depending on the experience they had whilst there. For Lawrence, the Annual Reports suggest that the years of hard work and dedication went into supporting a vulnerable part of society to improve lives, and whatever the regime at the time, the intention was always well meant. Faith and hope were always the driving principles at the Home, and without it, the sort of life the girls and children would have experienced remains open to question.

At least one part of St Faith's still remains in Bearsted. The statue of Our Lady and the Holy Child, given to Miss Tope in 1942, was amongst the contents of the chapel moved to Holy Cross church. It stands in the church as a gentle reminder of the loving charity and care given over many years by the dedicated staff to the girls of the Home.

Kathryn Kersey and Rosemary Pearce

27 The Women's Institute

The Women's Institute is almost universally regarded as quintessential to village life. However, it was not until 1918 that a branch opened in Bearsted. By this time women were beginning to benefit from the many different employment opportunities that had opened up to them during the First World War. Mrs Lucy Brook had particularly observed the change in the village due to the war. She noted that there were distinct social circles for the upper and lower classes, but there was no facility in the village for all the women to meet.

The Bearsted and Thurnham branch of the Women's Institute was founded by a group of ladies that included Lucy, Mrs Whitehead, Mrs Johnson, Mildred Higgins, Mrs W H Smith, Mrs Spenceley, Mabel Tasker and Alice Mendel. There are no specific details of the first meetings as the records do not commence until 1921, but it is known they were held in a large room at the White Horse. The organisation rapidly became known by the initials WI.

It did not take long for the founder members to realise that for the WI to flourish in the village, separate premises were required. In 1922, Walter Fremlin sold them some land situated close to Oliver's Row in The Street. The building firm of Cox which was based in Maidstone was selected to construct the hall at a cost of £675. The architect fee cost a further £45 so a huge amount of fund-raising was undertaken.

The WI's aims are to promote friendship, fun and education. These include the appreciation, promotion and preservation of local traditions and crafts. Classes have been run in dress making, smocking, rush and cane work, candle-wicking, tatting and soft furnishings.

Two members were responsible for developing a small business in the village. Mabel Tasker and Alice Mendel set up The Bearsted Fur and Glove Industry at Danefield house. Local families supplied materials such as bundles of cured rabbit skins to make the gloves and other families sewed them. Winifred Harris recalled that there was great excitement when they received an order for a pair of gloves for the Prince of Wales. Once the gloves were completed, nearly every worker tried them on before they were delivered to grace the hands of royalty! Due to the untimely death of Alice in 1941, the company was only in business for a few years.

In 1924 the West Kent federation of the WI held a pageant at Lullingstone Castle at the invitation of Lady Emily Hart Dyke. Bearsted was responsible for the section called 'The Coming of Christianity in AD 597'. These two photographs show some of the Bearsted cast from the pageant and include Mildred Higgins, Muriel Moss, Mrs King, Alice Mendel, Mrs Groombridge and Eileen Blandford:

Photograph courtesy of Jenni Hudson

Photograph courtesy of Jenni Hudson

A fresh round of fund-raising activities began when it was decided to extend the hall. Mrs Groombridge, even composed a poem about the villages of Bearsted and Thurnham in which she managed to include virtually every surname in the area. The poem sold very well indeed at three pence a copy. This is the first verse about Bearsted:

> There is a place of great renown,
> Bearsted, its name, not yet a town,
> With Dukes, and Deans, and Pearsons, too,
> Datsons and Pollards not a few.

A room was added to the hall and the kitchen enlarged. The work was completed in 1939. The hall has been used for so many activities since it was built that it is quite impossible to give a comprehensive list.

Many older residents will remember that during the Second World War the hall had a central role in the village. After the heavy raid on Detling airfield in August 1940, some of the wounded personnel were taken there for assessment and basic first aid.

In October 1940, the hall was turned into a canteen and a rest room for the troops stationed in and around Bearsted and Thurnham. An appeal in the parish magazine yielded sufficient cooking pots and other equipment to start the provision of hot meals. Books, magazines and board games were also donated by the village after another appeal.

Volunteer cooks reported to Mrs Daniell. The canteen staff were supervised by Mrs Grout and a hundred volunteer helpers included Mrs Colgate, Mrs Swift, Mrs Pollard and Mrs Croucher. In 1943 it was estimated that along with countless cups of tea, 76,696 meals had been served: an average of 211 a day.[1] Men were also recruited as canteen stewards, organised by Lance Monckton.

It did not take long for the WI to establish another facility so that the evacuee children in the village could receive a meal. This was slightly separate from the canteen service offered to the troops. The Methodist Chapel in Ware Street was used for the younger children while older children were accommodated in the WI Hall. Meals cost 3d a head and guaranteed substantial portions of meat and vegetables together with some bread. A second course of fruit, milk puddings, fruit pies or tarts was available. Seasonal donations of fruit were always welcomed.[2] This facility was supervised by Mrs Grout, assisted by Mrs Markwick.

In 1940 a Fruit Preservation Centre was set up by members of the WI. The scheme was based in a room at the former Thurnham vicarage, under the direction of Mrs Derrick. As the parish magazine recorded, the centre opened on 9 July and operated on Tuesdays, Thursdays and Saturdays during the fruit picking season. £60 was required for the necessary sugar and the money was lent by residents in units of £1. Fruit could be bought for preservation from the centre between 10 and 11.30am. Accounts were settled weekly.

Such was the success of the scheme that the centre opened a shop in the village. However, prices were governed by the Ministry of Food and were not competitive with the shops. When the vicarage was used for billeting of service personnel, the preserving centre transferred to the Mission Hut in Ware Street. The WI gave £5 to use the premises, subject to meeting the cost of all the gas used. Among many remarkable statistics for the WI during this time is that in six days, over 800lb of jam was once produced.[3]

Members of the armed services that were stationed in Bearsted appreciated that there was somewhere that could provide companionship and comfort in an environment similar to home. The warm welcome led to some kind comments by Rev E Bennitt, Chaplain to the Forces, when he attended the WI Canteen Committee Annual General Meeting in 1942. He recalled that he had been told that he was very lucky to visit the best canteen in Kent. Countless servicemen had told him how much they had enjoyed the wonderful atmosphere of the Bearsted canteen! It eventually closed on 22 November 1945 with a social evening and the remaining funds were donated to charity.[4]

Doris Britcher recalled that after the war, the WI held a concert for the children of the village which was very well received and raised £100.

This photograph shows the hall today:

Photograph courtesy of Malcolm Kersey

The hall has housed a lending library, provided accommodation for school lessons, children's clinics and playgroups. It has been a concert hall and a venue for dramatic productions. It continues to be available for hire by local clubs and it used for parties and wedding receptions.

One of the best-known services offered by the WI is that of a Country Market. Jean Spendley recalled that markets had been held since the First World War but it was not until 1976 that plans were made to open one in Bearsted. The first was held on 6 November and was a great success. Only home produced goods are sold including pies, cakes, bread and biscuits, preserves, eggs, garden plants and vegetables. A wide variety of craft work is also available for sale and to order.

This photograph which was taken in 1990, shows a busy trading session:

Photograph courtesy of Bearsted and Thurnham WI

In December 2003, Jean estimated that in addition to cakes, puddings and other food for Christmas, over a thousand mince pies were produced!

As with most success stories, the WI has continued to grow and enlarge. Bearsted Green WI was founded in 1980 and so is a relative newcomer. As Lesley Thorne recalled, the branch was set up as there was a long waiting list for Bearsted and Thurnham. The founder members included Lesley Thorne, Anne Seaton and June Clowes. The first meeting was held on 6 August 1980 with Ruth Charnock as the president. This illustration shows details of the first programme:

Wednesday, 7th January at 7.45 p.m.

Party

Coffee Hostesses — Mesdames Dickers, Dutton, Easeman, Elliman, Evans, Eady, Fletcher, Fenn. Flowers Mrs. Young.

Wednesday, 4th February at 7.40 p.m.

Mrs. M. Ridsdale. "Life as a fashion model".

Coffee Hostesses — Mesdames Farrin, Grogan, Horseman, Honeybone, Harden, Harris, Judd, Jack. Flowers - Mrs. Elliman & Mrs. Copp.

Wednesday, 4th March at 7.45 p.m.

Mr. W. Buck talking on "Silver".

Coffee Hostesses — Mesdames Jarnett, Kemp, Layton, Lines, Littlejohn, Lambert, MacFarlane, Morton. Flowers - Mrs. Harden.

Wednesday, 1st April at 7.45 p.m.

Mrs. J. Wyatt speaking on "Enamelling".

Competition for best home made Easter bonnet.

Coffee Hostesses — Mesdames Morrissey, Mills, Nicholls, Needham, Philpot, Pemberton, Pastides, Richards. Flowers - Mrs. Sopato.

REPRESENTATIVES

Craft	Mr. J. Clowes
Leisure & Trading Stall	Mrs. A. Seaton
Magazines	Mrs. L. Thorne
Press Rep.	Mrs. L. Warrington
Public Affairs & International	Mrs. P. Todd
Refreshments	Mrs. C. Trimmer

A.G.M. - June 4th at Royal Albert Hall.

Half yearly Council Meeting - 28th. Chatham Central Hall.

Reproduced courtesy of Bearsted Green WI

There are also branches of the WI at Roseacre and Madginford.

Kathryn Kersey and Rosemary Pearce

28 The Yeoman area of Bearsted

It took some time for the Yeoman area to be developed. The name is derived from the Kentish Yeoman public house on the Ashford road. At the start of the Twentieth century the land on both sides of the Ashford road was largely cultivated as fruit orchards and hop gardens.

The north side of the Ashford road

One of the earliest surviving records for the Kentish Yeoman lists Michael Stokes as the publican in 1839. Subsequent publicans include John Peters and Stephen Hicks.[1] Later in the Nineteenth century, the first of several generations of the Carr family ran the public house: Allan Carr held the license in 1891.

This photograph of the public house was taken in 1925:

Photograph courtesy of Allen Carr

It is believed that the property may once have been part of the premises for Otteridge Farm. Margery Gibson (née Pearce) recalled that behind this building was some spare ground. There were also several barns, and a stable where horses were kept. An oast house was sited where the Yeoman surgery now stands. In 1900, the property was owned by the Lushington family who sold it to the brewers, Isherwood, Foster and Stacey Limited for £2,200.[2] Subsequently it was owned by Fremlins brewery.

Allen Carr, grandson to the earlier licensee, recalled that his grandfather and father were master carpenters but ran the public house assisted by various members of the family. During the Second World War his father would get up before 6am, prepare the pub for opening, mop all the floors and 'bottle up'. Then he would go into Maidstone and work a full day at Tilling Stevens. When he returned home, there was just time for a meal before opening the pub for the customers.

This photograph of Kath and Allen Carr behind the bar was taken in the 1960s:

Photograph courtesy of Kent Messenger group

During the summer and early autumn, the main customers were Hoppers from the East End of London. The breweries operated a Rating System which was levied on barrelage. The more beer sold, the more the publican paid the brewery. Although it was the smallest pub in the village, the Carr family estimated that the Kentish Yeoman paid more in rates than any other local public house. Allen's father often used to say that they earned the brewery's living.

During the Second World War, in order to assist the local effort in the 'Dig for Victory campaign' Bearsted and Thurnham Produce Association was formed in 1943. The annual subscription was one shilling and sixpence. There were forty members and the benefits included cheap seeds and fertilisers. The Committee included Lionel Datson, Mr Abery and Bill Foster. A sty was also built on the spare ground at the Kentish Yeoman for a Pig Club. The club members included the Pearce, Harnett and Gregory families. A licence was required from the Ministry of Food to keep the animals. Evelyn Pearce (née Harnett) recalled that they were such lovely pigs that she used to sit on the wall and scratch them, not dreaming that the animals were going to be killed and eaten!

The Harnett family owned a gas-fired copper and every Sunday the Pig Club members would use it to prepare the swill for the pigs. This included all the unsold or old vegetables from their market garden and seemed part of the natural economy. When the pigs were slaughtered, the pork and bacon was a welcome change to the usual diet that was controlled through rationing.

Little changed for many years at the Kentish Yeoman. Allen rarely took holidays and it was not until the early 1960s that anything other than alcohol was sold on the premises. Once it was decided to introduce catering it was mainly in the form of pies and sandwiches.

For the greater part of the Twentieth century, there were two nurseries in the area. Frank Harnett opened a garden nursery and shop on fifteen acres of land between Roseacre Lane and Yeoman Lane that bordered the Ashford Road and which was near the Kentish Yeoman public house. The land had previously been cultivated as a hop garden and had become available due to a slump in the hop trade. For many years, the family lived in Bearsted Cottage by the Green, before moving to a house called Otteridge in Yeoman Lane. It backed on to the nursery.

Frank was married to Kate, who was the daughter of George Furber, a surgeon in Maidstone. They had three sons and two daughters.

These undated photographs show Frank and Kate Harnett in later life:

Both photographs courtesy of Kent Messenger Group

This shows a typical account from the nursery and is dated January 1923:

Reproduced courtesy of Roger Vidler

Evelyn Pearce (née Harnett), recalled that as the business began to develop, a florist shop was opened on the land fronting the Ashford Road. It catered for weddings and funerals, in addition to cut flowers and floral arrangements.

During the war years, only fruit and vegetables were grown as the nursery became a market garden in compliance with government orders. Land Army girls came to work in the fields.

After the war, a large area of land was made over to a rose nursery. A huge sign was erected which bore the words 'Harnett's for Roses'. Many older residents will recall that it did not take long for the sign to become a land mark feature in Bearsted and beyond.

This type of label, made from red card, was tied to every rose supplied by the nursery:

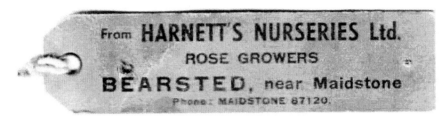

From **HARNETT'S NURSERIES Ltd.**
ROSE GROWERS
BEARSTED, near **Maidstone**
Phone: MAIDSTONE 87120.

Reproduced courtesy of Ian Payne

Like many companies after the war, when compared to the national chains of garden shops today such as Notcutts, there was little economy of scale. The business was still heavily dependent on the weather and seasons. Evelyn recalled that there were particular problems caused by a dock strike which held up a large order of rose root stock sent from Holland. Most of the order perished, causing financial hardship. In order to continue trading, some of the land was sold. The florist shop was enlarged to sell fruit, vegetables and groceries. Deliveries were made by van to local customers.

On his retirement, Frank sold the large family home, Otteridge, and had a chalet bungalow built on some of his land which he named Little Otteridge.

This is an undated, but recent photograph of Little Otteridge:

Photograph courtesy of Ian Payne

The business was restructured by Edward Harnett, who was known as 'Sam', and grandson of the founder, who had followed his grandfather into the nursery trade. Edward remained in control of the nursery until the development of modern marketing outlets for garden products led to a down turn in business. The land was eventually sold for development and housing in the 1960s. It seems appropriate that the new roads built in the area were called Otteridge Road and Nursery Avenue.

In the 1970s, a branch of Lloyds Bank. was built on land formerly part of Harnett's Nursery, on the left hand side of the Kentish Yeoman The bank continued to conduct business there for well over twenty years before closure. The building was later demolished and the site has now been incorporated into part of the new and enlarged Yeoman surgery.

This photograph was taken in 1986:

Photograph courtesy of Bearsted and District Local History Society

Harold Stringer's hairdressing business was slightly set back from Ashford Road, at the corner of Yeoman Lane. A typical short-back-and-sides haircut at Mr Stringer's shop cost 6d and Harold had a reputation for a swift service. He was able to cut the hair of the conductor from the 109 bus whilst the vehicle was turning round. The conductor would see the bus around the corner, then get off and have a haircut. By the time the bus was ready to leave five minutes later, the conductor was back on. A private garage now stands on the site of Harold's premises.

In the 1930s, the Yeoman Café was also located on the corner of Ashford Road and Yeoman Lane. The café had once been called The Firs Café but there were several changes of name. The café also sold newspapers. Mick Patterson recalled that he used to deliver newspapers on foot for the owners before he was promoted to a delivery round which included Church Lane. By taking on a larger round, he qualified for a shop bicycle with a big wicker basket on the front. Margery Gibson and Marjorie Cork recalled that The Firs seemed to be a very old-fashioned shop. It was so tiny that when there were more than three customers, it was an effort to get in and out the front door.

The site of the café was re-developed in the 1960s into a parade of shops called Yeoman Court. Hoods newsagents opened where the café had once stood. When Mr Hood sold the newsagents, the name changed several times and is now known as Bearsted News. Other shops to occupy parts of Yeoman Court have included an off-licence, a hairdressing salon on the first floor, a small Centra supermarket and latterly, a security and alarm business. This photograph of the shops at Yeoman Court and the Esso garage was taken in 1986:

Photograph courtesy of Bearsted and District Local History Society

The south side of the Ashford road

By the 1930s, some of the farmland on the south side of the Ashford Road, started to be developed. The Yeoman garage was well established and Yeoman nursery had just been built. Part of Spot Farm was sold for housing and became known as the Spot Farm estate. This was followed by the construction of Cavendish Way and Shirley Way.

It took some time for the residents in the new houses to assimilate into community life in Bearsted. Marjorie Cork had left school by the time her family moved into the village and because she did not join many clubs or societies, she had little social contact with the other village residents. She recalled that to begin with, her family only visited the main part of Bearsted in order to go to the doctor or to attend the Fayre. However, the Second World War was a great social catalyst. Many more people from the Yeoman area became involved in village life as their social circles widened through participation in local activities such as First Aid courses which were held at Bearsted House.

By the junction of Cavendish Way and the Ashford Road, were some small shops which have now disappeared or been altered. Brenda Ansett (née Mercer) recalled that in 1939 her family moved into Cavendish Way when her father, Len Mercer, took over the butcher's shop from Mr H Older. This was located where the bungalow stands that is now an office for the auctioneering firm of Clive Emson.

Nearby was also a grocery shop called Cavendish Stores which was run by Jim Cooper. It became a sweetshop run by Mr Sawbridge and later owners included the Stibey and Mortimer families. Joyce Bourne recalled that it was called The Regent Sweetshop, and even during the war and strict rationing, there always seemed to be a chocolate bar available for her!

Further up Cavendish Way was a bakery run by two sisters, the Misses Twort, who also sold cups of tea and coffee to accompany the cakes and buns. Joyce thought that the ladies always seemed very old and were not adverse to picking buns off the floor that they had dropped, brushing the dirt off them and then calmly offering them to customers that had witnessed their actions. Nearby, was a ladies hairdressers called 'Valerie's' and a Co-operative store. The latter was run by Mr Berefield.

The following two photographs of the area were taken in 1986. Since they were taken some of the shops have changed once more:

Photograph courtesy of Bearsted and District Local History Society

Photograph courtesy of Bearsted and District Local History Society

The Yeoman nursery was run by Mr Abery. Richard Hunt, who worked there for many years, recalled that the business was owned by a syndicate which included the Bodsham farm group and members of the Miskin family. This advertisement appeared in the parish magazine in 1929:

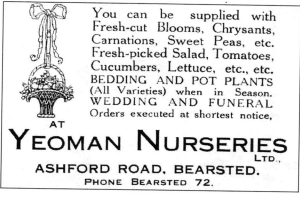

Reproduced courtesy of Jenni Hudson

When it first opened, the nursery comprised an enormous greenhouse complex with massive water pipes and some other smaller buildings. The pipes ran down a narrow cinder pathway alongside Yeoman garage.

This aerial photograph taken in the 1930s shows the first greenhouse to be built. It is the long building by the Yeoman garage. The property just visible behind the greenhouse was Mr Abery's bungalow:

Photograph courtesy of Martin Elms

The nursery greenhouses covered two acres of land. During the Second World War, under directives issued by the Ministry of Food, the nursery grew tomatoes. Joan Thorne recalled that the tomatoes were so popular that people used to queue the entire length of the greenhouse to buy them! When a bomb landed nearby, virtually all the glass in the greenhouses was shattered. The greenhouses were later refurbished and repaired by some German prisoners of war.

After the war, the nursery expanded with further greenhouses being built. Richard recalled that an immense quantity of flowers were grown and dried at the nursery. In addition to this, three-quarters of an acre of land was used to grow perpetual carnations, an acre was used to produce chrysanthemums and another quarter of acre for pot plants and tomatoes.

This photograph shows the extent of the premises around 1952:

Photograph courtesy of Audrey Fermor

After many years of successful trading, Yeoman nursery finally closed in the 1980s. The land was sold for housing. The site of the nursery is now occupied by Taskers Close, Bodsham Crescent, Button Lane and St Peter's church. This photograph was taken in 1986 and shows part of the original greenhouse. It was the last part of the nursery to be demolished.

Photograph courtesy of Bearsted and District Local History Society

Next to the nursery there was a further row of small shops. In 1946 the Mercer family butchers moved to 106a Ashford Road, the current location of Roseacre Launderette. Nearby is a shop that was run for many years as a florist, but latterly has become a branch of Regal Estate agents. Older residents will remember that it was once an electrical shop. It was built by Bob Filmer and run by Mr Don Black and his son, Roger. Prior to the shop opening around 1950, Mr Black traded from a smaller building which was further back on the same plot of land. In addition to electrical goods, the Black family also sold crockery and other household items. Mr Black's shop later became a cycle shop.

A mobile fish and chip shop used to visit the village. The van was owned by John Bradford before he opened a wet fish shop in Earl Street, Maidstone. The livery on the van was cream with green writing. Mr Bradford use to ring a hand bell to announce his presence in the village but the smell from the van was very distinctive. By 1959 a fish and chip shop had opened next door to Mr Black.

This photograph shows the launderette and other shops and was taken in 1986. The Ward and Partners estate agents office stands on the site of the Yeoman Nursery office and flower shop.

Photograph courtesy of Bearsted and District Local History Society

Mrs Hannah Collinson lived in a bungalow near the fish and chip shop. She was always regarded as quite a character, notable for her lively temperament and seemingly unaffected by her speech impediment. Mary Baker (née Palmer) recalled that Hannah never seemed to grumble about anything. Hannah was a Roman Catholic and as the nearest Catholic church was in Maidstone, walked there to attend Mass. As a child, she had walked into Maidstone from Staplehurst for the same reason.

In January 1977, Catholic services were held at the Memorial Hall. In less than a year, the Diocese agreed that there were enough people attending the services for the congregation to be classed as a parish. Whilst funds were being raised to build St Peter's church, Hannah used to donate some of her weekly pension. Father John Hines always tried to refuse it by saying that it was her money. Hannah was undeterred by this argument. Her reply was nearly always along the lines that it was really God's money. She wanted to obey God's will by doing something good and worthwhile with it. A site was found in Button Lane for the new church and it was consecrated 4 November 1984. Hannah lived to be 96 years of age and to see St Peter's church built and opened.

This photograph of the church was taken in 1986:

Photograph courtesy of Bearsted and District Local History Society

About 200 yards to the east of the fish and chip shop stands a property with eye-catching light blue roof tiles. This was once the site of the Bower Tea Garden, formerly a beer house. The 1851 census return describes Harriet Kirby, as running the business. Subsequent sellers of beer include James and Mary Richardson, and Charles Stamford.

The license for the Bower Tea Garden ceased after 1905[3] but the venue continued to be a popular and attractive place for motorists and cyclists to stop for tea. The location by the main road to Ashford and Folkestone allowed it to benefit from increasing volumes of traffic. After the Tudor House was built, the two premises competed for business as people used their leisure hours to travel. However, the Tudor House was able to offer bigger and better facilities so the tea garden closed.

Kathryn Kersey and Rosemary Pearce

29 Cross Keys estate

Before the Cross Keys estate was built, the land was cultivated as a cabbage field and a hop garden. Alan Croucher could recall his father, Ambrose, ploughing and sowing the land. The area took its name from Cross Keys Cottages which are on the opposite side of The Street. The cottages had once been an inn and are now listed as an historic building.[1] This photograph shows the cottages around 1900:

Photograph courtesy of Chris and Sue Hunt

This undated photograph shows the view from some of the hop gardens towards Holy Cross church:

Photograph courtesy of Margaret Morris

After the end of the Second World War, there was an acute housing shortage in the country. Houses destroyed during the war had not yet been rebuilt. Many young couples who were serving in the armed forces had married during the hostilities. They discovered when they returned to civilian life, that there was nowhere to live. Vera Banner (neé Croucher), recalled that after she married Bernard in 1943, they were in this situation as there was very little accommodation available or suitable for young families.

Vera's first married home was a renovated nissen hut that had been previously used by the Army. It was located in the parkland around Vinters House. However, the huts were not suitable for long term residence as they were very cramped, suffered from damp, and there were problems with heating. When Vera was offered one of the new houses in Cross Keys, she thought that she had been offered a palace!

Mary and Bernard Hirst were in a similar situation to Vera and her husband. Bernard Hirst had been born in Tower Lane, Mary Jarrett was his cousin, and they married in 1946 shortly after the war finished. Like many young couples, married life began with accommodation in one room of a relative's house. In this instance, it was 'Auntie Mill's' house at 6 Tower Lane, where Bernard's mother lived. The houses have since been re-numbered.

Bernard could remember his mother saying that their house was owned by Mr Whitehead. He had previously offered all the houses he owned in the lane to his tenants at £300 each. There was one condition: all the houses had to be bought by the occupiers at the same time. One tenant did not wish to buy so the sale did not proceed. The house was quite small. Auntie Mill insisted on various rules which made life very difficult, particularly as Mary and Bernard had two small children. The council particularly wanted families with small children to live in the new Cross Keys estate, so Mary and Bernard applied for a house. Both Vera and Mary's husbands were to spend the rest of their lives there.

Cross Keys was bordered by The Street and two fields beyond the lower part of the estate towards Sutton Street. The fields sometimes contained livestock, usually sheep or horses. The stream that ran through them eventually became 'the Lilk', and flowed into the lake opposite Otham Lane. In winter months it often flooded, covering a good part of the land, and of course the adjacent road. Eventually the culvert under the road was improved, and the problem addressed. The stream was edged by old pollarded willow trees, but very few survive. This photograph, taken from Cross Keys in 1960, shows Sutton Street, the flooded field and some of the willows:

Photograph courtesy of Rosemary Pearce

Mary and Bernard were the first of six families to be offered a house on Cross Keys. After they heard that their application had been successful, they regularly walked to the building site to look at the progress being made. It seemed an improbable dream that one day they would be living there with their children.

Two sets of ten houses around the outside of the estate were the first properties to be built, on the highest ground. A clear view of the oast houses and Bearsted House can be obtained from the back bedrooms of these houses. It was possible to see the traffic driving along the Ashford Road but the trees have now grown and obscure the view from the front bedrooms.

This undated photograph shows Mary by the front door of her house. Note the oast houses in the background:

Photograph courtesy of Mary Hirst

Mary and Bernard moved into 48 Cross Keys on 28 October 1950 after nearly four years in Tower Lane. They had very little furniture. Mary recalled that the front room was virtually empty, it had no carpet and was used to store the pram. However, what really mattered was that they were in their own home, at last. Two more children, Jacqueline and Carol, subsequently arrived to make use of the pram.

This photograph shows Bernard and Mary with their sons Christopher and Michael, in 1951:

Photograph courtesy of Mary Hirst

The first night in the new house at Cross Keys was particularly memorable: when Bernard switched on the electric light, nothing happened! They had moved on Saturday and the electricity was not due to be connected until the following Monday. Candles were used until the brand new electric lighting was available for use.

The house has changed very little. The property was known as a 'semi-detached corner house' as it was built on a corner plot, so the rooms are all of a substantial size. As a corner house, it was very slightly differently laid out to the rest of the estate. The first houses to be finished, numbers 45-48, all had flush-fitting doors with oval-shaped black bakelite handles.

48 Cross Keys had a garden to the front, back and side and two sets of steps; four at the front and eight at the back, to provide access. Three bedrooms and a bathroom, a front room, a sitting room at the back and a kitchen all provided a spacious living area for a family. There are still quarry tiles on the window sills and a substantial wooden-panelled staircase in the hall, which was specially varnished by Bernard to bring out the beautiful grain.

There was a gas supply to the house. The kitchen was already provided with a gas cooker in a specially designed alcove and the heating was via an open fire with a back boiler although it did not seem to be very efficient. Next to the kitchen was an outhouse with a copper and a coal cellar. The cellar was eventually removed when central heating was installed many years later and the kitchen was extended to include the outhouse. Hot water was supplied via a geyser but only for downstairs. If a bath was required, buckets of hot water still had to be carried upstairs.

The houses round the outside of the estate were completed first: the pavement finished just below Mary's garden gate. Mary recalled that there were two blocks of ten houses which were erected by Mr Filmer and his company. Mr Nichols and Mr Avery from the council oversaw the development.

The rest of the estate and Trapfields Close was built by Messrs Furnell from Cudham. During the subsequent building works, Mary was often visited by the workmen. They measured each room of her house and then made the other houses slightly smaller! The development comprised sixty four houses; twelve of these were two bedroom flats in blocks of four. The bungalows for elderly residents were built after the centre section of the estate was completed.

The middle of the estate was initially used as a store for building materials. All the children were told about the dangers of building sites but for some it seemed irresistible. Mary recalled that one day, her parents were due to visit. Christopher and Michael went out to play. They headed for the building site and met up with Richard Carcary who invited them to follow him through an obstacle course. This included crawling through a hollow barrel which still contained some tar. Mary was still removing the tar remnants from Michael when her mother arrived.

It seemed a long time before the heaps of building sand and bricks were finally cleared up as the houses were completed. Four houses along from Mary's house were Mr and Mrs Cork together with their sons, Lawrence and Andrew, who were roughly the same ages as Bernard and Mary's children. Mrs Cork's parents, Mr and Mrs Amos, were frequent visitors as Mr Amos had a car. On one occasion, one of the boys climbed into the car and inadvertently set it into motion. Mary was talking to a neighbour outside her house when the car went past. Before anyone could stop it, the car ran into a heap of the building sand. Fortunately, no damage to either car or occupant was sustained!

Several years after the house was built, the council decided that the estate needed landscaping and some trees arrived. Many of the trees planted by the council have not survived or have been removed by later owners of the houses. Of the three silver birch saplings were planted in the garden of 48 Cross Keys, only one remains.

Mary and Bernard were the first people on the estate to have a television. They were also the first to own a washing machine. Their black and white television cost just under £100 (more than £1,700 today) and was in a wooden cabinet that had two doors. The screen seemed very big at the time but now seems very small indeed. During the Coronation in 1953, seventy two people crowded into their sitting room to watch the ceremony. Mary recalled that on Cup Final days, there always seemed to be a crowd of people in their house to watch the match.

Trapfields Close was built between 1959 and 1960 on the site of Mr Stringer's market garden which had lain fallow for three years after his death. Mary is well aware of these dates as the council used six feet of their garden to construct a path. Once again she made countless cups of tea for the workmen.

Mary has seen many changes in Cross Keys. The majority of the houses are now privately owned, and those that are still occupied by tenants have been transferred to a housing trust. The social structure of the area has changed. When the estate was first built, only a few mothers had full time jobs. Many people had the time to stand and talk, either on the front door step or over the back fence. With changes in ownership many fences have been replaced by substantial hedges. Extensions or conservatories have been built in many back gardens.

Another change has been the decline in local tradesmen making regular calls. In the 1950s and 1960s the tradesmen included Mr Cicely, who sold groceries from a van and 'George', the Co-op Baker. Mr Wickens delivered milk, and Wakefield's supplied coal. An ice-cream van visited and 'Paddy' the road sweeper kept the estate roads clean.

Bernard's main leisure interests included gardening for which he won many prizes. However, Bernard and Mary are probably best known for their substantial support of the Men's Club over many years. He eventually became the President.

One of Mary's fondest memories concerns the catering arrangements of the Men's Club. Although the White Horse and the Royal Oak public houses offered hot meals, the facilities at the club did not really extend to providing food. She was aware that there might be a demand but there was no budget for catering. Mary sometimes organised what became known to members as 'plates of food' and charged a small sum to cover the costs. The catering began as an informal arrangement and depended on what ingredients, surplus to requirements, were given to her by members of the club and village. The food varied, but nearly always included a selection of sandwiches and cheese straws, small cakes and pastries. Mary is sometimes still asked by long-standing members of the club when they meet her in the village, whether she has any cheese straws available in her shopping bag!

Rosemary Pearce

Our new house had been used by the builders during the first phase of building. I seem to remember quite a few tea-stains up the walls when we first went to look, and Mother had to do quite a bit of scrubbing before we moved in.

My family moved into our three-bedroomed, semi-detached house at Cross Keys towards the end of 1951, just in time for my brother's fifth birthday. Although we had lived with Gran, and so did not have a lot of furniture, it still took some time to move in. Much of the furniture we did own bore the utility mark. The double bed came from Gran's house, and I remember seeing Dad carry the mattress round the road on his back, looking like an ungainly tortoise. At the end of the day we were not too tired to have a celebration, complete with an ice-cream cake, purchased from Datson's bakery earlier that day.

Prior to this, we lived with my widowed grandmother in Sutton Street. She had an outside toilet, but we now had a bathroom and toilet upstairs. We were under cover if we used the toilet in the outhouse, but it was very cold in the winter. The outhouse also contained a gas copper, so on washdays (usually a Monday) the little room was filled with steam. Sometimes the copper boiled over, and hot water spread out onto the path outside. There was no covering on the concrete floor, so there was no real damage. My father made a wooden rack to fit the copper so that my mother could use it to bottle fruit and tomatoes in Kilner jars. The jars had to be heated to cook the contents and create a vacuum to seal the rubber rings and glass tops securely to the jar. This form of preservation gave us fruit for pies and other puddings all through the year, even when the fruit was out of season.

Our new home had another luxury – electric light in all the rooms. In Gran's house there was gas lighting in the living room, the front room, and the front bedroom. The lighting and the range used for cooking made the living room very hot during the winter. We used candles to go to bed. If subsequently we needed to go outside to the lavatory, it was not easy on a windy night! In our new home we had a gas cooker in the kitchen, and hot water on tap, thanks to a back boiler. We children did not really know how lucky we were, but I am sure that my mother appreciated all the 'modern conveniences'. However, we had no fridge.

Dad made radio speakers that were extensions of the main radio set so that my brother and I could listen to programmes like 'Hancock's Half Hour' when we were in bed. However, this also meant that our parents could control how late we listened, or to what we listened as they unplugged the speakers at the end of our allotted time. We acquired a Dansette record player when we were a little older.

When Cross Keys was first built, there were two areas of rough grass where we could play on bikes or soap-boxes - the early go-carts. The larger area provided the space for several street parties and for community bonfires on Bonfire Night. We knew we were trespassing, but sometimes went over the fence or hedge to play in the field. The kingcups which grew on the edge of the stream were a big attraction for a small girl. Other people 'acquired' large stones for their rockeries from what were reputed to be Roman remains but were actually loose stones from the remains of a medieval, moated manor house.[2]

Two years after we moved in, the residents of Cross Keys held a street party on 4 June to celebrate the Coronation, as this photograph shows:

Photograph courtesy of Chris and Sue Hunt

At the street party, we children sat at the table wearing crepe paper hats in the patriotic colours of red, white and blue. We had tea, an orange, a bag of sweets and a chocolate wafer. Our mothers wore their pinafores during the meal and attended to our needs.

As the residents grew more affluent, garages were built on the smaller grass area. Initially there were around twelve, although this number was later increased. Much later, bungalows were built on the larger piece of rough ground, beside the road which was a cul-de-sac with a turning circle at the top. It was known to residents as 'The Frying Pan', from its shape. For many years the scout hut stood on the edge of the field which bordered this road. The field is now called the Elizabeth Harvie field, donated to the parish by a generous single lady with the interests of young people at heart. The scout hut was burnt down but was subsequently re-built at a different location.

Chris Hunt once told me that my family were always considered to be rich people because my father was the only white collar worker living there when the estate was first built. We were not the first to have a car, though. That honour, of course, went to Mr Amos, who was the grandfather of my friend Loll. Loll lived with his family at the top of the estate.

I have one further, but much later, memory of our house at Cross Keys. After many years there my widowed mother was making preparations to move when she discovered a Second World War shell in our coal hole. Not knowing quite what to do about it, she telephoned the police who alerted the bomb squad. Fortunately, the bomb squad declared that the shell was harmless but not before a full-scale alarm had been initiated! I can only think that my father acquired it with an idea of turning it into an artefact of some nature and then abandoned the idea along with the shell.

30 Four Fires in Thurnham Parish

This map shows the south part of Thurnham civil parish in the 1960s and the relative position of the four properties that suffered significant fires:

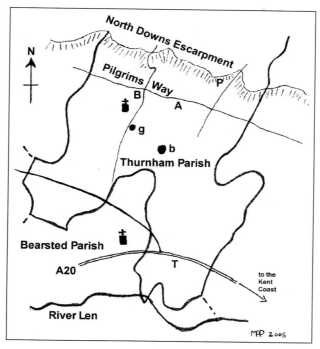

Diagram courtesy of Michael Perring

Key:

A – Aldington Court   B – The Black Horse
P – Pilgrims' Place   T – The Tudor House
g and b show the positions of the former Gore Pond and The Basin

By the end of the Second World War, the Kentish members of the National Fire Service were amongst the finest fire-fighting forces in the world. Fighting fires during the German bombardment of the county during 1940 and 1941 led to an experienced and disciplined force. Through the Fire Services (Emergency Provisions) Bill of May 1941, the National Fire Service was created in August. It comprised professional fire-fighters, volunteer Auxiliary Fire Servicemen and wartime-only firemen who had been recruited under the earlier Air Raid Precautions Acts of 1937 and the Fire Brigades Act of 1938. From May 1945 the National Fire Service was gradually contracted and from 1 April 1948 (as the result of a Bill of 1947) it was devolved to Local Authority control. The Kent Fire Brigade was able to continue using the former 30 Fire Force base at a former country house and estate called The Godlands at Tovil, Maidstone, as its headquarters.[1]

During the period of the fires being considered here, the Kent Fire Brigade was equipped with new appliances and a new Command and Control Centre at Headquarters was opened in 1984. It employs a computer-based communications and mobilising system. There is a database containing information on all known addresses in Kent, the nearest hydrants and water supplies, and the location and availability of appliances and staff.

Aldington Court

The parish of Aldington, which was annexed to the larger parish of Thurnham in the Sixteenth century, was recorded in the Domesday survey of 1086[2] as comprising two closely neighbouring manors. That to the west became known as Aldington West Court or Aldington Septvans (after the name of the resident family), the other as Aldington Cobham (now Cobham Manor).

In the early Eighteenth century, the house was remodelled in the Queen Anne style,[3] as this undated photograph shows:

Photograph courtesy of Jean Jones

The house was sited just below the Pilgrims Way beneath the escarpment of the North Downs. The southern approach was via a lake and avenue of trees, an outstanding feature on Eighteenth and Nineteenth century maps. In 1917 Charles Igglesden visited the house and described some of its external and internal features:[4]

> Aldington Court is built in the typical Queen Anne style, a feature being the elegant windows of that period. There is the original hall leading to a dais facing the front door. Upstairs is a room which was obviously a drawing-room...In one room on the ground floor is a delightfully artistic Queen Anne niche. Although Aldington Court was owned by many families of note in past days, it was, at one time, used as a farmhouse, but, comparatively recently, considerable alterations were made...On the east side of the house can be seen the remains of an old stone wall...On the other side of the house is a particularly quaint and picturesque wall with a handsomely designed coping in brick. It is dated 1703 and a peculiar guttering runs by its side...A plan of Aldington Court and the estate [shows] that there were two fine avenues leading up to the residence. The vista, as seen down the avenue of elms facing the front door, extends away down into Bearsted, and at the end is a glistening lake. We can conclude that this was always a green drive and that the actual roadway leading to the house was along the avenue of limes on the western side, an avenue that still exists...

At the time of Charles Igglesden's visit, the house was owned by the Lushington family. It remained in their possession until the fire in 1949 when it was being converted into three flats.

Nobody was in the house when the fire started before 4am, 15 December 1949,[5] but Mr Bird, the caretaker, was the first on the scene. The Maidstone Fire Brigade was called by exchange telephone and informed the Kent Fire Headquarters that a water tender had been sent out. Sub Officer Filmer, who was in charge, believed that it was a stack fire. Divisional Officer Moon was informed and left for Maidstone and then went on to Aldington Court.

A pump salvage tender was sent from Maidstone, but by 4.38am Sub Officer Filmer was requesting a full attendance at Aldington Court. A few minutes after that, Divisional Officer Moon requested four pumps and a hose-laying lorry. He advised that the ground and first floor were well alight and that the roof had gone, but there was now no risk to surrounding buildings. Water was pumped via an extensive relay from Gore pond in Thurnham Lane. Sub Officer Filmer then reported that the entire building was severely damaged and falling down, crews would be detailed for a considerable time and that more petrol, and an urn of tea were required. Divisional Officer Moon managed the relief crew. By 10.11am Sub Officer Filmer and Divisional Officer Moon, together with the pump escape and salvage tender, had returned to Maidstone.

At the peak of the fire, four appliances from Maidstone and one from Eccles were in attendance and three jets were in operation. On the following day, after an inspection by Divisional Officer Moon, a water tender and two men were sent to Aldington Court to damp down two pockets of buried fire.

This photograph of the fire-damaged house was published in a report about the fire in the Kent Messenger, 16 December 1949:

Photograph courtesy of Kent Messenger group

Pilgrims' Place

Pilgrims' Place was a little larger than Aldington Court, with fifteen rooms, but it is not shown on the 1870 and 1897 Ordnance Survey maps.[6] It seems to have been part of the Friningham Manor estate and was described in a property advertisement of 1936 as a 'secondary residence'.[7] It was shown on the Ordnance Survey maps of 1909 and 1939.[8]

This photograph of work being carried out on the building was taken around 1910:

Photograph courtesy of Norah Giles

By 1934 it was being used as a fox farm, owned and managed by Commander Stack. Fox Farm Cottages which were adjacent, appear on the 1937 Ordnance Survey map. This entry in a trade directory shows details of the fox farm:⁹

FOX FARMS.

STACK'S FOX FARM,
OWNER-MANAGER,
COMDR. C. M. STACK.

Member of the Silver Fox Breeders' Association of Great Britain & Ireland & of the British Fur Breeders' Association.

The nearest farm to London for silver & blue foxes.

FRININGHAM LODGE, DETLING, NEAR MAIDSTONE, KENT.

Stations, Maidstone or Bearsted & Thurnham.

Telephone & Telegrams, Bearsted 6218

Reproduced courtesy of Michael Perring

At the time of the fire, the house was owned by Mr Fredenburgh, a journalist and diplomatic correspondent. On 14 November 1954, he was taking pre-luncheon aperitifs with guests, when his son, Edward, alerted him to smoke in the room above. The roof and upper floor of the fifteen-roomed house were well alight and the Fire Brigade was summoned. Before they arrived, Mr Fredenburgh and his guests managed to save many of the valuables and furniture. A pump escape, a pump salvage tender and a water tender from Maidstone were in attendance. Water tenders from Eccles, Lenham, Loose and Sittingbourne were also in attendance and a main salvage tender from the London Salvage Corps was summoned. All of these vehicles had difficulty in negotiating the narrow lanes[10] and there was a shortage of water.

The fire was brought under control after two hours by one jet from a relay from open water (presumably Gore Pond or Aldington Basin), three jets from water tenders and four hose reel jets. The roof and top floor were severely burnt and damaged by smoke and water. Relief crews were sent for during the evening and Station Officer Stamper finally returned from the fire at 4.07am on the following day. Divisional Officer Moon and Assistant Divisional Officer Pearce inspected the wreckage of Pilgrims' Place later in the morning.[11] This photograph of the wrecked house was published in a report about the fire in the Kent Messenger, 19 November 1954:[12]

Photograph courtesy of Kent Messenger group

The Tudor House

Despite its name, the Tudor House was constructed in the late 1920s. The roadhouse was built by Mr A Eustace Short, who was one of the Short Brothers. One of the reasons for its construction was to provide employment for the skilled workforce at Shorts' barge factory in Rochester when demand for barges was declining rapidly.[13] The building was in the style of a Tudor mansion around a central court, constructed from seasoned oak timbers brought from Oakwood, Maidstone. Peg tiles came from Hollingbourne and Paddock Wood.[14]

These undated postcards show the central court and part of the tea room:

Photograph courtesy of Michael Perring

Photograph courtesy of Ian Payne

The Tudor House was situated to catch the increasing motoring public, at the edge of Milgate Park on the main Maidstone to Ashford road (A20). The facilities included a restaurant to seat 90 people, a ballroom and a banqueting hall which could accommodate a further 350 people. There were other function rooms and it was described as 'one of Kent's best known eating places and night spots'.[15]

This photograph of the Tudor House, taken in 1926, shows the early layout of the property:

Photograph courtesy of Chris and Sue Hunt

This undated postcard shows the ballroom:

Photograph courtesy of Martin Elms

The Tudor House was listed under the erroneous address of Ashford Road, Bearsted in 1930:[16]

Tudor Tea Rooms – Cornish Teas a Speciality. Parties catered for.

Similarly, in 1930:[17]

Tudor House Café, A.E. Short

The location was corrected in later directories to Thurnham. Thus in 1934:[18]

Tudor House Café

Mr Tomlinson owned the Old Barn Tea House in Hildenborough and after buying the Tudor House, Thurnham in the 1930s, he needed a car park attendant. In his words:[19]

...as we had a suit of armour hanging on the wall we decided [he] could wear the suit; a man in armour outside a Tudor Mansion being quite appropriate.

He advertised in Maidstone for a thick skinned man to wear the suit:[20]

Maidstone is full of thick-skinned men, scores applied.

The successful applicant, Mr Maskell, later featured in a postcard advertising the facilities:[21]

TUDOR HOUSE, MAIDSTONE. CAR PARK ATTENDANT.

Photograph courtesy of the Gordon Ward collection,
Kent Archaeological Society

The property changed ownership in 1978 for a sum that was rumoured to be £350,000. Planning permission was sought for the addition of a motel with 54 bedrooms and outline permission for an eighteen-hole golf course immediately to the south. The new owners, Mr and Mrs Ferid Hickmet, intended to go ahead with these projects and planned to upgrade the existing facilities.[22]

This aerial photograph shows the layout of the building around 1980:

Photograph courtesy of Chris and Sue Hunt

However, Mr and Mrs Hickmet's plans were not realised: the Tudor House had a somewhat tarnished reputation by the early 1980s. According to some local opinion, it was a place to be avoided late at night, although there are few recorded instances of disorder. Other changes had also been made as it was disclosed in April 1983, during a prosecution for food hygiene offences, that the owners were a company called Vrumsol and Ferid Hickmet was a director. The company was fined £3,475 by magistrates.[23]

In contrast to the other fires, that at the Tudor House on 16 July 1983, was caused by arson.[24] Forensic experts confirmed that there had been a break-in less that two hours after the Friday night disco had finished and that there were at least two places where fires had been lit. The arsonists could not have chosen a better time because meteorological records show that June was an exceptionally dry month. July was the driest month on record; the maximum temperature on 15 July was only slightly lower than that on the hottest day of the year, which was the following day.[25]

The fire started at about 3am. Police were alerted by an automatic burglar alarm and they called the Fire Brigade, who found the restaurant well ablaze and repeatedly called in support.[26]

The fire was brought under control in two hours. Over sixty fire-fighters from many parts of Kent, with ten appliances, including turntable ladders, a hose-laying lorry and an emergency tender, fought the inferno using ten jets and a monitor. However, most of the building was destroyed. One difficulty was the low water pressure due to the dry weather. The Water Board was unable to increase it and lines had to be laid to a pond a quarter of a mile distant.[27]

The Black Horse

A map of Thurnham dated 1709, shows that James Fuller owned the site of the Black Horse in the early Eighteenth century.[28] It was inherited by his son, John, and in a conveyance of 1751, the property was described as 'The Black Horse'. The conversion to an inn was probably accomplished by the tenant, Richard Catt, between 1744 and 1751. It is situated on the south-western corner of the crossroads of the Pilgrims Way and Thurnham Lane leading to Castle Hill. It changed little over many years.

This postcard of the Black Horse is undated, but was probably taken in the early years of the Twentieth century:

Photograph courtesy of Martin Elms

In the decade before the fire, the landlord, Leslie Broughton, his first wife Marion (who died in 1986), and second wife, Carole, turned the public house and restaurant into one of the busiest establishments in the area.[29]

This fire started on 28 November 1988,[30] probably by a smouldering cigarette end that had either fallen onto, or was close to, a settee in the bar of the public house. Fortunately, the flames burnt the cable of a burglar alarm and set it off at 2am. The noise woke Les Broughton in his bedroom above. Les saw smoke coming through the floor, and flames flickering outside the building. He and wife Carole ran up to wake Carole's teenage son, Christopher, and daughter, Fleur, on the floor above. The family escaped from a first floor window and slid down an extension roof into the garden. Fleur was slightly injured during the descent. Les then forced open the back door to rescue his two dogs, but smoke had killed the cat.

Meanwhile, the Fire Brigade arrived having been summoned by a neighbour. Two appliances from Maidstone and another from Larkfield were sent. The fire-fighters arrived to find the family tackling the blaze with a hose. The fire was under control after two hours and the fire-fighters stayed until lunchtime. Relief crews cleared the contents from the building, which was gutted, apart from the restaurant, and had lost most of its roof.

The Aftermath

Neither Aldington nor Pilgrims' Place was rebuilt. They had outlived their usefulness and were not replaced. In the earlier part of the Twentieth century, it was desirable to own a large country house. When they were not available, they were constructed; Pilgrims' Place was one example of this, and so was Thurnham Keep, which stills stands, further to the west. Sometimes, because of this fad, existing buildings were adapted: Thurnham's forge was enlarged to produce Thornham Friars.

The upkeep of these large establishments required servants and other staff such as gardeners. This pattern of life continued until the end of the Second World War. The social effects of the war and new political ideas meant that people were now less willing to become servants. Inheritance taxes and increasing maintenance costs turned these large houses into liabilities. Personal income could not even be boosted by farming foxes. The fashion for wearing animal skin coats or a fox skin around the neck, a paw secured by a clasp hidden in the dead animal's mouth, which was prevalent in the 1920s and 1930's, had become abhorrent. Today, Pilgrims' Place is just a few stones in the woodland beside the North Downs Way long distance path.

Even before the fire, Aldington Court was being converted into flats. The outbuildings became 'Thurnham Keep Farm', which is shown on the 1987 Ordnance Survey map.[31] In 1959, the construction of the M20 motorway severed a direct track (the tree-lined drive mentioned earlier) from Aldington to Bearsted. Neither bridge nor tunnel was provided and this route was impeded by a diversion to Water Lane and back. In due course, Hubert Batchelor acquired the farm and brought in new methods of cultivation. These included the destruction of trees, hedgerows and the ancient trackway. The land was drained and Gore Pond and The Basin below Aldington were emptied. There is still a bridlepath which passed across sticky clay until its recent diversion to the west bank of the Lilk Stream. It is intended that this route will be landscaped to provide a wildlife habitat.

It is ironic that the demise of Aldington Court has ultimately denied future fire-fighters the sources of open water which had been successfully used to contain the fire. The extinction of the two large residences also significantly depleted the sparse population of the Ecclesiastical Parish of Thurnham — effectively the northern half of the Civil Parish since 12 April 1945.[32]

The brewing company Whitbread funded the rebuilding of the Black Horse and a new hotel on the Tudor House site. The police made extensive enquiries in the week following the Tudor House fire, appealing to the public for information on cars parked nearby and running footsteps heard close to the site at the time of the fire.[33] A week later, the police were offering a £5,000 reward for information leading to the conviction of the arsonists. The damage was estimated at over £0.5 million. Matters were not helped by thieves breaking into a store on the site and stealing some wine. There were also insinuations of the involvement of the management in the fire which were denied by Alan Hickmet, the banqueting manager.

A 'shell-shocked' Ferid Hickmet returned from France, where he had been celebrating his birthday, immediately after the fire and dismissed a report that the property destroyed was worth £1.5 million.[34]

The arsonists escaped detection, and in 1985 the ruins were demolished prior to a re-development. An artist's impression of the new Country Club Hotel and Golf Course appeared in the local paper in 1986.[35] The Mayor of Maidstone, Councillor Mrs Sarah Haskett, cut the first sod of the £8 million development with the chairman of Thurnham Parish Council, Norman Macpherson, amongst the guests.[36] The new complex with seven conference rooms, four syndicate rooms, 117 bedrooms, a leisure club with a swimming pool and an eighteen-hole golf course opened in 1988. The dream of 1978 was more than realised, but the Hickmets had gone.

The story of the Tudor House also reflects the changing pattern of life in the Twentieth century. At first, the area was part of the parkland surrounding Milgate House. When the mock Tudor restaurant was built, it became a popular destination for a walk, a bus ride, or an outing by 'motor', for morning coffee or afternoon tea, or for a club or society to hold a lunch or dinner dance.[37] It was well placed to entice the rapidly expanding middle class population, mainly in the 'ribbon' development along the Ashford Road. It was a good place in which to be seen.

After the Second World War, the Tudor House was equally well placed to attract the rapidly expanding population of motorists making their way to and from the coast at the weekends. Then progress brought catastrophe! The Maidstone by-pass, which opened early in the 1960s, also by-passed the Tudor House and rejoined Ashford Road near Eyhorne Street. A grand new hotel called 'The Great Danes', complete with indoor swimming pool, was erected near this junction. Market forces were firmly against the Tudor House! Due to the fire, jobs were lost, but were eventually regained. The facilities at the new Country Club are more than adequate to satisfy the needs of the exercise-starved salesmen, commuters and executives now living in Bearsted and Thurnham, and alleviate the increasing demand for golf. The Tudor Park Hotel contains conference meeting rooms, three of which are appropriately named 'The Thurnham Suite'. Thurnham Parish Council has met there since April 2005.

Immediately after the fire at the Black Horse, the Broughton family left the hamlet to live with friends, but soon returned and lived in a mobile home in the car park while the builders were at work. Just over a year after the fire, the Black Horse re-opened. Apart from a few beams, it looked much the same as before.[38]

This photograph from 1989 shows Leslie and Carole Broughton outside the re-built Black Horse:[39]

Photograph courtesy of Kent Messenger group

The Broughton family moved out in 1990 and were succeeded by Frank Wyldbore and in 1996, by Mrs Sandra Yates. In 1998 John and Julie Freeman took over and have expanded the restaurant trade. Their successful bed and breakfast venture, utilising rooms built in the garden, has resulted in planning consent for a further eight rooms.

The role of public houses has changed during the Twentieth century. They have moved from slaking the thirst of the local population (predominantly farm hands and armed servicemen camped nearby in both World Wars), to providing meals for people driving into the parish from the surrounding area. The fire cut off one good restaurant for a while, but the bar meals trade continues to be highly competitive and the public is always fickle!

The organisation of the Kent Fire Brigade, their equipment and communications system have improved immeasurably during the Twentieth century. Although they had little chance of saving the buildings in the above fires, they contained the flames. No woodlands or neighbouring properties were damaged, and some were very close.

The stories of the fires emphasise the lack of water. This has become even more acute with the demands caused by recent population expansion outstripping supply. Fire-fighting in Thurnham today could be even more hampered by lack of water, especially as there is less open water now.

Michael Perring

31 Thurnham and Bearsted in the late 1960s and early 1970s

Whilst on our way to my grandmother's house in Rainham, we took a wrong turn and ended up by the Green. My parents were enchanted by the view. They were looking for somewhere to live as my father started a new job. He had previously been employed as a Safety Advisor on motorway construction. This involved what is known today as 'short term contracts' and included building the M6 motorway. For a time, there were no more motorways to be built, and so we returned to Kent. We rented 62 Ware Street from Mrs Martin. Her mother, Mrs Watkins who lived next door gave kind and generous advice.

No one in my family realised the age of 62 Ware Street, also known as Oak Cottage. It certainly seemed to be an old house which had many beams with intriguing shapes. More curious, however, was the 'flying freehold' arrangement which meant that one of the back bedrooms was actually located in part of 64 Ware Street, which was adjacent. It could only be accessed via a doorway from our house. The attic was reached from a door in the front bedroom and a steep flight of stairs. It was well worth the climb though as the attic space extended the entire length of the building.

This photograph of 62 Ware Street was taken in 1999. The lower roofline is part of a modern extension. All the windows are modern replacements of a different design to the original fittings.

Photograph courtesy of Malcolm Kersey

In the kitchen there was another curious arrangement: a ceiling panel could be removed allowing you to look right into the bedroom that was part of the flying freehold. It was many years later before I discovered that the house bears a Grade II listing. Parts of it are estimated to date from 1667.[1] Some of the arrangements I once considered to be curious were the result of alterations. It is certainly one of the oldest surviving properties in Ware Street.

The daily routine was punctuated by the sound of trains as they travelled along the line behind Rosemount farmhouse which lay behind our house. Dad was nearly always the first up in our household as he was now employed as a Safety Officer at the Marley Foam factory in Lenham and it took a while to travel there. The factory produced the plastic fronts of car dashboards that were filled with rigid foam. They were known as 'crash-pads'. Dad always knew when a new type of car was about to be launched.

Ware Street was rather quieter than today as there were fewer cars using the road. The first houses on Sandy Mount were just completed. A favourite occupation for some of the children who lived there was sitting on the earth bank whilst watching the traffic. There was always a chance of spotting a car that had been featured as stolen on Shaun Taylor's 'Police Five' television programme. There were many occasions when I joined some of my friends in this pastime. A hedge was eventually planted on the bank.

It did not take me long to get to school every day: the route involved walking up the hill in Ware Street and then down to Chestnut Place. I enjoyed looking in each shop window at Chestnut Place: Mr Wood's, the butcher; Mr Page's shop and drapery; the Post Office and Taylor's newsagents, where my brother had a newspaper round.

Further down The Street was a chemist shop that also sold wool. Bearsted Stores were on the corner of the Green opposite the Royal Oak pub. My mother met me from school and then we would walk down past the Royal Oak to Wakefield's coal merchants' office to place an order, when more coal was required. A tray of samples for the different types of fuel they could supply always looked interesting. Once the order was placed, we then went next door to Datson's bakery for bread and there was always the possibility of purchasing some 'New Penny' chocolate and biscuit wafers which tasted wonderful. Nearly opposite the bakery was Holly House Stores.

I appreciated being able to play on the Green during school lunchtimes in the summer. Daisy chains and 'gym practice', which involved cartwheels and handstands, were favourite occupations. I vividly remember trying my very first, rather wobbly handstand, under the steady gaze of Alfred Mynn, forever depicted playing cricket on the wooden village sign.

Whilst on the Green, one of the best things to do was to sit underneath some of the fir trees at the Church Lane corner. I cannot remember ever being supervised on the Green, although I am almost sure that even in those innocent days, we were. If the dinner ladies were in evidence it was either Mrs Austin (known as Ozzie) or Mrs Martin (known as Marty). Both ladies seemed to have endless patience and time to share with small children.

I liked to sit and look at some of the oldest houses that bordered the Green and try to imagine what it must have looked like when they were first built. In the heat-heavy days of summer I used to imagine a lady looking remarkably like Anne Boleyn at Bell House. She was always a tragic figure in my young mind, already heavily influenced by R J Unstead's view of history! The elegant front of Bearsted House inspired the idea of a graceful lady in an Empire-line dress arriving in a carriage driven by two immaculate horses. The property accommodated Eylesden Court Preparatory School at this time. Sometimes, the splashing sound of the swimming pool being used on a hot summer day was tantalising.

Just before Bearsted School re-located in 1972 to a new building in The Landway, we moved to a house on the south side of the Ashford Road. Daniel T Jackson Limited, who were builders based in Colchester, Essex, had bought the land in 1968. The development was initially called Spot Lane Estate. It did not take long for the roads to acquire their official names of Greensand Road and Ragstone Road.

The 'show homes' were 1, 3, 5 and 7 Greensand Road. There were three types of semi-detached property constructed. All the houses were built with either electric or gas-fired warm air central heating. Customers could also specify paintwork finishes, the colour of the ceramic wall tiles for kitchen and bathroom, and the vinyl floor tiles, using charts supplied. The extent of each property was marked by two interwoven panels and 'fencing' which in reality comprised wooden posts and two strands of plain round wire. Our house was built on Plot 33 and cost the huge sum of £6,300.

My parents decided to apply to the building society for a mortgage to assist them in the house purchase. However, it was by no means certain that the building society would agree. Social unrest, failing governments and the arrival of the three-day week made uncertain times.

Our house was the last to be finished as the construction company was undergoing financial problems. These certainly showed in the quality of the finishing details of the house and garden. The building schedule was also affected by a wet winter and spring, which meant that the decorators had great difficulty in achieving a final finish to the painted walls. The garden was fenced, but had been abandoned for some weeks prior to the handover of the property. There was no sign of the promised turf for the lawn and a heavy crop of weeds had begun to grow.

Once we had moved in, my father spent a great deal of time endeavouring to remedy the faults in plasterwork and the ceilings. Eventually, my parents decided that the house was finished to an acceptable standard, but just before this, the building company was declared insolvent. We were advised that no further remedial work could be undertaken. When my parents landscaped the garden, a massive amount of rubble and building debris was unearthed. There was a sufficient quantity of bricks and breeze blocks to lay the foundations of a patio and a brick built step.

These two illustrations show part of the information distributed by the builders and the original layout of the estate:

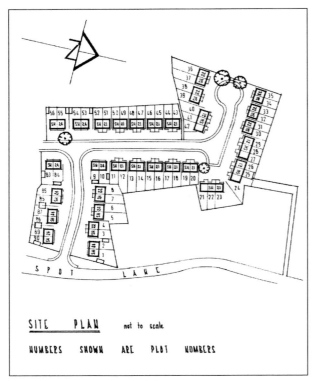

SITE PLAN not to scale

NUMBERS SHOWN ARE PLOT NUMBERS

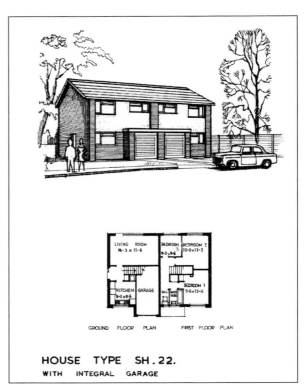

HOUSE TYPE SH.22.
WITH INTEGRAL GARAGE

Reproduced courtesy of Malcolm Kersey

Due to the company's insolvency, the development of the land at the bottom of Ragstone Road was suspended. It changed hands several times with various proposals and schemes. Many designs were rejected due to a lack of provision for flooding which it was felt had to be included due to the close proximity of the river Len. It was not until the middle of the 1970s that construction began again and Gault Close was built.

Our local shops were now those in Egremont Road, Madginford. As there was a variety of retailers, these seemed quite sufficient for the immediate needs of our family. There was the Pricerite supermarket which later became the International Stores. It also had the sophistication of a 'Home and Wares' section which sold items such as plastic buckets and washing up bowls.

Next door to the supermarket was a newsagent called The Newsbox. This shop had confectionary displayed on trays which were then protected by an enormous curved cover made out of transparent perspex. There was also a butchers, a hairdressing salon, a branch of Stonham chemists, a greengrocer and the Egremont Do-It-Yourself shop that sold practically everything in timber and ironmongery that could ever be required.

At the end of the parade of shops was one unit that was occupied by a variety of small businesses which seem to trade for short periods before closing. The first shop in this unit was the Bearsted Cassette Library, then it became a Sports Shop and a boutique, before achieving rather more permanence as a veterinary surgery run by Mr Margett.

In 1975 Madginford Library opened, and I wasted no time in becoming one of the first junior members. I looked forward to Saturday mornings when I could change my books as I now had a valid excuse for not accompanying my parents on shopping trips into Maidstone. In the library, in addition to a wide choice of books, there was a small range of musical scores and some books that had been specially produced in large print. There was also a small glass fronted cabinet in which the trophies awarded by the Madginford

Residents Association were kept. Two years later, the residents association wound up their activities and the trophies were placed on permanent display.

Until the 1980s, from Ragstone Road you could look over to wooded and disused ragstone quarries. Spot Lane ran alongside the lower edge of the quarries, then up a quite steep slope before connecting with Church Lane by St Nicholas church, Otham. The quarries were interesting places to explore and were a good source of shellfish and plant fossils which could easily be found. Our garden was decorated with several enormous lumps of ragstone with fossils lodged in them that I brought home precariously balanced on my bicycle. The edges of the quarries were carpeted with wild flowers through the spring and summer: bluebells were prolific in some areas.

This undated photograph below is a typical view of the quarry area looking towards Madginford standing just below St Nicholas church in Church Road, Otham. Although this part of Church Road still exists as a footpath, Horton Downs, Foxden Drive and Reinden Grove were later built on the land in the left hand side of the photograph. The land directly behind the line of wooden fencing on the right hand side was incorporated into some of the gardens in Frithwood Close.

Photograph courtesy of Peter Green

At the bottom of Spot Lane were the remains of a watermill which at one time had been known as Otham corn mill. The ownership of the mill can be traced back to 1782 when Edward and Thomas Pine were named in some sale particulars.[2] By 1972 the mill had long fallen into disuse and the buildings were rapidly becoming ruinous. A fragment of apple orchard survived together with the remains of the channels for the water. There was an abundance of wild flowers in the orchard and I can recall the excitement of once finding a Common Spotted Orchid.

The surviving part of the mill buildings, together with the site of the orchid, were razed to the ground and completely cleared during the late 1970s but I cannot remember an exact date. It is possible that their demolition was part of the Gault Close development. One part of the mill remains: the ragstone bridge over the main water channel.

191

This photograph of the bridge was taken in 1986:

Photograph courtesy of Bearsted and District Local History Society

Eventually, whilst I was away at college, the quarries began to be backfilled and then built upon. Every holiday I returned to a little more development in the area as the first houses were built and occupied in Horton Downs, Longham Copse and Foxden Drive. The Downswood housing estate had arrived.

Kathryn Kersey

Notes to the Text

1 A brief overview of Bearsted and Thurnham

1   *The History and Topographical Survey of the County of Kent*
Edward Hasted
E P Publishing 1972

2   For further details see pp.x-xi
A History of Bearsted and Thurnham
The Bearsted and Thurnham History Book Committee 1978

2 Ware Street, Thurnham around 1900

1   Conversation with Jean Jones, 12 February 2004
also see 1742 Memorandum concerning the purchase of a house and two acres of meadowland adjoining Ware pond by Henry Rand.
CKS Reference U1401 Z4

4 Sandy Mount farm, Thurnham

1   i   Lease re Windmill in Berstead 1777-1862
CCRC Reference T003: Church Commissioners capitular estate 1349-1946
Nos 103621 103623 103623-103645 149587-149591

      ii   1841 census return for Thornham
NA Reference HO 107/463/2

2   Tithe Apportionment Schedule for Bearsted, compiled 1842
CKS Reference P18/27/2-3

3   i   *Ibid.* Lease re Windmill in Berstead

      ii   *Monckton's Trade Directory 1854*
KAS Library

4   Bearsted entry in *Watermills and Windmills*
William Coles Finch, published by Arthur Cassell 1933

5   Edward Pretty FSA Kent Etchings/Drawings
P18, sketch 37
Maidstone Museum

6   *Op. Cit.* 1841 census return for Thornham

7   Tithe Apportionment schedule for Thornham, compiled 1843
CKS Reference IR 29/17/39

8   1851 census return for Thornham
NA Reference HO 107 1618 98-111

9   Particulars and conditions of sale of some Freehold Estates 1858
CKS Reference U1569 T15

10   Sale of Hersts Lane 1858-1859
Letter dated 21 December re Armstrong sale
CKS Reference U248 T7

11   1891 census return for Thornham
NA Reference RG 12 524 101-116

12   1871 census return for Thornham
NA Reference RG 10 946

13   i   1881 census return for Thornham
NA Reference RG 11 0933 118 2

      ii   1891 census return for Thornham
NA Reference RG 12 691

14   'everything found' is a phrase used in these circumstances to indicate that the clothing for work, payments for board and lodgings and utilities were paid by the employer and were therefore not included in the wages

7 John Perrin's enterprise: the shops at Chestnut Place

1   Kent Fire Office Insurance Reports
13 January 1900

2   *Ibid.*

3   p.122
A History of Bearsted and Thurnham

4   Photograph from the collection of Yeandle Papers·
CKS Reference U1401 Z12-13

5   Entry for Bearsted in *Kelly's Trade Directory for Kent* 1899

6   Undated conversation with the late Jessie Page

7   Entry for Bearsted and Thornham
Pigot & Co Trade Directory 1826

8   *The Postal History of Maidstone and the Surrounding Villages*
Sidney J Muggeridge
The Postal History Society 1972

9   *Ibid.*

10   Entry for Bearsted in *Kelly's Trade Directory for Kent* 1855

11   *Op. cit. The Postal History of Maidstone and the Surrounding Villages*

8 A Crotal Bell: land holdings and local farming practises

1   Abstract of the Title of the Right Honourable Charles, Earl of Romney to a messuage or tenement, lands and heredits in the parishes of Bearsted and Boxley in the County of Kent taken in exchange from the Sadler's Company 1834.
CKS Reference U289 T39

2   Will of Edward Hill, made 20 December 1645 and proved 29 October 1646
NA Reference PROB/11/197

3   For more detailed information about livery companies see *The Livery Companies of the City of London*
Corporation of London Public Relations Office, 1997 Guildhall.

4   The term 'mystery' comes from the Latin *misterium* meaning 'professional skill'.

5   A cordwainer was someone who made shoes.

6   Unpublished correspondence dated 1 October 2003 between author and Company Archivist of Saddler's Company.

7   *Op. cit.*
Abstract of Title of the Right Honourable Charles, Earl of Romney 1843

8   1803 Court Minute Book
Saddlers Company, held at Saddlers Hall, 40 Gutter Lane, London E2V 6BR

9   Tithe Apportionment map for Bearsted 1842, schedule dated 1844
CKS Reference P18/28/2-3

10   1861 census return
NA Reference RG 9/499 43-56

11   Report of the Royal Commissioners on the Livery Companies of the City of London 1880-1884
Copy held at Saddlers Hall

12   1871 census return
NA Reference RG 10 939

13   1881 census return
NA Reference RG 11 0926 46

14   Photograph of the Green, Bearsted from the collection of Yeandle Papers
CKS Reference U1401 Z12-13

15   The cottages bear a Grade II listed status and it is believed the buildings date from 1600-1669
National Buildings Record 8524 ID 503375

16   *Op. cit.* Bearsted Tithe Apportionment

17 Sale particulars 1858
CKS Reference U1569 T15

18 *Op. cit.* entry for 18 August 1897
Court Minute Book, Saddlers Company

19 Entry for Bearsted, *Kelly's Trade Directory for Kent* 1899

20 *Op. cit.* entry for 18 August 1897
Court Minute Book, Saddlers Company

21 i   *Ibid.* entry for 20 July 1898
Court Minute Book

ii   *Ibid.* entry for 29 September 1898
Court Minute Book

22 7 March 1918 log book entry (volume covering 1908 to 1921)
Bearsted Church of England School
CKS Reference C/ES 18/1/4

23 9 February 1927 log book entry (volume covering 1922 to 1959)
Bearsted Church of England School
held at Roseacre School, The Landway, Bearsted

24 Letter dated 6 March 1929
District Valuer to Clerk for Maidstone Rural District Council
CKS Reference P18/30/16

25 Letter dated 25 July 1966
Clerk of Bearsted Parish Council to Kent Association of Parish Councils
CKS Reference P18/30/20

26 Letter dated 25 July 1968
Messrs Day, Rooke & Bradfield, re Mrs Wright and sale of land to Bearsted Parish Council
CKS Reference P18/30/20

27 Letters dated 16 March 1968
i   Bearsted Parish Council to Messrs Day, Rooke & Bradfield

ii   Bearsted Parish Council to Messrs Monckton, Son & Collis
CKS Reference P18/30/20

28 Letters dated 5 July and 12 August 1968
Messrs Whitehead, Monckton and Co. to Bearsted Parish Council
CKS Reference P18/30/20

29 Letter dated 19 August 1969
District Valuer to Bearsted Parish Council
CKS Reference P18/20/17

30 Letter dated 13 October 1969
CKS Reference P18/30/22

31 Further information in bundle of documents
CKS Reference P18/30/22

32 i   Letter dated 12 July 1968
Bearsted Parish Council to Messrs Turton & Blackford

ii   Account dated 25 August 1969
Messrs. Turton & Blackford to Bearsted Parish Council
CKS Reference P18/30/20

33-34 i   Letter dated 12 March 1969
J Belsom & Sons to Bearsted Parish Council concerning estimate

ii   26 September 1969 Account from J Belsom & Sons to Bearsted Parish Council
CKS Reference P18/30/20

iii   E M Harden, listed as an allotment holder, is Ted Harden the village watch and clock repairer mentioned on p.119

35 Sketch map of allotment and named holders
CKS Reference P18/30/20

9 The Village Blacksmiths: Charles Tester and Eustace Thwaites

1   'to clinch' - to fasten a nail by bending and beating down the point

2   Charles Tester ran the forge from 1920 to 1946

3   Vanner – a horse suitable for a van

10 Baroness Orczy in Bearsted

1   *Links in the Chain of Life (Autobiography)*
Baroness Emmuska Orczy 1947

2   Photograph from the collection of Yeandle Papers
CKS Reference U1401 Z12-13

3   *Op. Cit. Autobiography*

4-5   *Ibid. passim*

6   Letter from Baroness Orczy to the Editor of *Kent Messenger*
Published 14 September 1914

7   *Op. Cit. passim Autobiography*

8   Faculty for reservation of grave re Montague Barstow 1913
Holy Cross church
CKS Reference P18/6/57

9   Surrender of Faculty for reservation of grave re Montague Barstow 1913
Holy Cross church
CKS Reference P18/6/51

12 Bearsted Green Bakery

1   *Ye Olde Bearsted Green Bakery*
Rowland Powell
Bygone Kent, Volume 21, Number 12 December 2000
Meresborough Books

2   i   Tithe Map and Apportionment Schedule 1840-1842
        CKS Reference P18/27/2, 3

       ii   *Kelly's Trade Directory for Kent* 1855

3   *Kelly's Trade Directory for Kent* 1867, 1874

4   Bearsted Vestry Minutes
CKS References P18/8/3 and P18/8/13

5   5 October 1898
Burial Register for Holy Cross 1871-1936
CKS Reference P18/1/8

6   1901 Census return for Bearsted
Reference RG13/764

7   Information contributed by Trevor Cleggett and Chris Hunt

8   *Op. cit.* Rowland Powell

9   Information contributed by Chris Hunt

14 Garages and Mechanics

1   *The Centenary Magazine 1839-1939*
Robert Skinner 1939

15 Thornham Friars

1   1843 Tithe apportionment map and schedule for Thornham
CKS Reference Dcb/TO/T6r,IR 29/17/39

2   i   1871 census return for Thornham
        NA Reference RG 10 946 p.41

ii   1881 census return for Thornham
NA Reference RG11 0933 128 p.21

3   Letter from Percy Wigan to Herbert Waring 9 April 1901
Thurnham file, Gordon Ward collection
KAS Library

4   *Ibid.*
Letter from George Hampson to Herbert Waring 7 August 1901

5   *Ibid.*
Letter from Percy Wigan to Herbert Waring 20 August 1901

6   *Ibid.*
Letter from Alfred Watkinson to Seymour and Waring 27 September 1901

7-8   *Ibid.*
Letters from Percy Wigan October 1901

9-10   Conversation with Geoffrey Fletcher concerning previous owners

11   *Ibid.*
Unsourced press cutting showing advertisement for the sale of The Friars, 1926

12   Conversation with Geoffrey Fletcher concerning previous owners.

13   Conversation with Michael Perring concerning previous owners.

14   Conversation with Geoffrey Fletcher concerning previous owners.

15   *The Pilgrims Way: camera studies and descriptive text*
Nellie Kirkham
Frederick Muller Ltd 1948

16   Conversation with Geoffrey Fletcher concerning previous owners

17 The Walkling and Bromley families

1   p.149
A History of Bearsted and Thurnham

18 Snowfield Cottage

1   i   1841 census entry
NA Reference HO 107 456 7

      ii   Tithe Apportionment map and schedule for Bearsted 1840, 1842
CKS Reference P18/27/2, 3

2   1851 census entry
N A Reference HO 107 1616

19 From butcher to baker: The Old Bakery

1   National Monuments Record for Bearsted
Monarch Uid 8545

2   p.89
World Without End
Helen Thomas
Faber 1972

3   Sketch by Edward Pretty, F S A
Mr Pretty was the first curator of Maidstone Museum
CKS Reference U1401 Z12-13

4   For further information on Helen Allingham, see the website: www.helenallingham.com
also *Helen Allingham's Cottage Homes Revisited*
Annabel Watts 1996

5   Herst Lands 1858 - 1859
Abstract of Title re. Armstrong estate
CKS Reference U248 T7

6   Entry for Bearsted
Pigot & Co, Commercial Trade Directory for Kent, 1829

7   Entry for household in 1841 census returns
NA Reference HO 107 456 7

8   1842 Tithe Apportionment for Bearsted
CKS Reference P18/27/2,3

9   Entry for household in 1851 census returns
NA Reference HO 107 1616 416

10   i   Entry for Bearsted
Monckton's trade directory 1854

       ii   Entry for Bearsted
Kelly's Trade Directory for Kent 1855

11   1858 Sale of property
CKS Reference U1569 T5

12   *Op. cit.* Herst Lands 1858-1859

13   *Kelly's Trade Directory for Kent* 1859

14   i   Entry for Bearsted
Kelly's Trade Directory for Kent 1867

       ii   1871 census entry
NA Reference HO 10 939 50

       iii   Entry for Bearsted
Kelly's Trade Directory for Kent 1874

       iv   1881 census entry
NA Reference RG11 0926 48 8

       v   Entry for Bearsted
Kelly's Trade Directory for Kent 1882

       vi   1891 census entry
NA Reference RG 12 685 104

15   Private correspondence held by Roy Datson, dated 24 August 1994, concerning the history of the building.

16   Entry for household in 1901 census returns
NA Reference RG 13 764 17

17   *Op.cit.* Roy Datson

18   1954 Abstract of Title in papers held by Jackie Nicholas

19   *Op. cit.* Roy Datson

20 Over a Century of Travellers Tales

1   p.107
Edward Thomas: a portrait
R. George Thomas
Oxford University Press 1985

2   *Ibid.* p.113

3   p.12
Maidstone in Old Photographs
Irene Hales
Alan Sutton Publishing 1990

21 Caring for the Community: doctors, nurses and nursing homes

1   Information from Dr Martin Moss and an undated leaflet concerning Yeoman Surgery.

2-5   *Ibid.*

6   Entry for Bearsted in *Kelly's Trade Directory for Maidstone* 1934:

> Rose mount Nursing Home
> Miss Clara Sayers, State Registered Nurse, Matron
> Telephone 6327

7   The original list is in the file for Bearsted: Miscellaneous I-III
Maidstone Reference Library

8   p.159
A History of Bearsted and Thurnham

9   *Op. Cit.* Dr Martin Moss and leaflet

22 Growing up in Bearsted in the 1930s and 1940s

1   Many residents of Bearsted can still recall feeling stunned by the loss of Pamela and husband during the Second World War. Pamela was killed 16 January 1943, a few months after marrying George Lawrence. For further details see:

> *Dutifulness and Endurance:*
> *Bearsted and Thurnham 1914-1948, 1939-1945*
> Kathryn Kersey 2005

23 'Artily': A Smallholding on the Spot Farm Estate

1   p.32
The Postal History of Maidstone and the surrounding villages
Sidney J Muggeridge
The Postal History Society 1972

24 Bearsted in the Second World War

1   Bearsted Planning and Development Correspondence, 1937
CKS Reference P18/30/5

2   Undated conversation with Roger Vidler.

3   18 December 1942 log book entry (volume covering 1922 to 1959)
Bearsted Church of England School.

25 Binbury, Thurnham and Detling during the Second World War

1   For more information about Daphne Pearson see the following website: www.gc-database.co.uk

26 St Faith's Home

1   Messuage and land 1750-1835, including copy of will, Catherine Watts, widow, of Thornham
CKS Reference U82 T151

2   *Ibid.*
Mr Edward Watts to Mr William Twopeny, 2 January 1752

3   *Ibid.*
Mr and Mrs Armstrong to Mr Barnes, 19 November 1800

4   Herst lands 1858-1859 Abstract of Title re. Armstrong sale lots 5, 8 and 9
CKS Reference U348 T7

5   A great deal of land held in Kent was subject to gavelkind. Gavelkind was a system of inheritance in which the land was equally divided between the heirs on the death of the parent. This was intended to further equal inheritance. However, by the 18th and 19th centuries, the system actually meant that the equal shares of inheritance were being divided into smaller and smaller amounts, with 'one share' being held by many people. Gavelkind practice led to many disputes concerning the right to inherit, particularly if people died intestate, or were under the age of 21 and so were considered to be an infant, or minor. It was not unusual for people to obtain credit and borrow money secured on their interest in land holdings.

6   Sale of Lands 1858
CKS Reference U1569 T15

7   Herst Lands 1858: conveyance of freehold messuage, lands and hereditaments situate in the parishes of Bearsted and Thornham, 18 December 1858
CKS Reference U348 T7

8-11		*Fifty Years of St Faith's 1898-1948* Rev H Yeandle CKS Reference U1401 Z1
12		1902 Annual Report for St Faith's Home The reports are currently held at Robert Runcie House, 2-3 Bedford Place, Maidstone
13		*Fifty Years of St Faith's 1898-1948*
14		1914, 1915, 1916 Annual Reports for St Faith's Home
15-16		*Fifty Years of St Faith's 1898-1948*
17-18		Research by Laurence Allen 29 July 2002
19		There is very little information available about the Kay Carlton Hill Film Studio. However, I am indebted to the City of Westminster Archives Centre which advised that the Kay Carlton Hill Film Studios traded between 1951-1974 in London NW8. The premises were a recording and photographic studio which had once been the Carlton Hill Presbyterian Chapel.
20		*Fifty Years of St Faith's 1898-1948*
21		1954 and 1957 Annual Reports for St Faith's Home
22		Notes 29 July 2005 from Lawrence Allen
23		1952 Annual Report for St Faith's Home
24		'a churching' was a short service of thanksgiving for a safe delivery of a child sometimes held in a church. Occasionally, in some parts of Britain, this was held either in the church porch or in the church just before the baptism of a child.

27 The Women's Institute

1		Holy Cross magazine 1939-1942 CKS Reference P18/28/19
2-3		*Ibid., passim* Holy Cross magazine, December 1945 CKS Reference P18/28/20
4		*Op. cit.* Holy Cross magazine 1939-1942

28 The Yeoman area of Bearsted

1	i	Entry for Bearsted *Pigot & Co.* 1839
	ii	1851 census return NA Reference HO 107 1610
	iii	1881 census return NA Reference RG11 0926 52
2		Sale of Kentish Yeoman, 1900 CKS Reference U716 T2
3	i	Harriet Kirby: 1851 census return NA Reference HO 107 1610
	ii	James and Mary Richardson: 1861 census return NA Reference RG9 499
	iii	Charles Stamford 1871, 1881 and 1891 census returns NA Reference RG10 939 1871 NA Reference RG11 0926 55 1881 NA Reference RG12 685 1891
	iv	Register of Licences 1903-1926 Petty Sessions, Bearsted Division CKS Reference PS/BL 3

29 Cross Keys estate

1		National Monuments Record listing for Bearsted Monarch Uid 8538

2 National Monuments Record listing for Bearsted
Monarch Uid 417970

30 Four Fires in Thurnham Parish

1 pp.139-245 Parts 3-4
To Fire Committed: The History of Fire Fighting in Kent
Harry Klopper
The Kent Council of the Fire Services Benevolent Fund 1984

2 Entry for Aldington Section 5, 68
The Domesday Book – Kent
Edited P Morgan
Phillimore, Chichester 1983

3 *Aldington West Court ye Seat of Richard Sheldon Thirty Six Different Views of Noblemen and Gentleman's Seats in the County of Kent. All Designed upon the Spot by the late T Badeslade Esq., Surveyor and Engraved by the Best Hands*
H Chapelle
London c. 1720

4 pp.64-65
A Saunter through Kent with Pen and Pencil Volume 14
Charles Igglesden 1920

5 i 16 December 1949, report in *Kent Messenger*,

ii Entry in Kent Fire Brigade Occurrence Book, 16 December 1949

6 i 1870 Ordnance Survey Map Scale 25 inches to 1 mile

ii 1897 Ordnance Survey Map Scale 25 inches to 1 mile

7 Thurnham file, Gordon Ward Collection

8 i 1908 Ordnance Survey Map Scale 25 inches to 1 mile Sheet 32

ii 1939 Ordnance Survey Map Scale 25 inches to 1 mile Sheet 32

9 p.967
Kelly's Trade Directory for Maidstone 1934

10 i 19 November 1954, report in *Kent Messenger*

ii 14-15 November 1854
Entries in Kent Fire Brigade Occurrence Book

iii p.15
Kent Fire, March 1955

11 *Ibid.*

12 *Op. Cit.* 19 November 1954 *Kent Messenger*

13 *Short Brothers Break Out*
J M Preston
Bygone Kent, Volume 21, Number 4
Meresborough Books

14 22 July 1983, report in *Kent Messenger*

15 *Ibid.*

16 *Kent Messenger Directory for Maidstone* 1930-1931

17 *Kelly's Trade Directory for Maidstone* 1930

18 *Kelly's Trade Directory for Maidstone* 1934

19 p.45
Tales from a Road House
A W Tomlinson, privately published 1979

20 *Ibid.*

21 Thurnham file
Gordon Ward collection

22 22 July 1983, report in *Kent Messenger*

23   *Ibid.*

24   *Ibid.*

25   pp.69-73
East Malling Research Station Annual Report for 1983
M F Wickenden 1984

26   *Op. Cit.* 22 July 1983, report in *Kent Messenger*

27   *Ibid.*

28   Estate map of Thornham, 1709
CKS Reference U588 P1

29   15 December 1989., report in *Kent Messenger*

30   i   *Ibid.*

         ii   Photographs from *Kent Messenger* seen in the Public Bar of the Black Horse

31   Definitive map of the Public Rights of Way: County of Kent
Sheet TQ 85 NW Scale 6 inches to 1 mile 1 April 1987

32   Rev W H Yeandle, vicar of Bearsted
CKS Reference P18/8/11-12

33   22 July 1983, report in *Kent Messenger*

34   *Ibid.*

35   8 February 1985, report in *Adscene* newspaper

36   21 July 1986, report in *Maidstone Borough News*

37   Tudor House list of dances, 1935 - A W Tomlinson; Noted by John N Hampson
Gordon Ward Collection

38   15 December 1989, report in *Kent Messenger*

39   *Ibid.*

31 Thurnham and Bearsted in the late 1960s and early 1970s

1   62-64 Ware Street
National Monuments Record for Thurnham
Monarch Uid 503597

2   For further details about Otham corn mill see
The Len Water Mills
 R J Spain
Archaeologia Cantiana Volume 82 KAS